IMAGES
of America

KITTITAS COUNTY

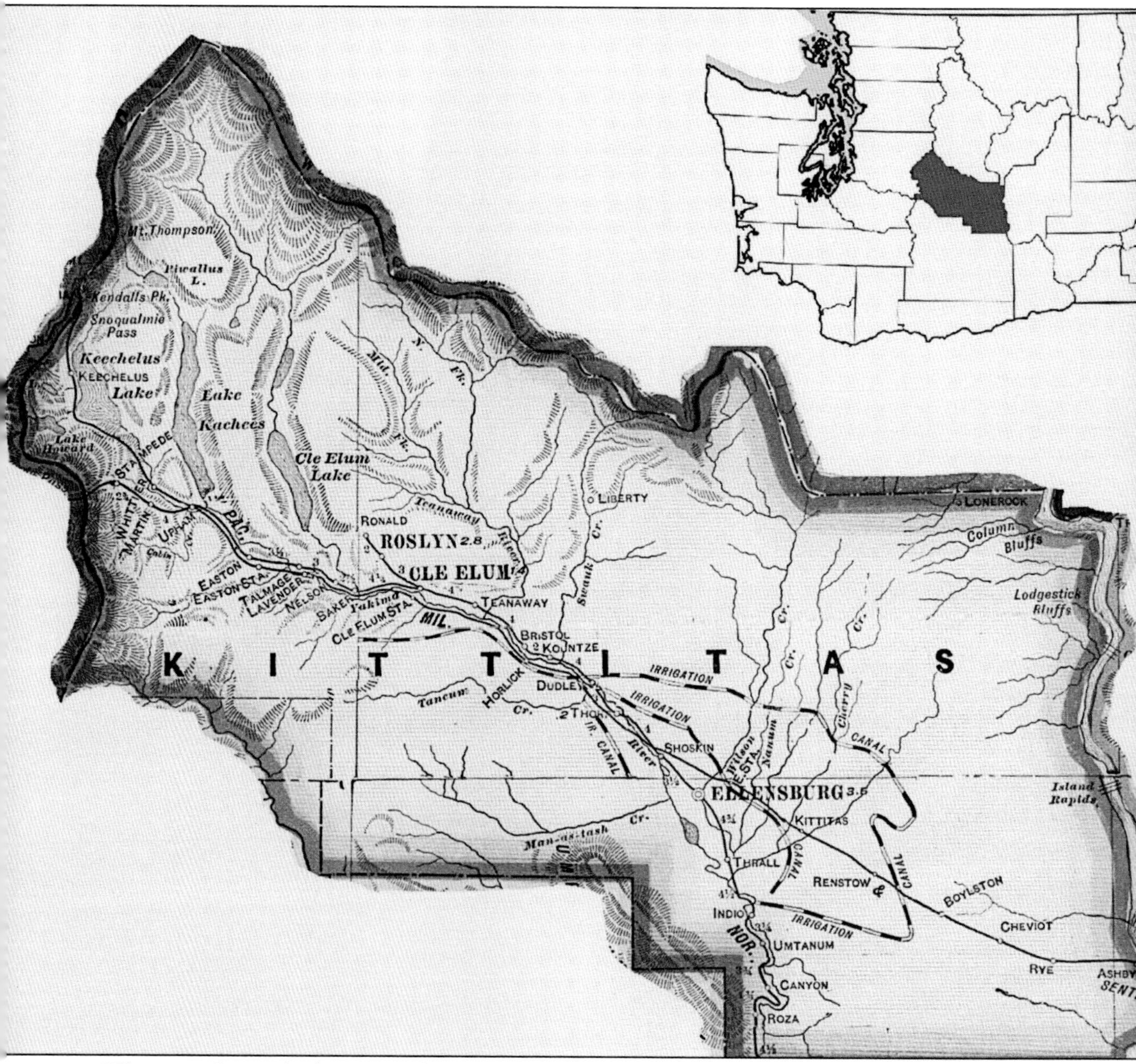

This map shows the location of Kittitas County in the state of Washington and a detailed outline of the county as it looks today. Most major cities and areas are included, but for clarity's sake, minor details have been excluded, as have rivers, lakes, streams, and mountains. (Ellensburg Public Library.)

ON THE COVER: Pictured is the Modern Woodmen of America (MWA) refreshment booth in Thorp around 1903. Each summer, members of the MWA in Central Washington and the Royal Neighbors of America would meet in Cle Elum for an annual logrolling contest. Communities such as Thorp would host events as well. These men are wearing MWA jackets, which had the picture of an axe on one side and a splitting maul on the other. (Ellensburg Public Library.)

IMAGES
of America

KITTITAS COUNTY

Andrew Caveness

ARCADIA
PUBLISHING

ISBN 978-0-7385-9588-7

Published by Arcadia Publishing
Charleston, South Carolina

Printed in the United States of America

Library of Congress Control Number: 2012937081

For all general information, please contact Arcadia Publishing:
Telephone 843-853-2070
Fax 843-853-0044
E-mail sales@arcadiapublishing.com
For customer service and orders:
Toll-Free 1-888-313-2665

Visit us on the Internet at www.arcadiapublishing.com

This book is dedicated to my wonderful wife, Melissa. She made far more sacrifices than I in the completion of this project, and I could not have done it without her enduring support and faith in me.

Contents

ACKNOWLEDGMENTS

There are several people that I would like to thank for helping me complete this book, for without their help, it would not have been possible.

Thank you to Sadie Thayer, Rocky Hively, and the Kittitas County Historical Museum (KCHM) Board of Directors in Ellensburg for their support. From discussing local history to generously allowing me to research on short notice, the KCHM staff was encouraging and supportive from the beginning. Sitting among Kittitas County historical items while researching gave me a real sense of my purpose here. I cannot thank the KCHM enough.

At the Ellensburg Public Library (EPL), director Debby DeSoer and local history librarian Milton Wagy were as supportive of this book as they were my first. After volunteering at the EPL for the last two years, I have come to appreciate the work that Milton has put into establishing, preserving, and organizing the local history collection. In addition, Milton's suggestions and corrections were very useful.

The Roslyn Museum allowed me to set up my laptop and scan pictures at will. Special thanks go to Joe Neiland; he was informative and helpful in many ways. For those of you who have not visited the museum, I encourage you to do so. Their collection is impressive, and the staff is more than willing to answer any questions you have.

Stephen Hussman at the Central Washington University Archives was supportive of my project and willing to have his graduate assistant, Talea Anderson, scan pictures for me on short notice. The Frederick Kruger Collection is housed there, and it is a treasure trove of Upper Kittitas County photographs and ephemera.

Finally, I would like to thank my wonderful family: Melissa, Nicole, Eliza, and Emily. They are always supportive and understanding of my work, especially when I am busy researching or writing. I am so lucky to have them in my life.

The images in this book appear courtesy of the Kittitas County Historical Museum (KCHM), the Ellensburg Public Library (EPL), the Roslyn Museum (RM), and the Central Washington University Archives (CWU), unless otherwise noted.

INTRODUCTION

Kittitas County, located in the geographical center of Washington State, is a diverse landscape that contains mountains, lakes, forests, rivers and streams, farmlands, shrub steppe semiarid land, and the mighty Columbia River, which carries water from Canada to the Pacific Ocean.

The area that we now call Kittitas County has a storied past. For many years, the county has been home to various bands of Native Americans. Principally, the Kittitas band of the Yakama Nation was the main inhabitant of the Kittitas Valley as well as Upper Kittitas County (the northwestern portion). The Kittitas Valley was abundant with camas, kouse, fish, and deer, while Upper County was rich in fish, berries, deer, and elk. The majority of the Native Americans who came into Kittitas County did so seasonally, returning to their home in the Yakima Valley during the winter months. There were, however, some year-round residents in Kittitas County who lived in small villages, usually along rivers or creeks. The Kittitas Valley also held a large meeting and council grounds, called Che-lo-han, where Native Americans from all over the region would convene and gamble, trade, sing, dance, and socialize. The Native Americans that resided in Kittitas County had little contact with Euro-Americans until the mid-19th century, other than fur trader Alexander Ross's visits in 1812 and 1814, when he was in search of horses.

In 1847, the chief of the Kittitas band, Chief Owhi, traveled south to the mouth of the Yakima River and visited Father Ricard of the St. Rose Mission. Chief Owhi was inquisitive about the mission, and in 1848, the Immaculate Conception Mission was established on Manastash Creek in the Kittitas Valley by Fathers Charles Pandosy, Chirouse, and G. Blanchet. Soon after, Pandosy began to travel and live with Chief Owhi, building himself a cabin on Naneum Creek. This was the first documented instance of a non-Native American residing in Kittitas County, although it is true that fur traders had traveled into the county in the 1830s and early 1840s. The mission work was a success for the most part, yet after the Yakama Indian War of 1855–1858, the governor of Washington Territory suspended all missionary work in the Yakima and Kittitas Valleys, and Pandosy left for a different mission in the Okanogan Valley.

In 1855, Chief Owhi was part of the delegation from the Yakama Nation who signed the Walla Walla Council Treaty with Washington territorial governor Isaac Stevens. Washington Territory was established in 1853 when it broke away from Oregon Territory, and Stevens was appointed the first territorial governor. This treaty took much of the land away from the Native Americans in eastern Washington Territory, establishing reservations and paving the way for future settlement on the now-available lands. However, many of the Native Americans who signed the treaty were not aware of the exact wording of the agreement, nor were they complacent when settlers encroached on their lands in search of gold and furs. The Yakama Indian War resulted in the Yakama losing about 90 percent of their lands, and they were confined on a reservation near Yakima, removing almost all Native Americans from Kittitas County.

In 1863, the Washington Territorial Legislature established Ferguson County, which encompassed most of what are Kittitas and Yakima Counties today. It was short lived, as there were only about 100 people living in the new county and none wanted representation. In 1865, the act establishing Ferguson County was repealed. However, the legislature and the governor wanted some sort of representation, so they created Yakima County in 1867, which included the current Kittitas County, and established F.M. Thorp's residence near Yakima as the county headquarters. About this time, the first permanent settlers were entering the Kittitas Valley, and over the next decade, the population grew steadily. John A. Shoudy came to the Kittitas Valley in 1871 and bought a small trading post, dubbed "Robbers Roost," from A.J. Splawn. Soon, Shoudy platted the town of Ellensburg and sold the lots at a reasonable price to encourage business growth. By 1874, there were enough settlers in the Kittitas Valley that the citizens began building the Manastash ditch, which was the first irrigation canal in the valley. By the end of the 1870s, Ellensburg was big enough that the residents felt either it should become the county seat of Yakima County or it should break away and become its own county. At first, there was limited support of this idea, but by 1883, most everyone living in the county agreed that Ellensburg should become the county seat of its own county. In November 1883, the Washington Territorial Legislature officially established Kittitas County.

Other than the Kittitas Valley, Kittitas County saw little other growth at all until the mid-1880s. Miners and trappers had been in the Upper County, but no real settlement occurred until 1883, when Thomas L. Gamble staked off a homestead in present-day Cle Elum. Gamble was originally from Pennsylvania, and by chance, a friend of his, Walter J. Reed, happened to be living in North Yakima at the time. Gamble convinced Reed to come stake a claim of his own, which Reed did, first building a cabin and then constructing the Reed House Hotel in 1887. Gamble platted Cle Elum in 1888, establishing himself in the present-day Cle Elum, while Gamble occupied eastern Cle Elum, known as Hazelwood at that time. Around the same time, a sawmill was established at the mouth of the Teanaway River by H. Witters, from which boards were cut and sent to Ellensburg and Cle Elum. Also, in 1883, the first coal deposits were discovered near present-day Cle Elum and Roslyn, yet it was not until 1884 that coal mining began to show promise. George Virden and William Brannon had discovered a large vein of coal on the site of what would become the No. 3 mine in Roslyn. Virden and another man, "Nez" Jensen, brought a sack of coal into Ellensburg to test its purity in a blacksmith shop. When the coal was found to be of good quality, word quickly spread.

In 1885, the coal deposits near Roslyn caught the attention of the Northern Pacific Railroad surveyors, and after sending a group of men to test the coal, the railroad decided it wanted to act. In 1886, the Northern Pacific Railroad was completed through Yakima to Ellensburg, which doubled the population of Ellensburg in two years. Work continued on the rail line towards Cle Elum, then through a tunnel in Stampede Pass in 1888, connecting the Puget Sound area with Kittitas County. The Northern Pacific had depots in Ellensburg, Cle Elum, Roslyn, and Easton and flag stops at Thrall, Thorp, Dudley, Bristol, Teanaway, and Nelson. Without the railroad, the expansion of Kittitas County, especially the Upper County, would have been severely limited. In 1886, the railroad brought drills and other tools to Roslyn, and their test holes proved that it would be worth it to mine the area for coal. The railroad began buying up settler's land, as they wanted to own the entire area and have exclusive rights to the mines. Some settlers were paid very well for their land, but others fought the powerful railroad, even legally. The railroad began the Northern Pacific Coal Company, which owned most of the mines, and the Northwestern Improvement Company with three retail stores in Roslyn, Ronald, and Cle Elum. Cle Elum and Roslyn experienced a rapid population boom, going from essentially no population in 1882 to roughly 337 and 1,500 people, respectively, by 1890.

Early miners in Roslyn were not without complaint; under the guise of the Knights of Labor, many coal miners went on strike in August 1888, demanding shorter workdays and a better working environment. The mining company, instead of giving in to the demands, brought in black miners as strikebreakers from Illinois by train under heavy guard and enlisted 40 armed men to guard the mines while they worked. After much tension, Washington territorial governor Eugene Semple told the mining company that their guards were not allowed and sent the Kittitas

County sheriff Samuel Packwood to Roslyn to disperse the guards and settle tensions. The governor, though, did not intervene in the labor dispute, nor send the strikebreakers away, and miners had to return to work without gaining rights, or find work elsewhere. The black miners stayed, and more came to work the mines, increasing Roslyn's black population to 22 percent by 1900. Many other nationalities also came from around the world to work in the Roslyn and Cle Elum mines, and Roslyn quickly became one of the most diverse cities in the Northwest. There were over 26 different ethnic groups represented in Roslyn, which is still evident today in the culturally separated cemeteries.

In 1873, gold was discovered in the Swauk area between Ellensburg and Cle Elum, and news quickly spread. A little bit of gold was discovered before this in 1867, but the find in 1873 was large enough to whet the appetite of many other miners. Soon, the Swauk Creek Mining District was organized, and claims were staked. However, the gold was not as easily found as it had been initially, and many miners left not long after they arrived. By the end of the 1870s, though, it began to pick up again, with Chinese miners finding some of the biggest lodes in 1877, much to the chagrin of other miners. In 1884, miners in the Swauk district decided to reorganize and enact new laws, which defined the boundaries and banned all Chinese laborers from mining in the district. Meaghersville, which became the town of Liberty, was the hub of all activity in the Swauk district, but many claims and miner cabins dotted the countryside along the hills and road leading towards Blewett Pass.

With Kittitas County flourishing, Ellensburg had high hopes that it would be selected to become the state capital. As a territory, Washington's capital was in Olympia, chosen due to its proximity to Fort Nisqually and Puget Sound. When Washington was selected to be designated a state, most felt that Olympia should remain the capital. However, others felt that Seattle, North Yakima, or Ellensburg would be a better choice; the latter two because of their centrality in the state and promise as growing towns. Ellensburg had a plat drawn out, including a capital square at the end of North Water Street, and the Craig brothers' completion of a governor's mansion on Craig's Hill. Unfortunately, on July 4, 1889, a fire destroyed the entire downtown district of Ellensburg, which essentially ruined any chance the town had of securing the capital. Just four months after the fire, in November 1889, Washington Territory became Washington State and Olympia was declared the capital. Ellensburg was, however, selected to be the location of a state Washington State Normal School, which opened its doors in 1891, first in the Ellensburg Public School building, then in Barge Hall in 1893. The town quickly rebuilt and was once again thriving. Many of the buildings in Ellensburg's downtown today were constructed shortly after the fire.

On May 9, 1892, there was an explosion in the No. 1 mine in Roslyn that killed 45 miners. The deep mine had exhaust shafts to ventilate the mine from deadly methane gas, called firedamp, which would naturally accumulate from underground sources. Miners were working to cut between levels when the firedamp ignited, killing the miners either directly or from asphyxiation due to the explosion consuming all of the oxygen. The tragedy left 29 women widowed and 91 children paternal orphans. After the bodies were recovered, there was an investigation launched, led by Justice Thomas L. Gamble of Cle Elum. Held in the Roslyn Town Hall, Judge Gamble appointed a jury of four businessmen and two miners to examine all of the evidence and determine whether the Northern Pacific Coal Company was at fault. It took over a week of deliberation and examination of the facts, but in the end, the jury decided that the company was partly at fault for not adequately ventilating the mine. The company agreed upon a compromise and paid out settlement money to the families of the miners killed.

The Chicago, Milwaukee, & St. Paul Railroad (alternately called the CM&StP or the Milwaukee Road) came through Kittitas County in 1909, adding a second rail line connecting the county to the east and west. The Milwaukee Road established substations in Doris, Kittitas, Ellensburg, Thorp, South Cle Elum, and Hyak in Kittitas County. Also, the Milwaukee Land Company platted the town of Kittitas in 1908 and established a depot and refueling area for the locomotives, as well as a storage yard and maintenance shop. Kittitas had two stores and a church by 1910; the Kittitas State Bank opened in 1911, and many other businesses and residents moved in around this time. Also along the Milwaukee Road was South Cle Elum, in which a depot, roundhouse, maintenance shops, railroad workers' bunks, and other buildings were constructed. South Cle Elum, incorporated in 1911, showed promise as a young city; however, its proximity to Cle Elum, as well as its isolation on the south side of the Yakima River, hindered any serious growth. The new Milwaukee Road consisted of six tunnels in the county, 121 miles of track, trestles spanning gulches, and nearly 12,000 feet of tunnel connecting Hyak and Rockdale through Snoqualmie Pass. Pre-tunnel, the Milwaukee Road used an alternate route around Snoqualmie Pass, and in 1911, it offered service between Seattle and Chicago. The tunnel through Snoqualmie Pass opened in 1915, establishing a more direct line from Ellensburg to Seattle than the Northern Pacific did. The Milwaukee Road became fully electrified in 1918, and it remained that way until it finally closed in 1980 due to lack of train travelers and better interstate systems for car travel. Today, the Milwaukee Road is the John Wayne Pioneer Trail, a portion of which is called the Iron Horse State Park Trail and runs along the old rail bed from the Columbia River to North Bend. Many hikers, bikers, and horseback riders enjoy the trail and its scenic views.

Vantage began when W.D. Van Slyke and his family came down the Columbia River from Trinidad, Washington, in search of new home. They landed at Vantage, and in 1914, the Van Slyke family started the ferry service between Kittitas and Grant Counties. A small store soon opened, and the town of Vantage began to grow. In 1917, both counties took over the ferry operation, and with highway improvements, traffic increased dramatically. In 1927, a bridge was completed across the river, ending the ferry service and establishing Vantage as a crucial stopping-off point for drivers in Kittitas County. Highway construction near Vantage unearthed a large field of petrified trees, and in the 1930s, Gingko Petrified Forest State Park opened. The interpretive center was built near the highway, and trails were constructed to lead people on a walking tour of this Miocene Epoch wonderland.

When the US Army needed a large area to practice bombings and shooting large guns during World War II, it turned to Kittitas and Yakima Counties. Originally, the Army leased 160,000 acres, but that increased to 260,000 in 1951. The Yakima Training Center, as it is called, now comprises 327,000 acres, a large portion of which is in Kittitas County. The training center is the largest expanse of shrub-steppe in the Northwest and is still actively used by the military, which arrive in convoys from Joint Base Lewis-McChord via Interstate 90.

There is much more to the history of Kittitas County, as told through the following pages. Kittitas County has come a long way since its beginning, yet the county has maintained a firm grip on its past, preserving the pictures and stories for future generations.

One

EARLY COUNTY

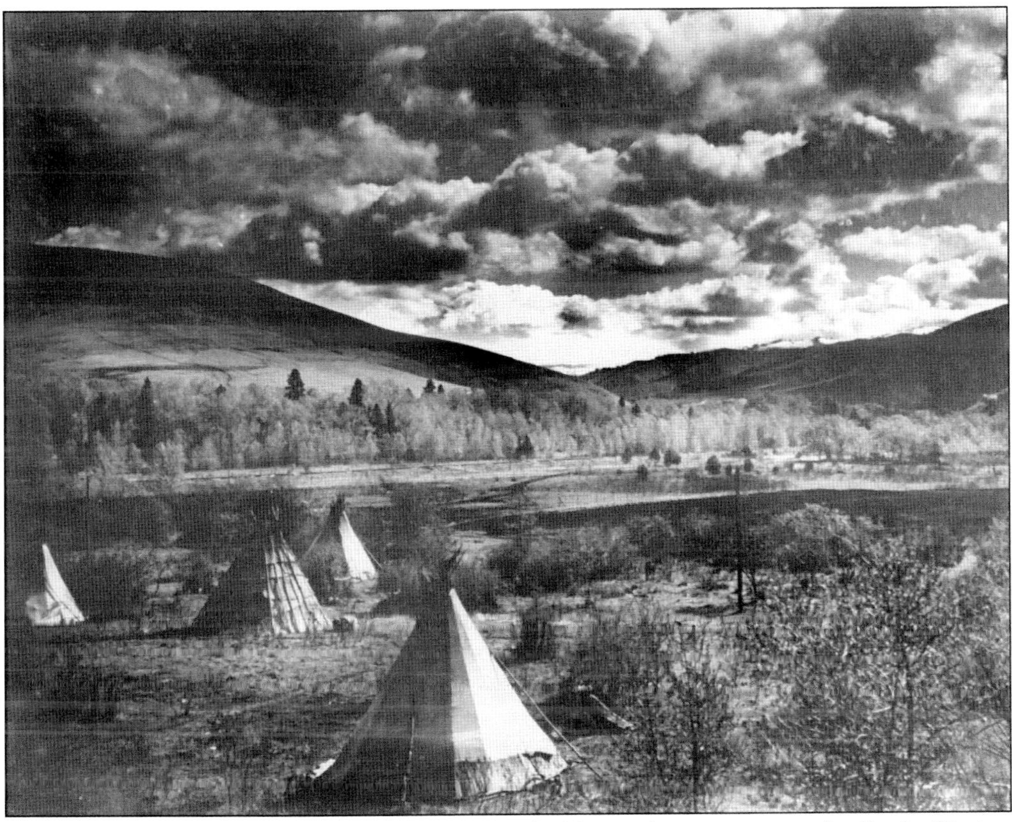

The earliest inhabitants of Kittitas County were the Native Americans, specifically the Kittitas band of the Yakama Nation. There were many Native American settlements in Kittitas County, with some villages containing up to 500 residents. After the reservations were established, most of the Kittitas band moved south to the Yakama Reservation, though a few families remained in the valley and some still came up during the summer months. (EPL.)

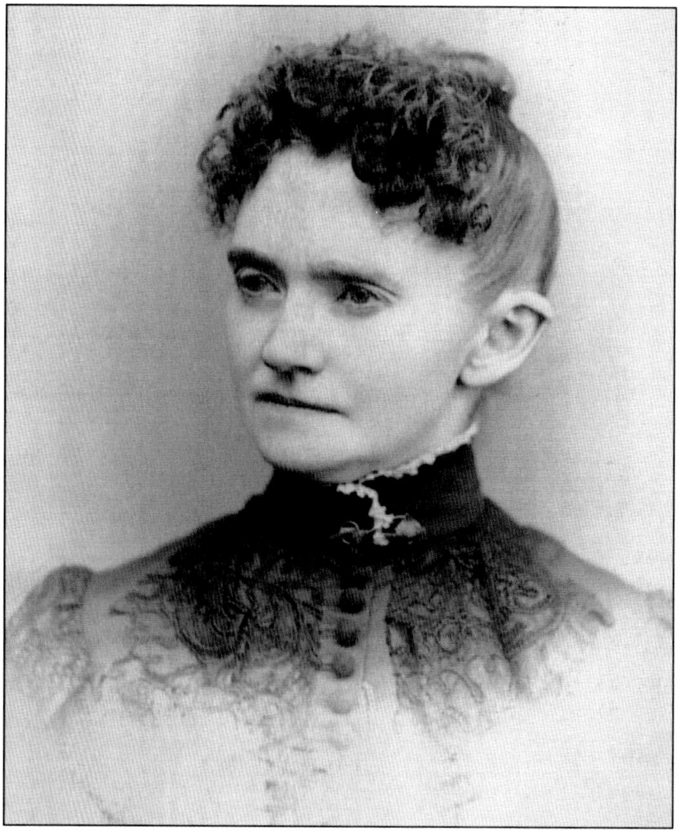

John Alden Shoudy was born in Illinois in 1842 and served during the Civil War for three years. After the war, he moved to California with his brother-in-law Dexter Horton, where he met and married Mary Ellen Stewart. They moved to Seattle in 1868, and Shoudy came to the Kittitas Valley and bought A.J. Splawn's store in 1871. In 1875, he platted a town and sold plots to settlers and businesspersons, naming the town Ellensburg for his wife, Mary Ellen. He was a member of the Washington Territorial Legislature in 1883 and was instrumental in the formation of Kittitas County. He was also a member of the state Constitutional Convention in 1889 and tried to have Ellensburg named the state capital. (KCHM.)

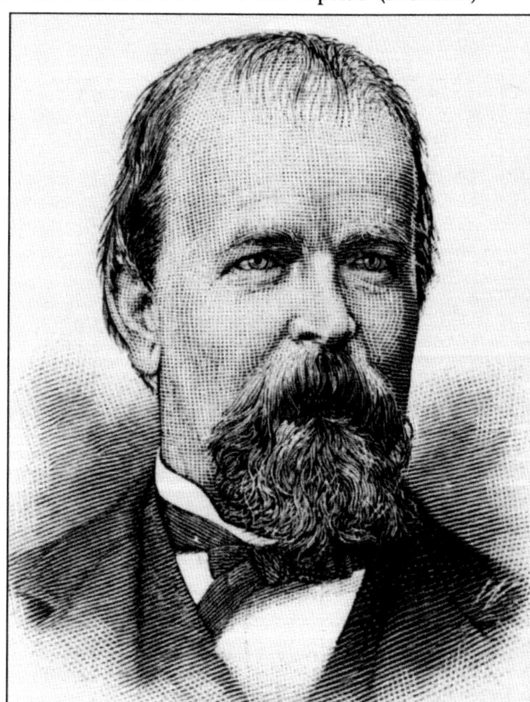

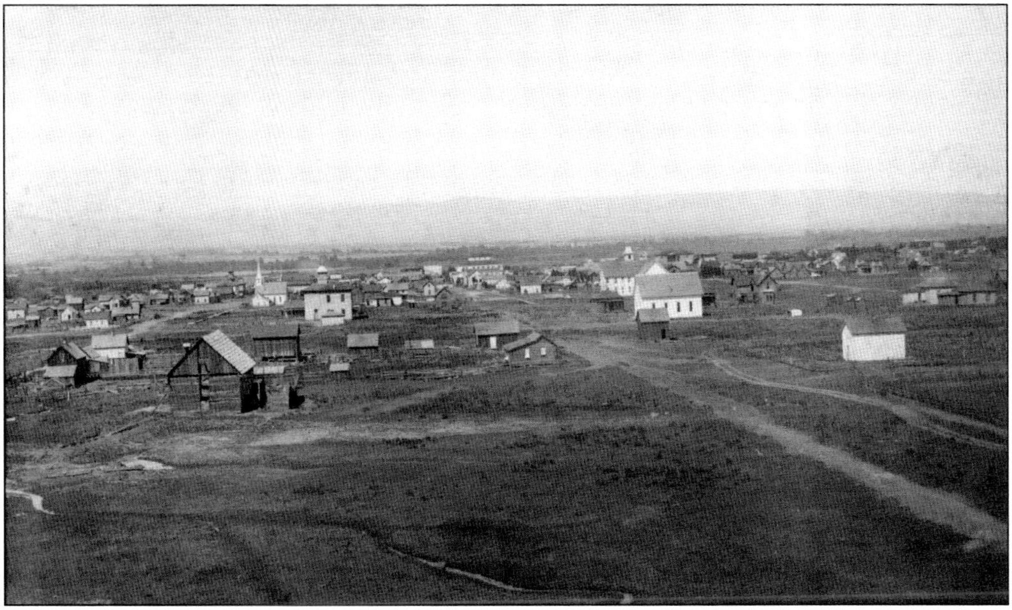

This view looking west across the valley from Craig's Hill shows Ellensburg before the fire of 1889. On the right, the Ellensburg Academy is the white building with the bell tower. It was the first school in the downtown area. In the center of the picture is the Johnson House Hotel, the three-story white building on the corner of Fourth Avenue and Pearl Street, which burned in the fire. (KCHM.)

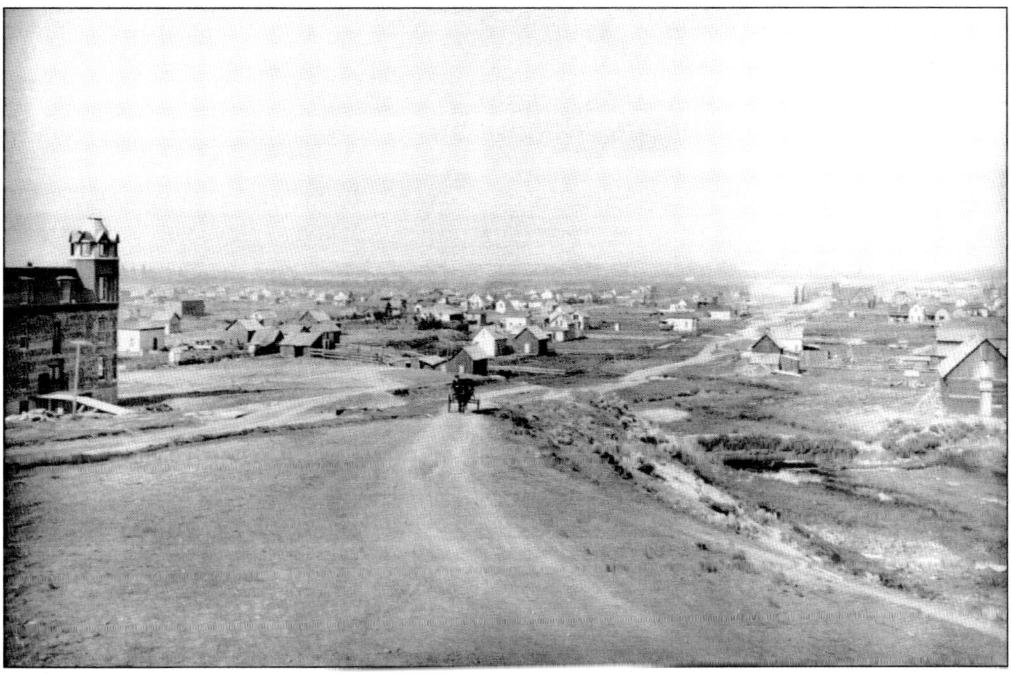

Looking west down Third Avenue from Chestnut Street, it is clear how sparsely populated and treeless Ellensburg was in 1890. On the left is the Craig mansion, built by brothers Britton and Samuel Craig, which was intended to serve as the governor's mansion had Ellensburg became the state capital. Today, the building still stands with a castle motif and serves as apartments. (EPL.)

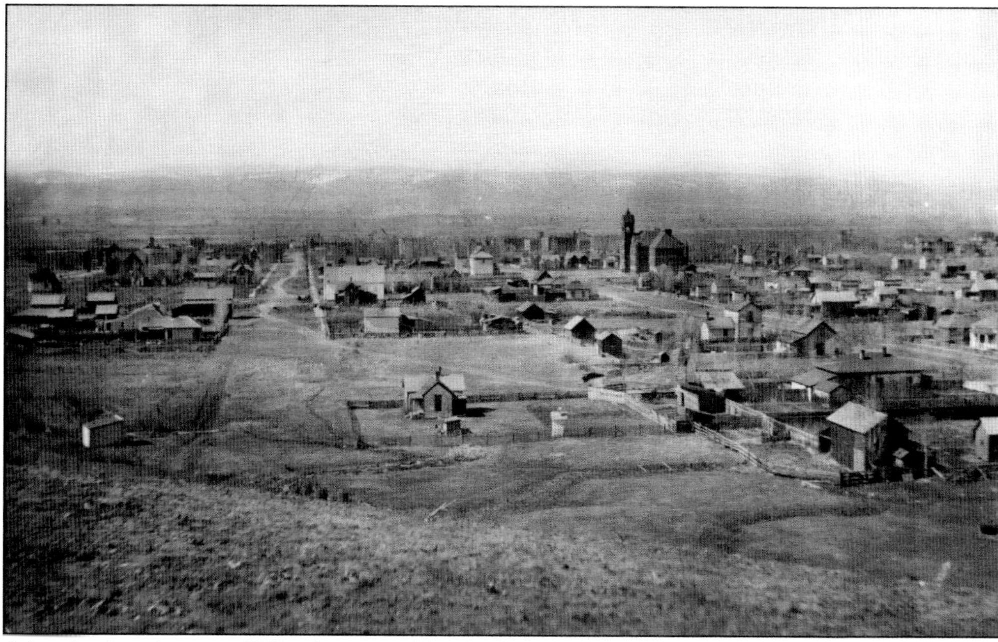

After the fire, the city of Ellensburg quickly rebuilt. Looking west Fourth Avenue from Craig's Hill, on the far left in the background, is the Cadwell Building, which now houses the Kittitas County Historical Museum. In addition, the cupolas of the Kriedel (left) and Davidson (right) buildings can be seen. The public school building, constructed in 1890, stands on the right. (KCHM.)

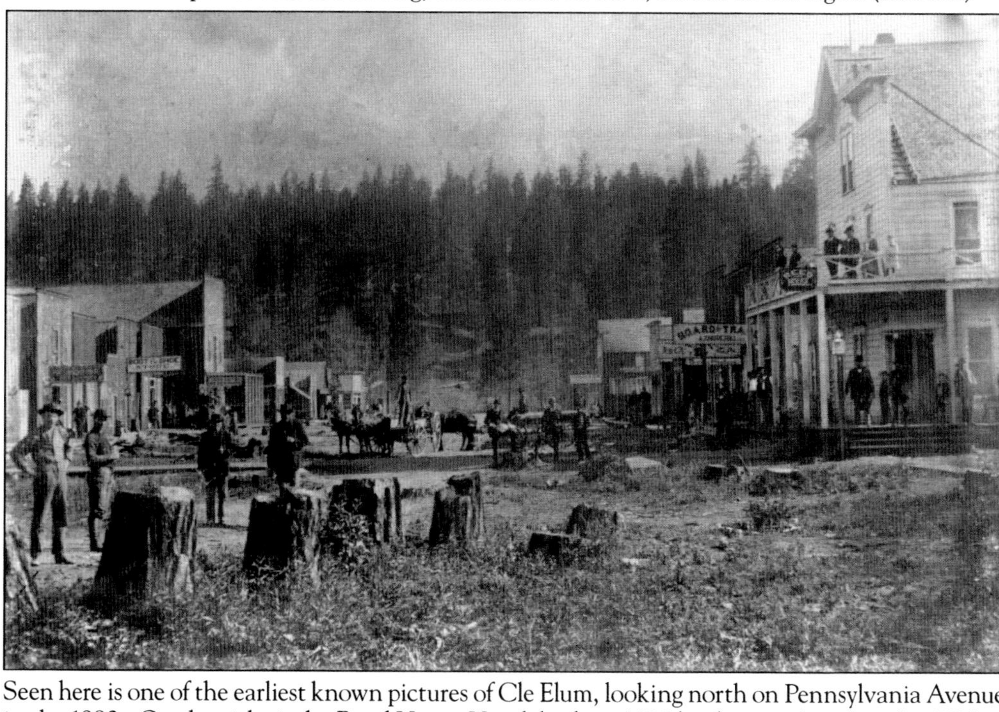

Seen here is one of the earliest known pictures of Cle Elum, looking north on Pennsylvania Avenue in the 1880s. On the right is the Reed House Hotel, built in 1886 by the town's cofounder, Walter J. Reed. Reed built a cabin at the west end of Second Street. The Northern Pacific Train Depot sat very close to where this photographer was standing. (EPL.)

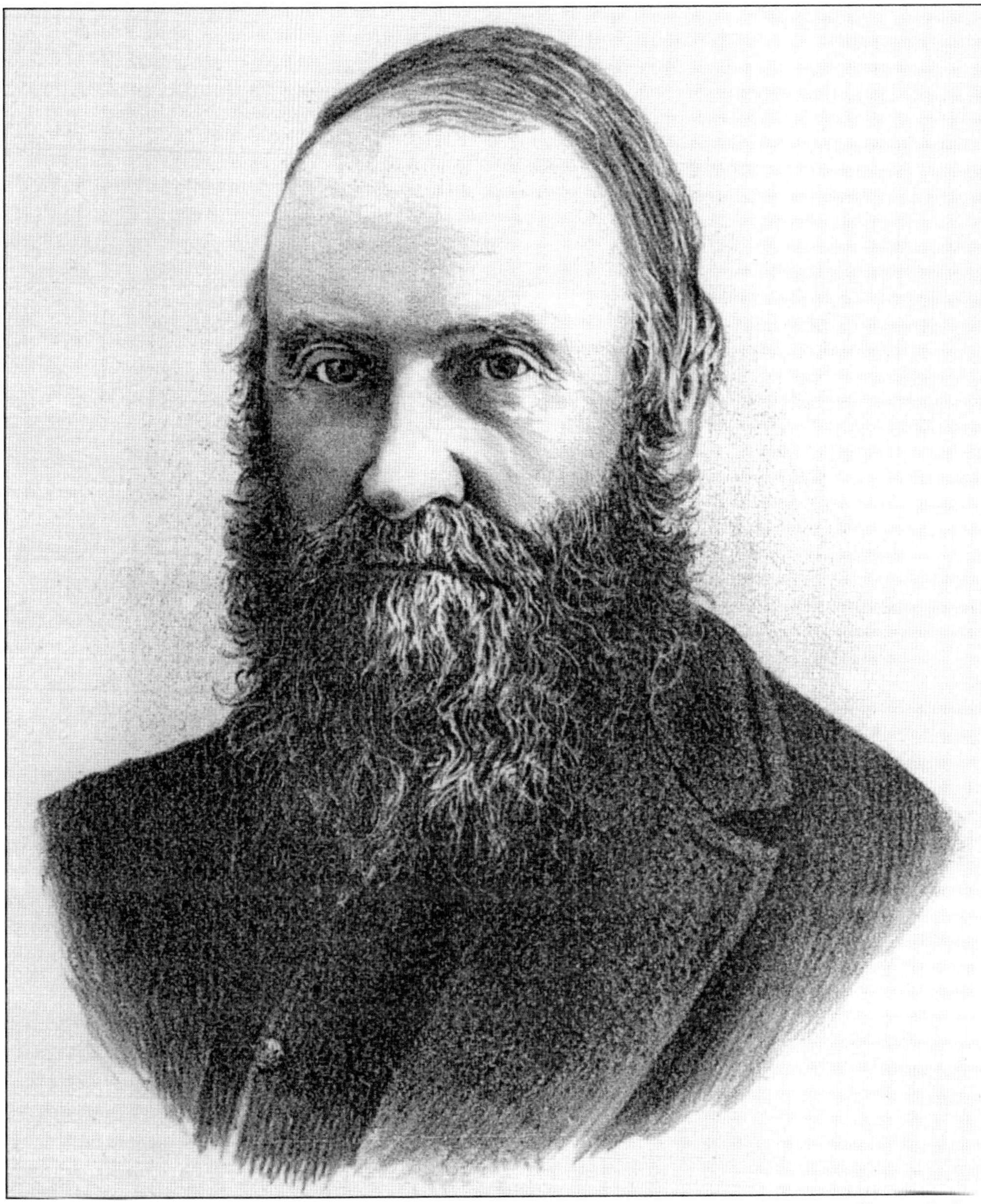

Born in Pennsylvania in 1827, Thomas Gamble came west in 1878 and eventually settled in what would become Cle Elum in April 1883, before there was even mention of a railroad coming through. Gamble, who knew Walter J. Reed from Pennsylvania, contacted Reed and told him to come to Cle Elum and homestead with him. In 1888, Reed filed the townsite plat for Cle Elum, and a few weeks later, Gamble filed his plat for Hazelwood, which is eastern Cle Elum today. In 1889, Gamble was elected county commissioner, and he also served as road supervisor. Gamble made several additions to the town. Twelve families moved in, and Gamble and Reed organized a school district with Gamble as the first clerk, a position he held until 1897. In 1894, Gamble discovered coal on his farm and leased the land to the coal companies on a royalty basis. Large mines were developed, and Gamble made a lot on royalties. Gamble was vice president of the State Bank of Cle Elum until his death in 1907. (EPL.)

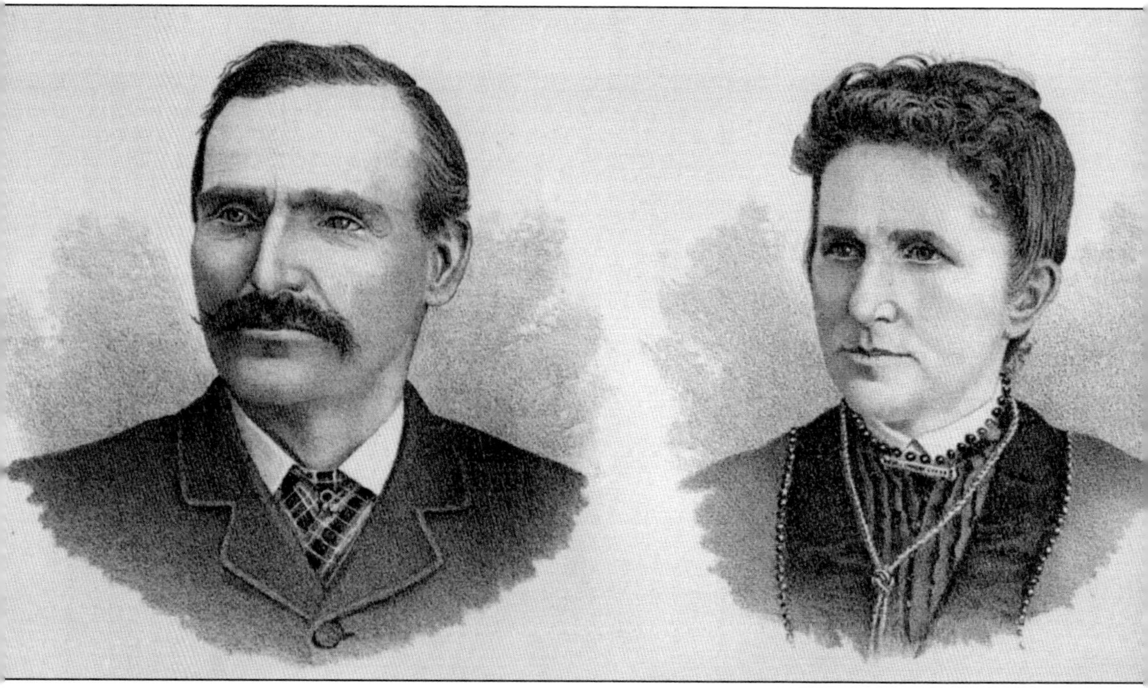

Born in Scotland in 1842, Walter J. Reed came to America with his parents in 1848, locating in Ohio. After school, he mined coal before joining the Army of the Potomac Infantry in 1861 during the Civil War. He was discharged from the Army in 1864, married Barbara Stiener, and returned to coal mining in Pennsylvania. Seeking a milder climate for his wife, they headed west, first to Oregon, then California, and in 1879, they came to the Washington Territory, settling in North Yakima. After five years of farming and raising stock in North Yakima, they decided to go to Cle Elum on advice from Thomas Gamble. There, they built a cabin, then the Reed House Hotel in 1887. Along with Gamble, Reed also discovered coal near Cle Elum and Roslyn. Reed was a member of the Independent Order of Odd Fellows, served as a state senator in 1904 (defeating A.J. Splawn), and was mayor of North Yakima, where he retired. He died there in 1908. (EPL.)

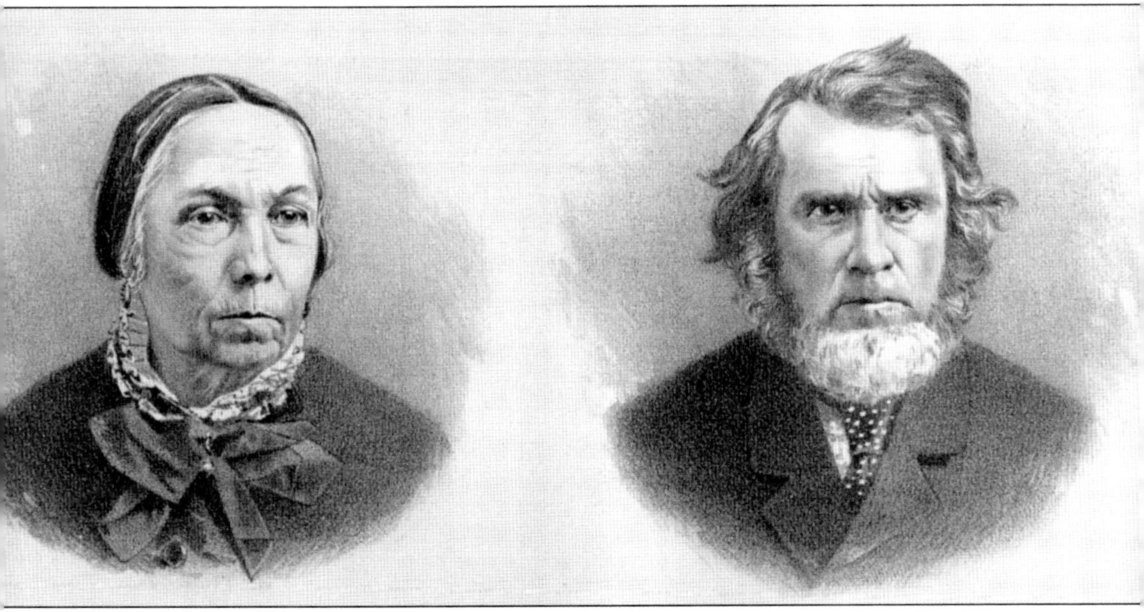

Born in 1822, Fielden M. Thorp left Missouri in 1844 for the Pacific Coast, crossing the plains in a 26-man, 12-wagon train. Following the early Oregon Trail and crossing at the South Pass, the group came into Oregon Territory to the Columbia River. From there, they floated down from The Dalles, landing near present-day Portland. Thorp went out into the Tualatin Plains and got work splitting rails. He and his wife, Margaret, resided in Benton County, but the Willamette Valley grew too populous for his liking, and in 1861, F.M. went to the uninhabited region of the Yakima, making a new home in the Moxee Valley, ranching and cattle ranging until 1869. In 1869, he again moved, this time to the Taneum Creek area near Ellensburg, becoming one of the first settlers in the county. The Thorps had nine children, but only six survived past infancy. F.M. Thorp lived out his days in the Taneum and died in 1893. He and his wife are buried in the small Thorp-Splawn Pioneer Cemetery that is visible from Interstate 90. (EPL.)

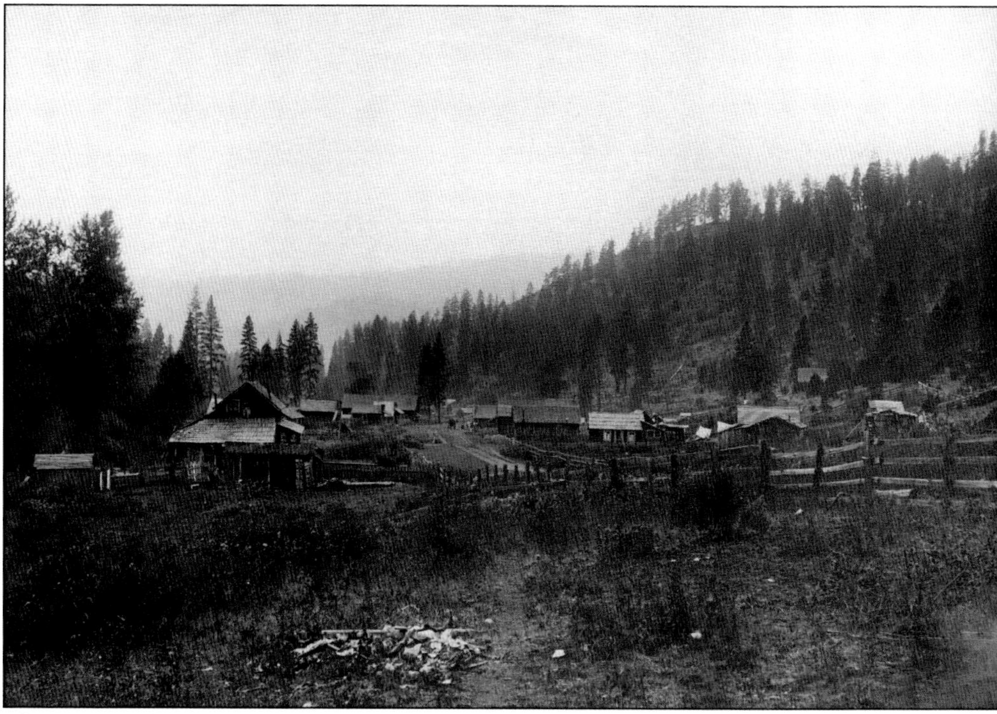

Thomas Meagher came to the Swauk area and staked a claim on Williams Creek, as did others, and a small mining camp began. The miners called the area Meaghersville after Meagher, and the name was used until about 1916. The woman seen below is Mamie Caldwell, standing on the porch of her grocery store in the old town of Liberty around 1912. This town was on the Swauk Creek near the current Highway 97 and was a stop for the stagecoaches and freighters before heading over Blewett Pass. Not long after this photograph was taken, the townsite was abandoned and moved to Meaghersville. The newly consolidated town was named Liberty to appease the postal department. (KCHM.)

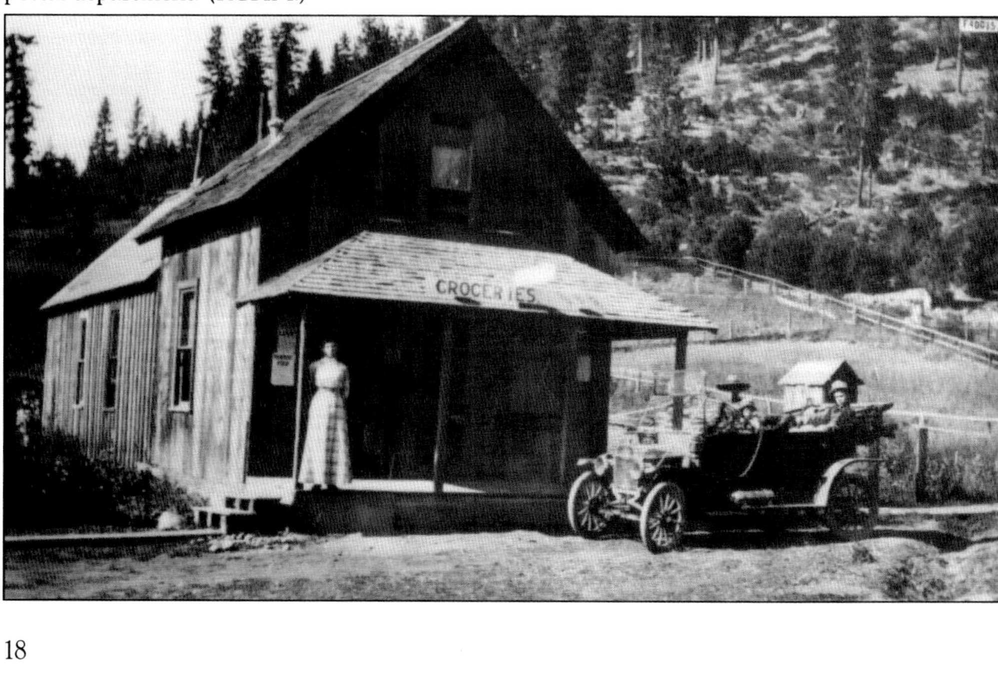

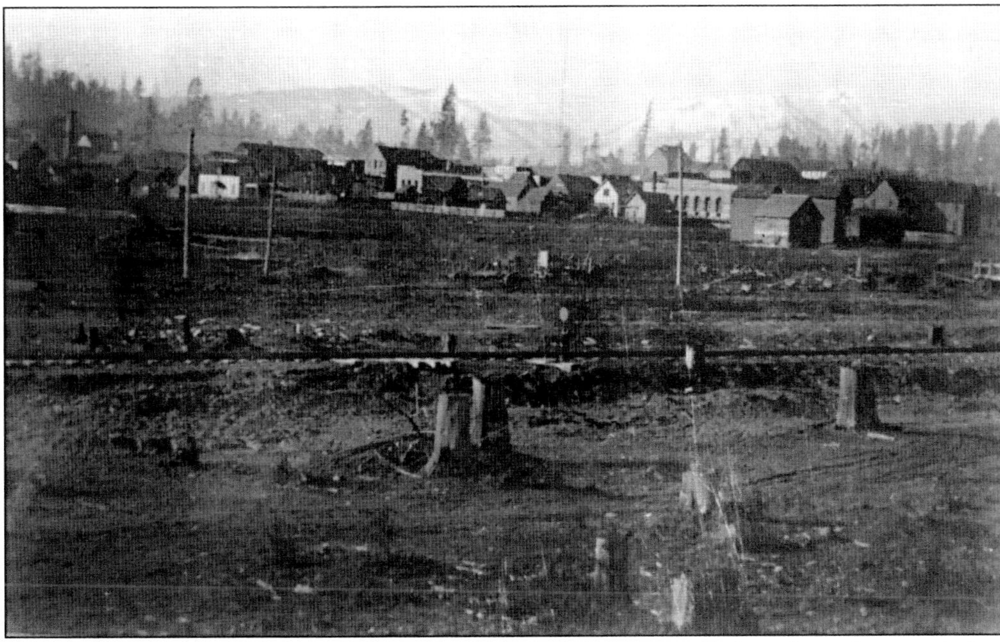

With stumps still dotting the landscape, this early Roslyn photograph shows how the town looked in the 19th century. The tracks belong to the Northern Pacific, which ran through town and up past Ronald and carried the coal from the mines down to Cle Elum. The snowcapped peak is Mount Baldy, which towers above Lake Cle Elum northwest of Roslyn. (EPL.)

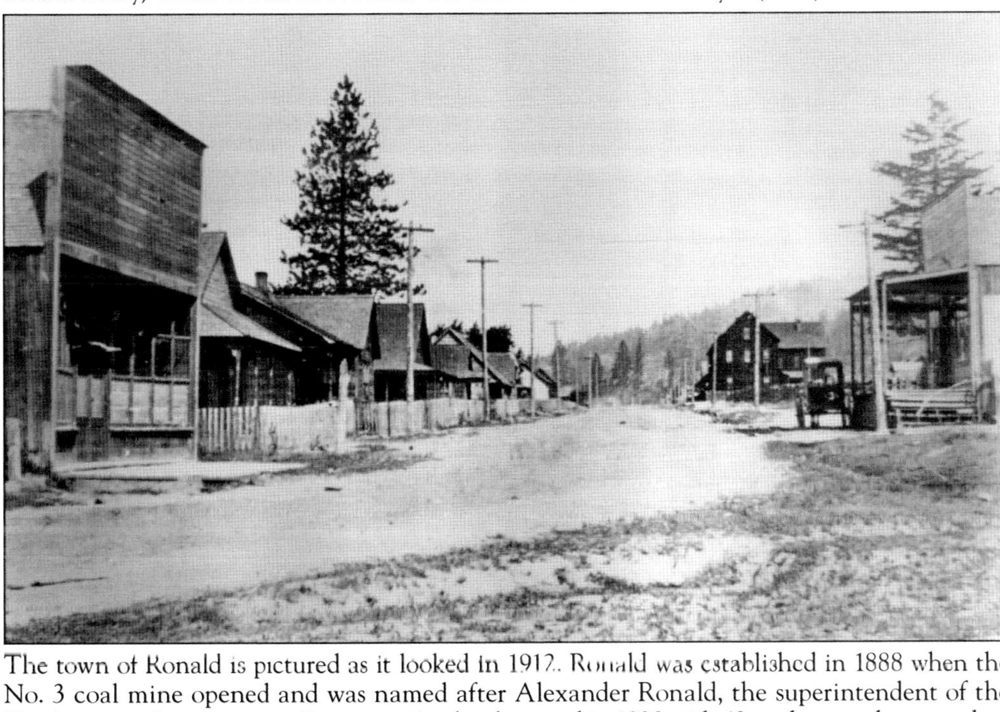

The town of Ronald is pictured as it looked in 1912. Ronald was established in 1888 when the No. 3 coal mine opened and was named after Alexander Ronald, the superintendent of the Northwestern Improvement Company. A school opened in 1890 with 49 students and one teacher. At its peak, Ronald had 11 businesses, including one of the three Northwestern Improvement Company stores in the Upper County. (EPL.)

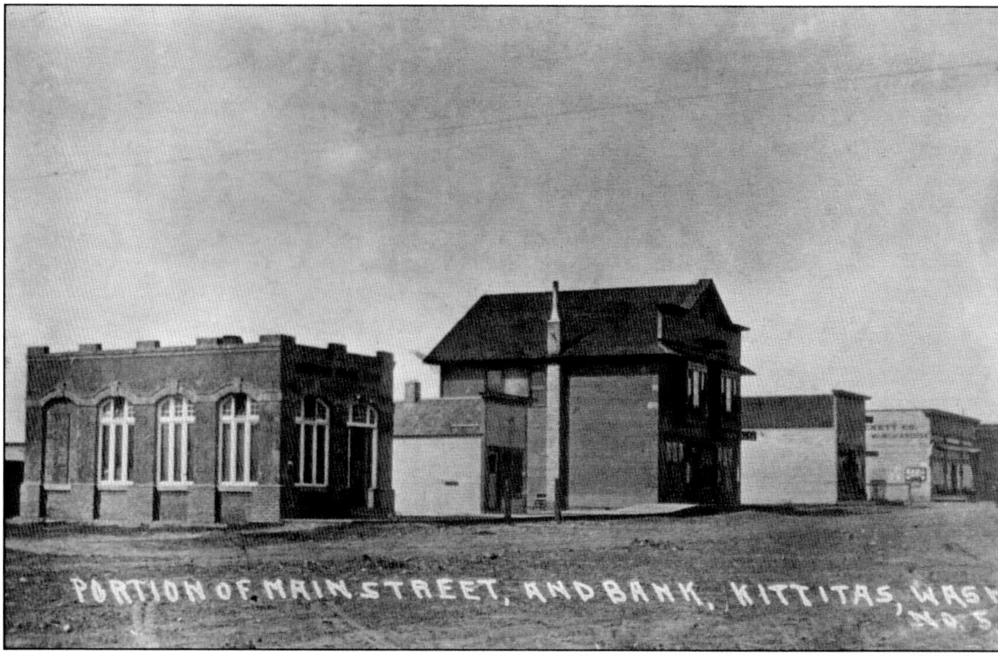

Kittitas had residents in the area in the 19th century, but it was not until the Chicago, Milwaukee & St. Paul Railroad came through in 1908 that a town was platted. After a depot was built and the town was laid out, it did not take long for people to come to that new town. Within a few years, Kittitas went from sagebrush to a promising town, with a church, stores, and a bank by 1911. This c. 1922 photograph shows the west side of Main Street. From the intersection of First Street and Main Street are, from left to right, the Kittitas Bank, DeVine Shoe Repair, Carrico Barber Shop & Drug Store (with rooms to rent), Yeldell Butcher Shop, Crockett Co. Merchandise Store, and a hotel. When the Chicago, Milwaukee & St. Paul Railroad came through the Kittitas Valley, a depot, water tower, and railroad yard were built, and the town of Kittitas grew. (EPL.)

Two

PEOPLE OF THE COUNTY

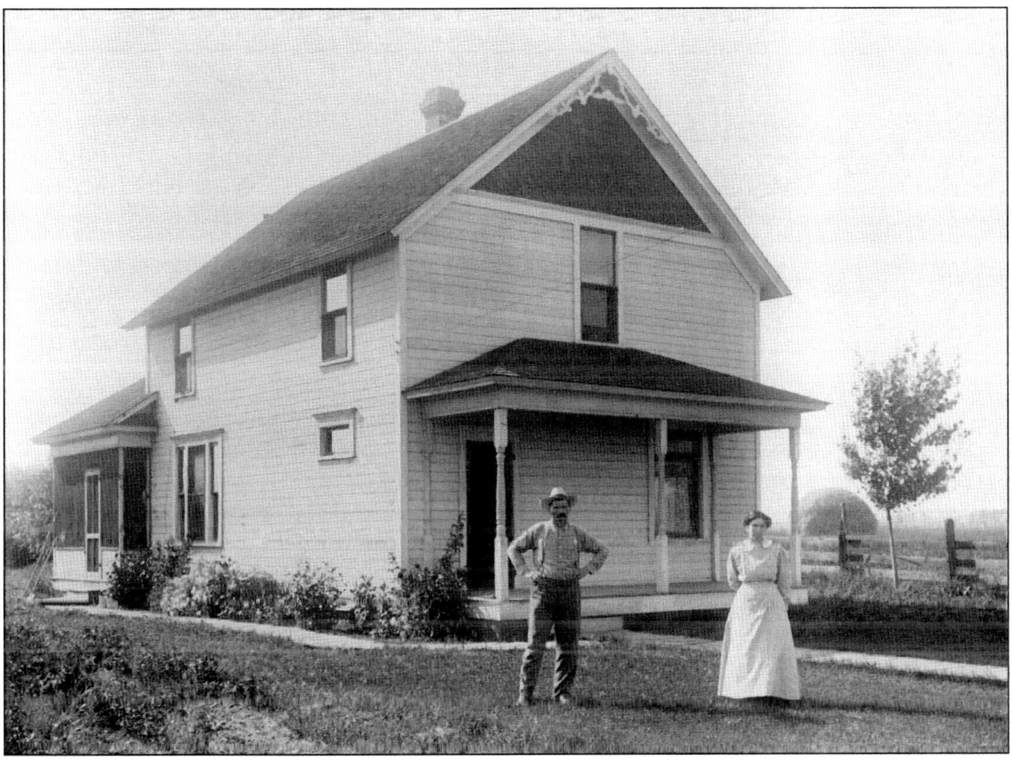

Minnie and Otto Kohler stand in front of their house on Tjossem Road in the Kittitas Valley. Otto came to the United States from Switzerland in 1882 when he was 10 years old and moved to the Kittitas Valley with his uncle Karl O. Kohler. Otto was a farmer until about 1920, when he retired with his wife to a house closer to town. (KCHM.)

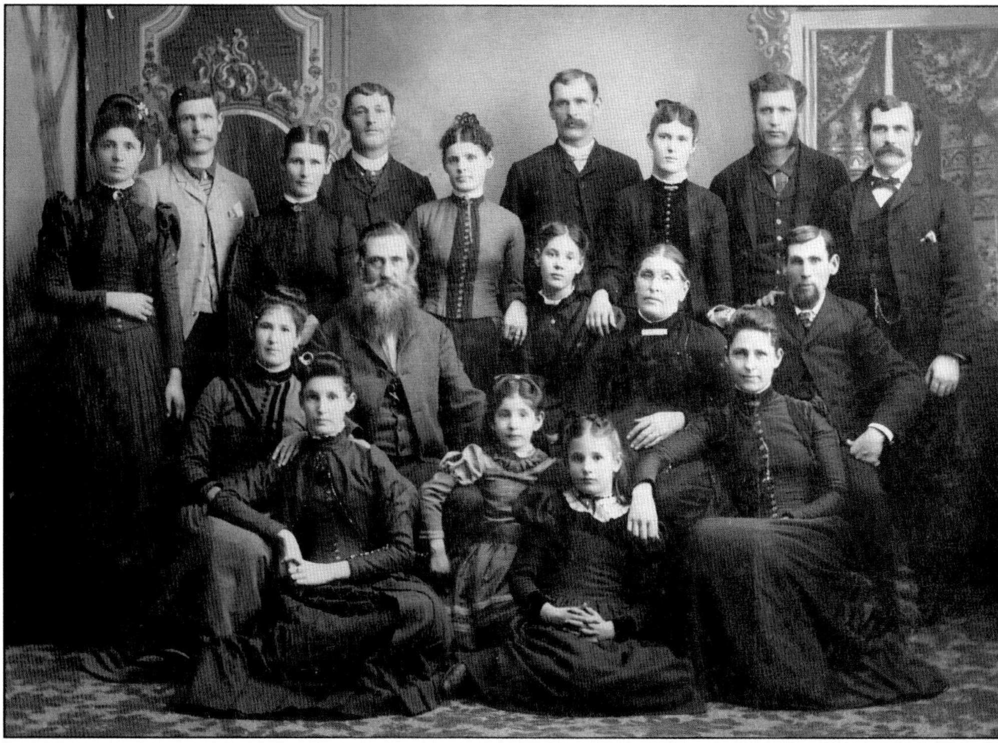

In 1872, Dr. John Robbins came to the United States from England with his wife Elizabeth and their 12 children. Initially settling in the Portland area, Robbins and his oldest son came to the Kittitas Valley on horseback in search of a new place to live. Robbins fell in love with the valley and moved his wife and children (now totaling 14) to a farm north of Ellensburg. (KCHM.)

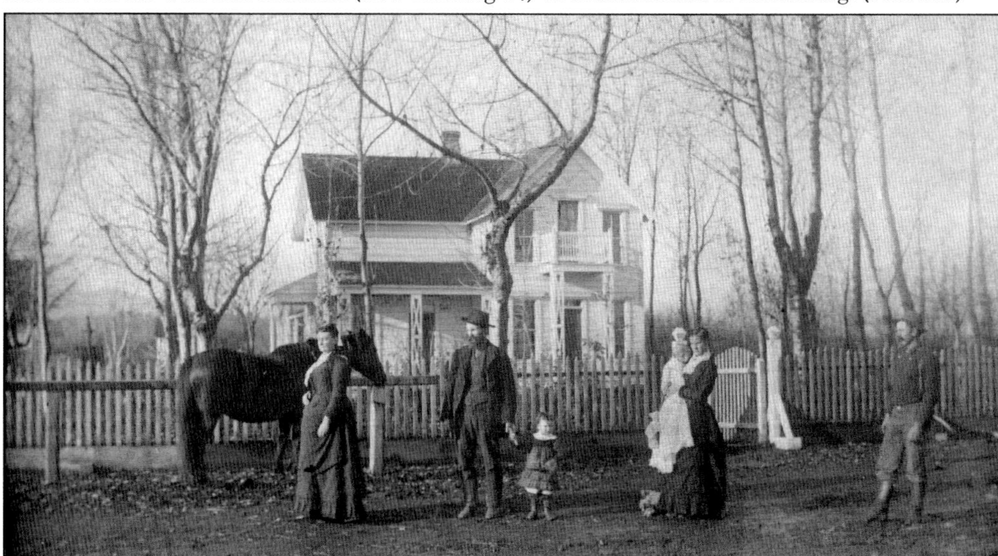

Pictured here is Charles and Jessie Kineth's home in the Kittitas Valley. Charles was born on Whidbey Island in 1855, his father being one of the first settlers of Coupeville. He moved to the Kittitas Valley in 1878, married Jessie Drake the following year, and homesteaded three miles west of Ellensburg, raising livestock. (KCHM.)

Antoine Bertram and his wife, Lucy Pahofta, resided in Thorp. Antoine came to the Thorp area with F.M. Thorp and Charles Splawn and worked on their farms. Antoine was first married to Lucy's sister Emma Pahofta, but she passed away. Lucy and Emma were the daughters of Indian John, a Yakama who is the namesake for Indian John Hill. Antoine and Lucy remained together until they died, and they are buried in the Holy Cross Cemetery. (KCHM.)

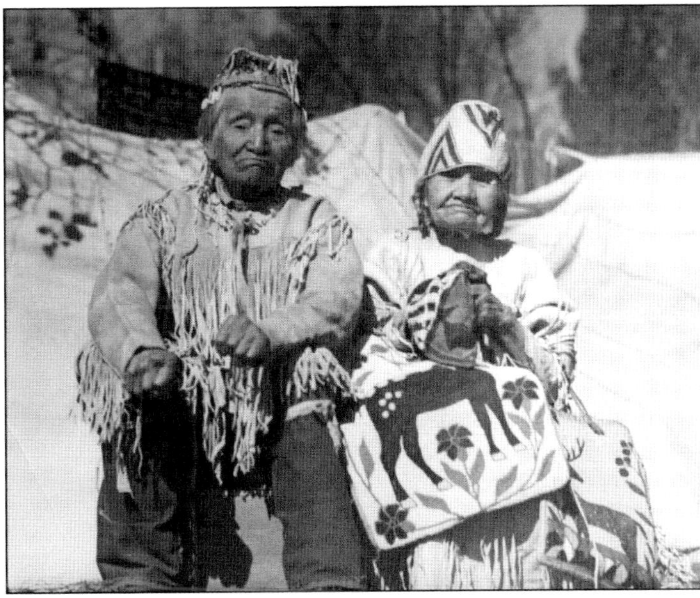

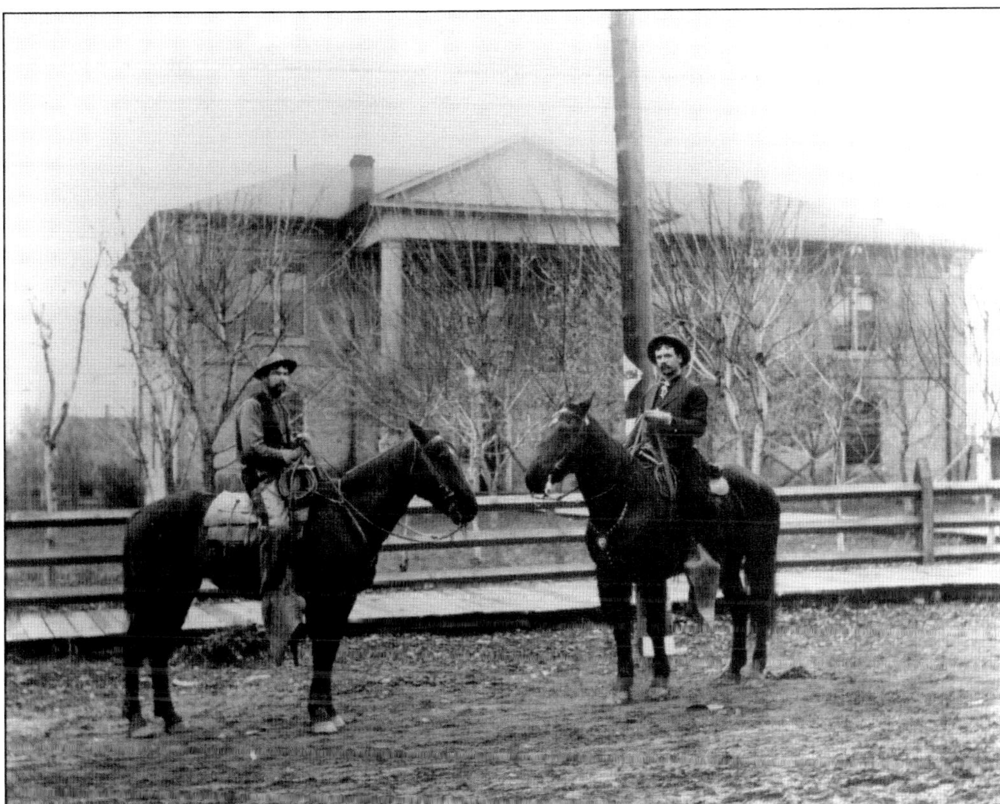

James Ives (left) and John Bowers pose atop their horses in front of the Kittitas County Courthouse in Ellensburg in 1898. James Ives, who was 15 when he came to the Kittitas Valley, was a cattleman and freight hauler. John Bowers, born in California, came to Ellensburg with his parents when he was little. (EPL.)

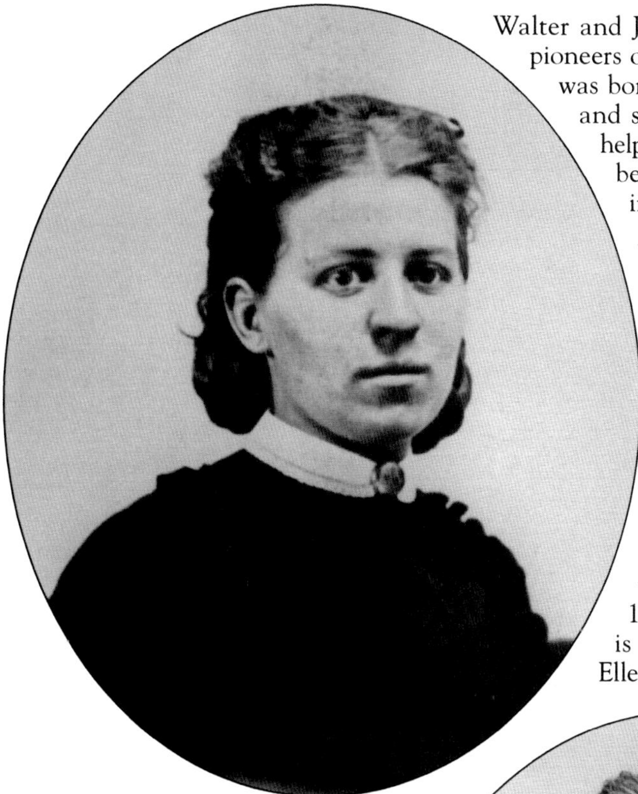

Walter and Jennie Olmstead Bull were early pioneers of the Kittitas Valley. Walter Bull was born in Albany, New York, in 1838 and served during the Civil War. He helped build the Union Pacific Railroad before coming to the Kittitas Valley in 1869 and settling on a large farm. Jennie Olmstead Bull came to the valley in 1871 with her family and was related to the namesakes for Olmstead Place State Park. She was a schoolteacher until she married Walter in 1873. Bull was the biggest landowner in Kittitas County at one time; his massive ranch comprised around 1,700 acres southeast of Ellensburg. Jennie died young, in 1885, leaving Walter and his five children widowed until Walter remarried in 1889. Walter Bull died in 1898 and is now buried next to Jennie in the Ellensburg IOOF Cemetery. (KCHM.)

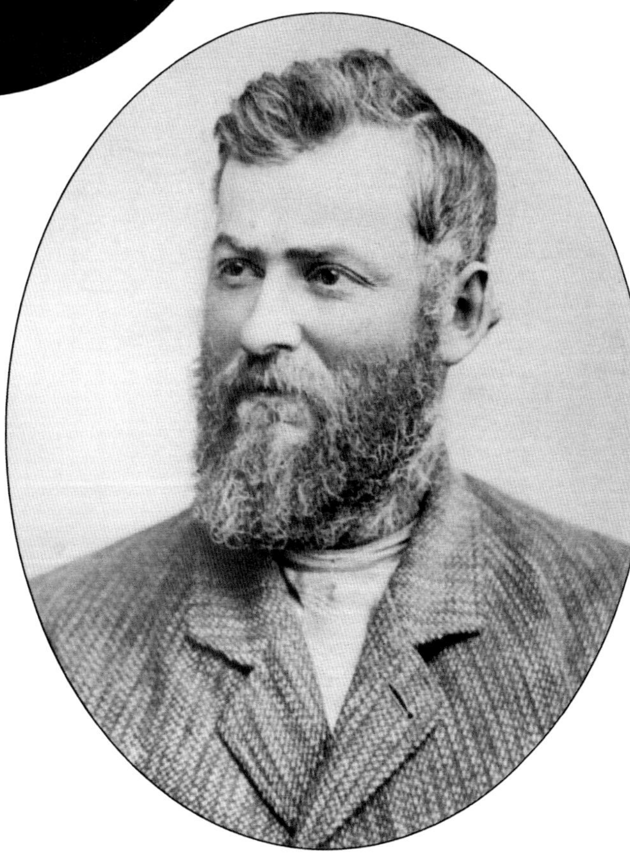

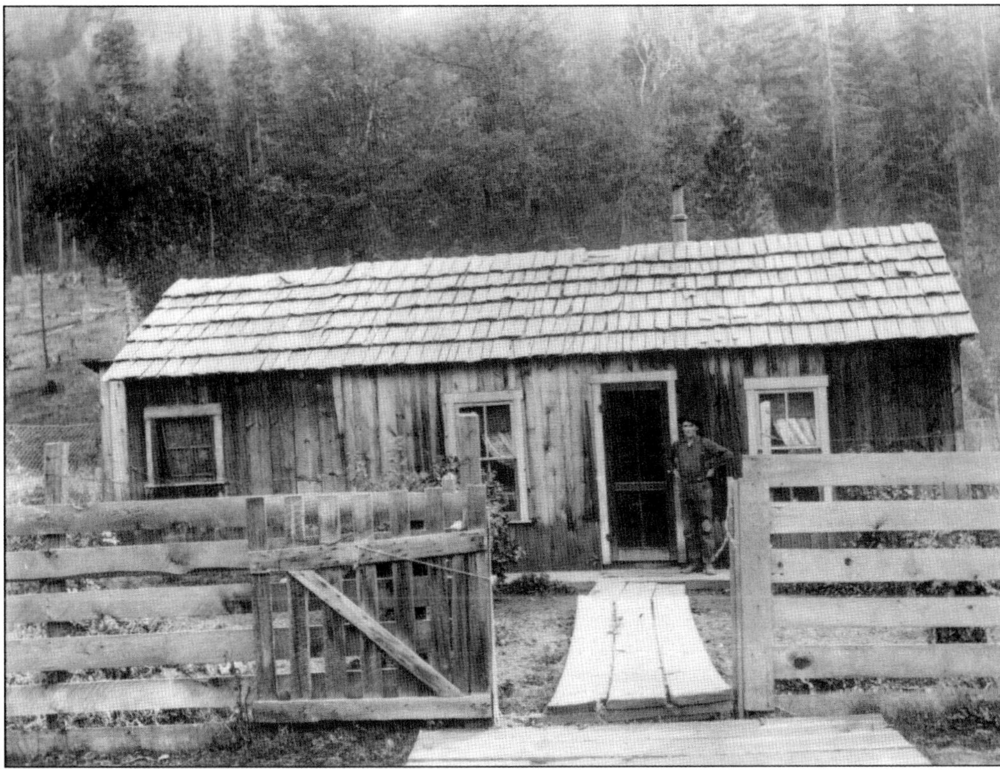

Ben Killson stands on the porch of his cabin in Meaghersville, the future site of Liberty. Killson came to the Swauk Mining District in the 1890s and set up shop as a storekeeper. Killson was also a miner, a notary public, and a mining recorder. Two of Killson's neighbors, Thomas F. and Elizabeth Meagher, were namesakes of the townsite. (EPL.)

Yakama Indians play what appears to be blackjack, using sticks or bones as gambling chips, near Ellensburg in the early 1900s. Standing are a woman named Molly and her nephew, palm out and holding a blackjack hand. Molly did not want to be photographed, and when her nephew was killed by rustlers shortly after, she felt his death was a result of the picture being taken. (EPL.)

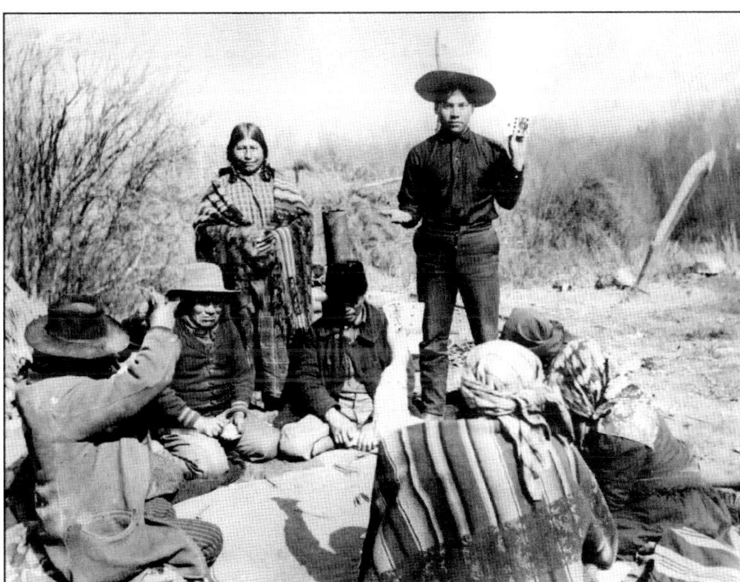

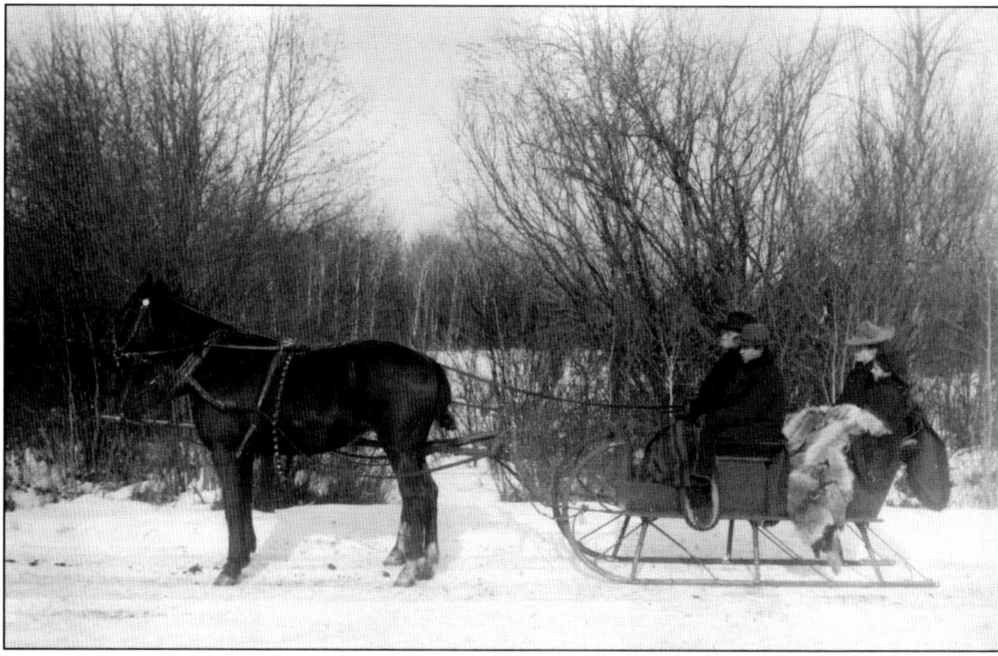

Ellensburg attorney Austin Mires and a few family members are out for a sleigh ride in the Kittitas Valley; this photograph was taken by his wife, Mary Mires. Mary (Rowland) Mires was born in Oregon in 1862 and came to Kittitas County with her family in 1874. Mary and Austin married in 1884 and raised their children at the family home on Ruby Street in Ellensburg. Mary was only an amateur photographer, but she took many historical photographs of people and places around Kittitas County, and today, her photo collection is a valuable resource for early Kittitas County history. Austin Mires came to Ellensburg in 1883, opened a law practice, and became very active in Ellensburg and Kittitas County development. Austin was the first mayor of Ellensburg, a member of the Washington Constitutional Convention, and a Superior Court judge in 1928. (EPL.)

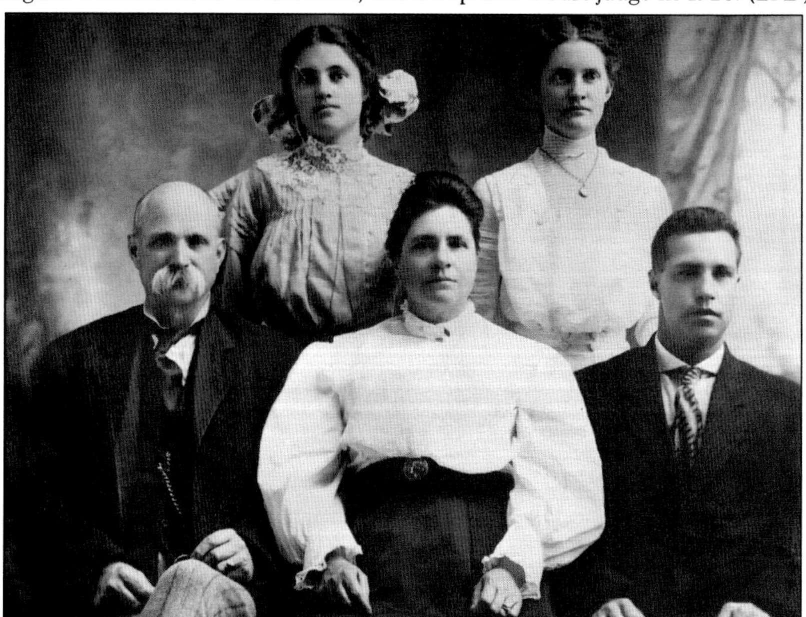

Nancy and Old Toby walk along Ruby Street in Ellensburg in the early 1900s. Toby aided the early white settlers in the Kittitas Valley, especially when problems arose between the settlers and the Native Americans in the area. Nancy was from the Yakama Nation and married Toby, a Coastal Indian, and they lived in Ellensburg. Toby was blind, and Nancy helped him get around town using a rope that he held. (EPL.)

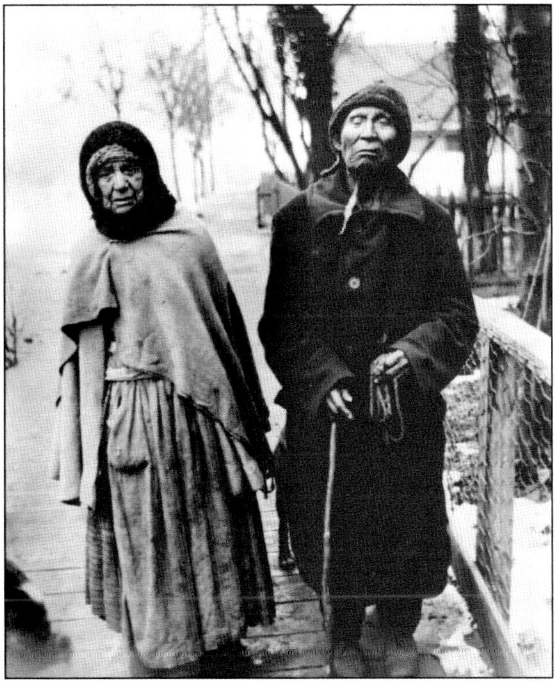

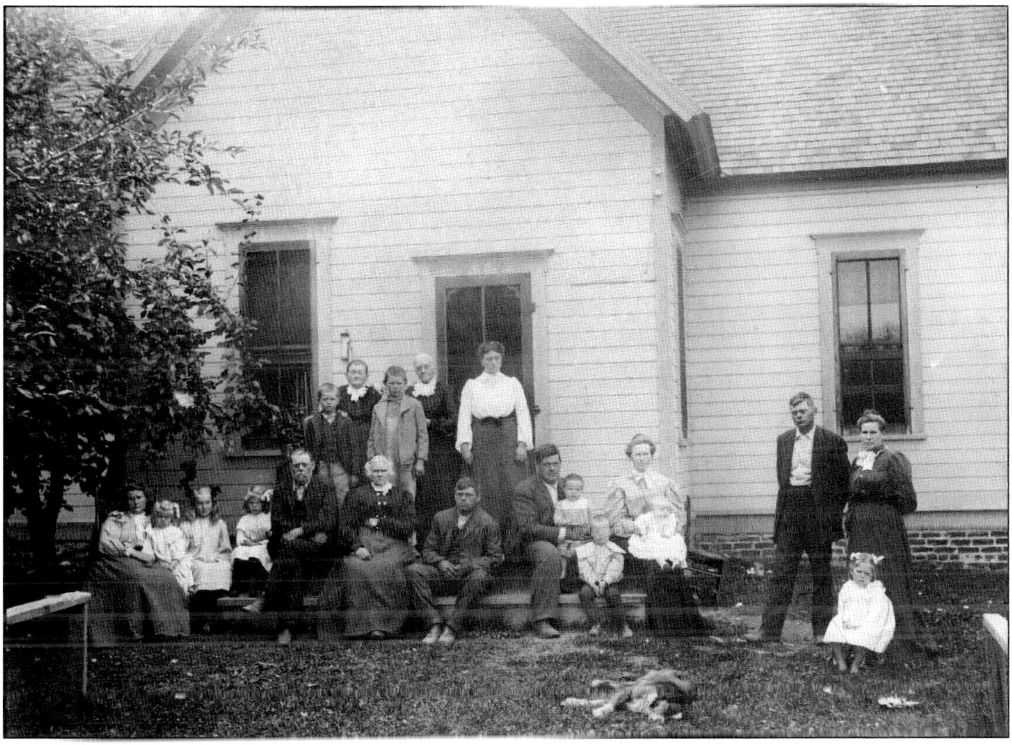

S.R. Geddis, born in Pennsylvania in 1838, came west on the Oregon Trail in 1846. His family came to Kittitas County in 1869 and homesteaded near Ellensburg. His farm grew to over 800 acres, and with the irrigation in the valley, he grew very prosperous. Geddis constructed the Geddis Block as well as the S.R. Geddis building, both still standing today in Ellensburg. (KCHM.)

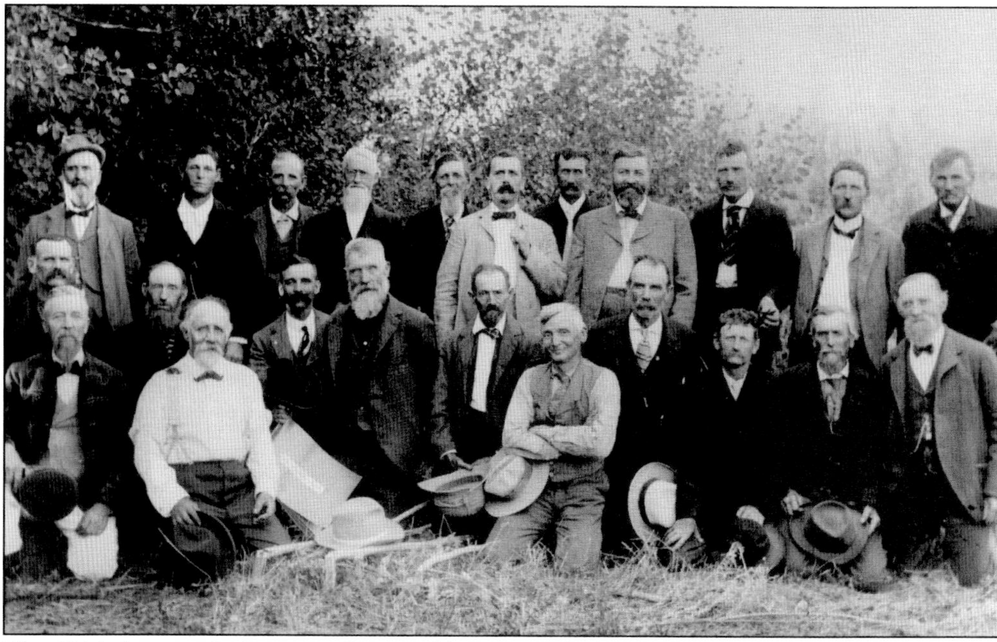

This 1904 photograph shows a gathering old-timers and pioneers in Ellensburg that consisted of 23 men who came to the Kittitas Valley in its early days and were respected members of the county. While there are too many to name here, Tillman Houser (first row, far right) came to the valley from Renton in 1868; his was the first white family to reside in Kittitas County. (EPL.)

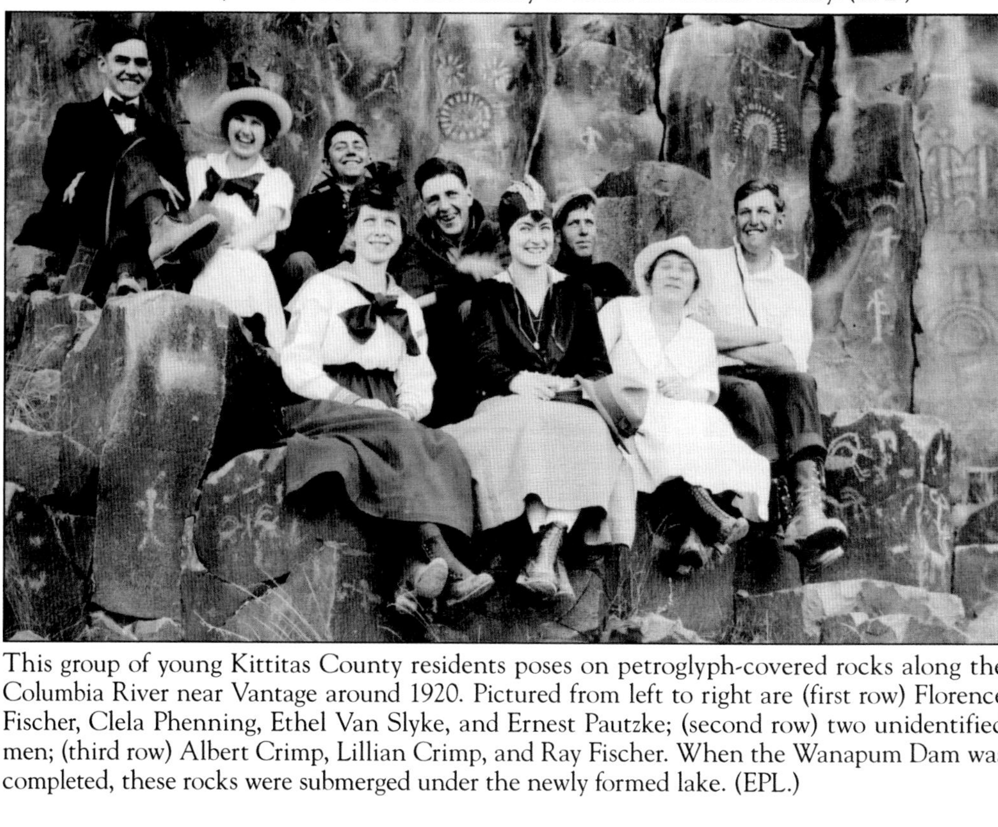

This group of young Kittitas County residents poses on petroglyph-covered rocks along the Columbia River near Vantage around 1920. Pictured from left to right are (first row) Florence Fischer, Clela Phenning, Ethel Van Slyke, and Ernest Pautzke; (second row) two unidentified men; (third row) Albert Crimp, Lillian Crimp, and Ray Fischer. When the Wanapum Dam was completed, these rocks were submerged under the newly formed lake. (EPL.)

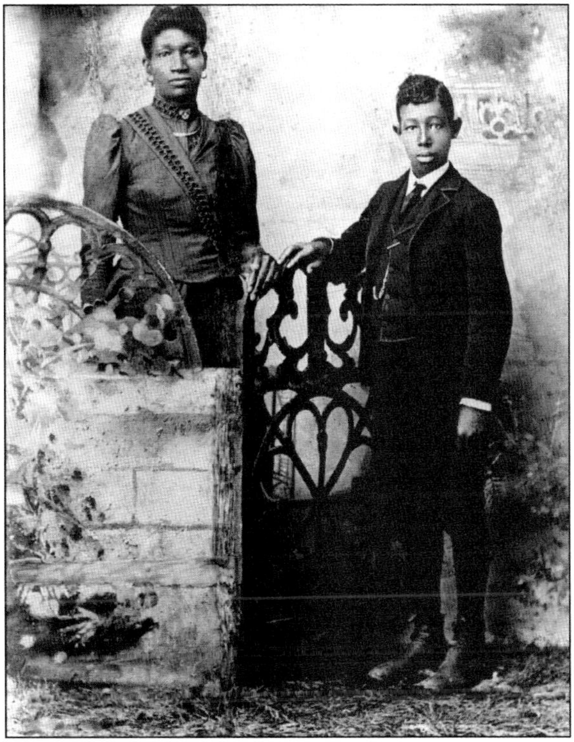

Pictured here are Lucy Breckenridge and her son John in Roslyn in 1889. Lucy, born into Slavery in Virginia in 1855, gained her freedom after the Civil War and moved with her husband Henry and their son to Roslyn in 1888. They came to Roslyn because Henry was brought in to work the mines during a strike by the white miners. After the strike ended, the family remained in Roslyn until 1898, when they moved to Spokane. (RM.)

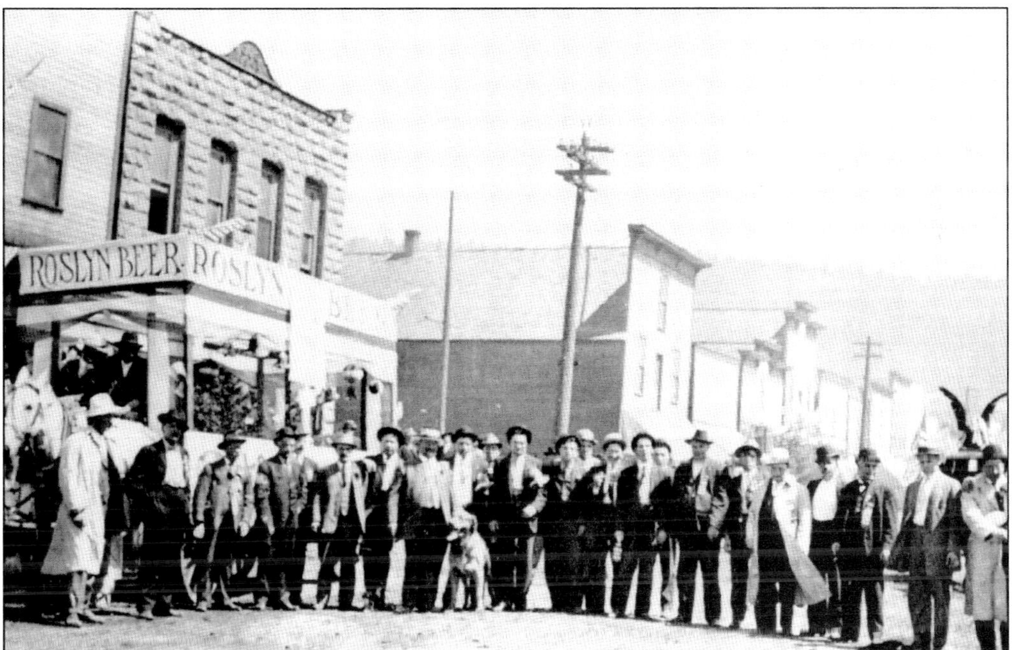

A group gathers on the street next to a wagon converted into a Roslyn Beer parade float. The stone building behind them now houses the Roslyn Café, which was a meat market and butcher shop at the time. Many of these buildings still stand today, and Roslyn Brewery still makes beer not far from where the photographer is standing. (EPL.)

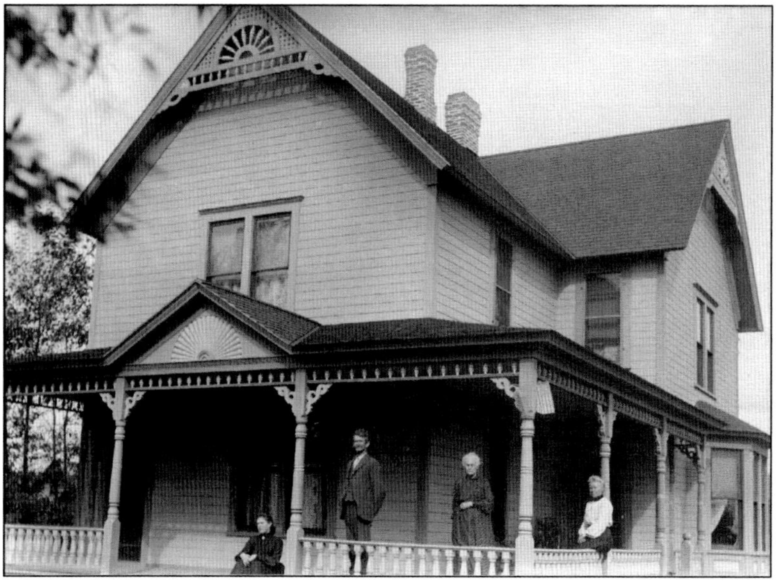

James L. Mills came to the county in 1878 from the Puget Sound area and settled near present-day Thorp; he later built this house. In 1879, he diverted water from the Yakima River and used it to power his sawmill. The water was also used to power the Thorp gristmill and feed a pond used to cut ice blocks in the winter. (KCHM.)

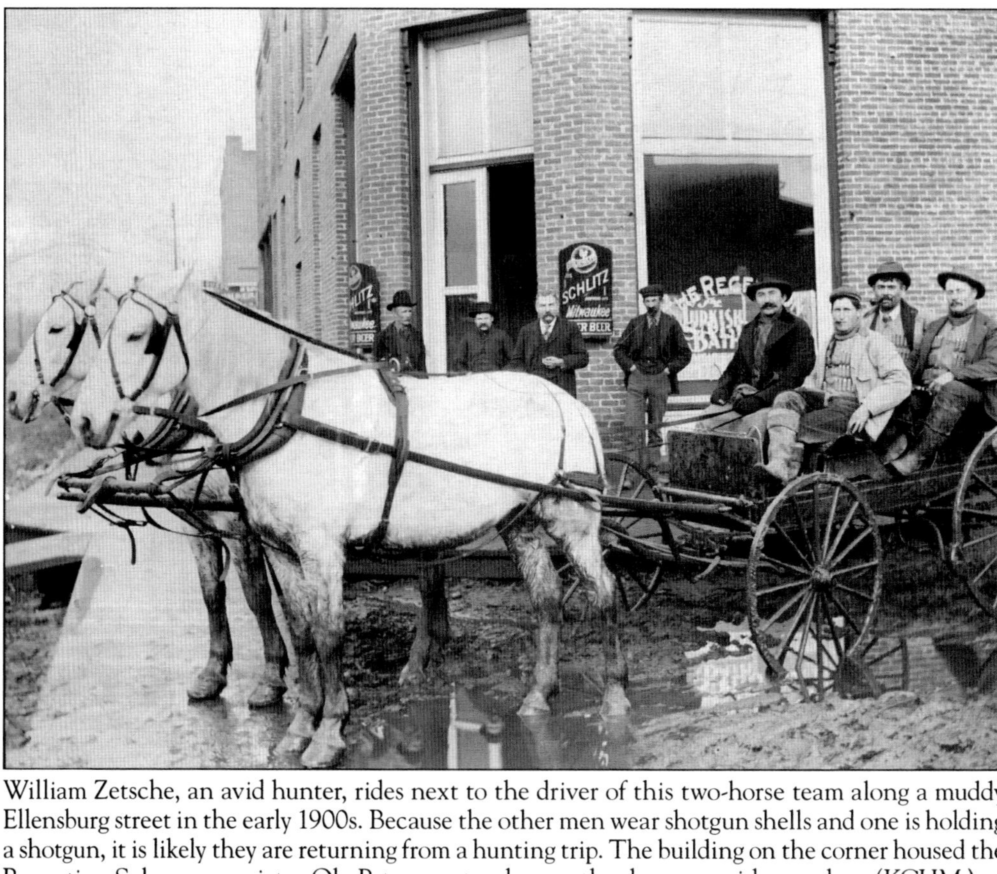

William Zetsche, an avid hunter, rides next to the driver of this two-horse team along a muddy Ellensburg street in the early 1900s. Because the other men wear shotgun shells and one is holding a shotgun, it is likely they are returning from a hunting trip. The building on the corner housed the Reception Saloon; proprietor Ole Peterson stands near the doorway without a hat. (KCHM.)

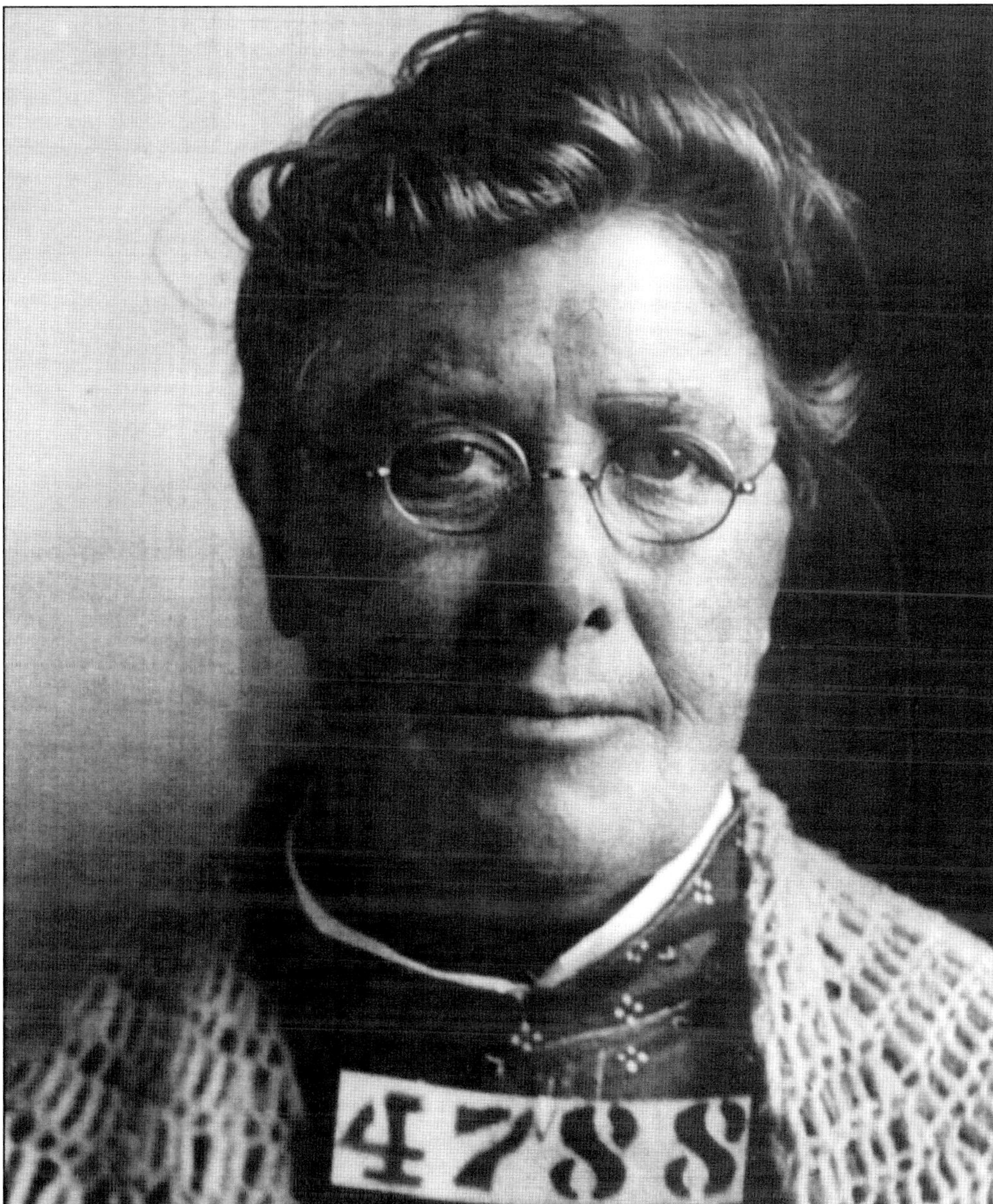

Mamie Norris lived with her husband, James, on Sprague Street in Ellensburg, renting out rooms to young men. Always known to be a little "off," most likely due to a horse kicking her in the head when she was nine, Mamie became infatuated with one tenant, Tom Murray, and became possessive of him. Oftentimes, she would claim that Tom was her son and could not be told otherwise. Whenever Tom would leave, she would pace around and wait for him to return. Tom went to high school at the public school building, which Mamie could see through the spyglass she kept by an upstairs window, and she would always watch to see whom he was talking to. After Tom told her he was moving to Yakima, Mamie said she would rather kill him than let him leave. On January 18, 1908, the day before he was to leave, she entered his room and shot him in his sleep, then tried to kill herself. She was convicted of the murder and sent to an insane asylum at Medical Lake, of which she escaped and was never seen again. (EPL.)

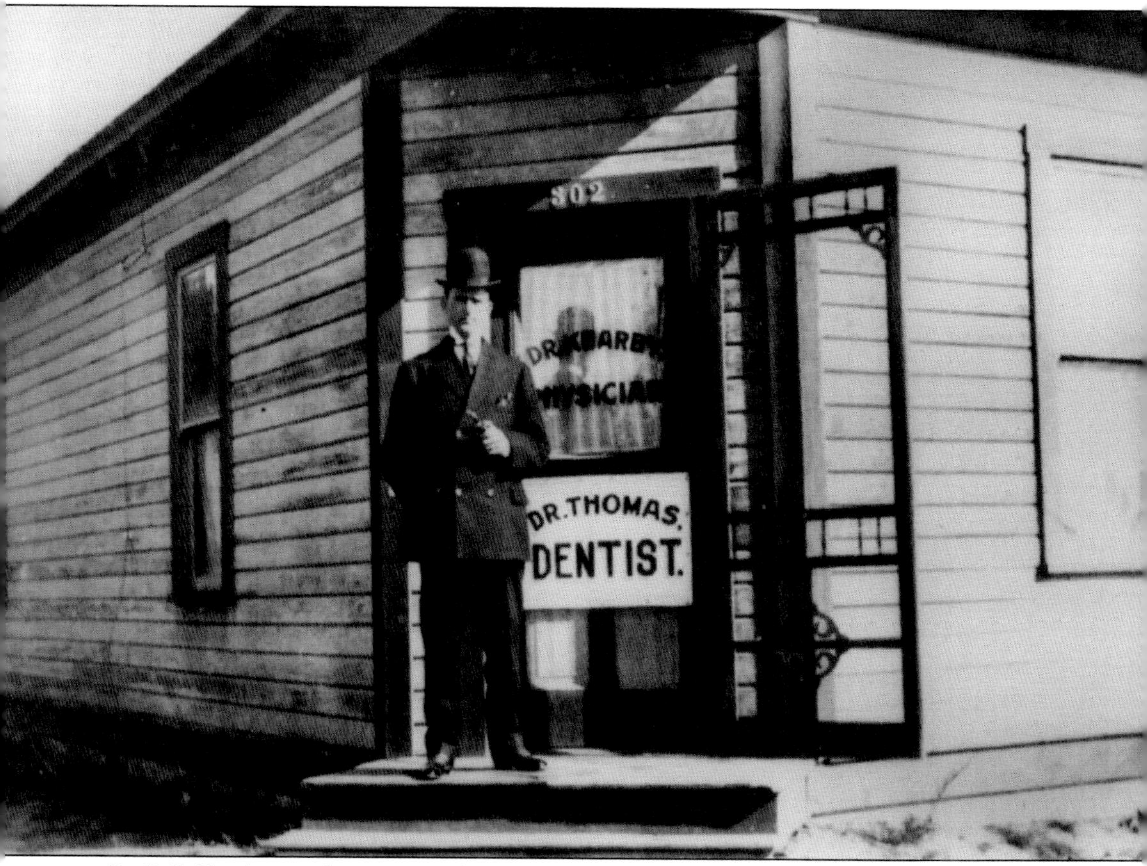

Dr. D.O. Kearby was the contract physician for the workers during the construction of the Chicago, Milwaukee & St. Paul Railroad through South Cle Elum. He also shared this medical and dental office with a dentist in Cle Elum in 1906. Kearby was on duty in 1907 when five men were killed and four injured while working on a tunnel for the railroad. (EPL.)

Three

BUSINESSES

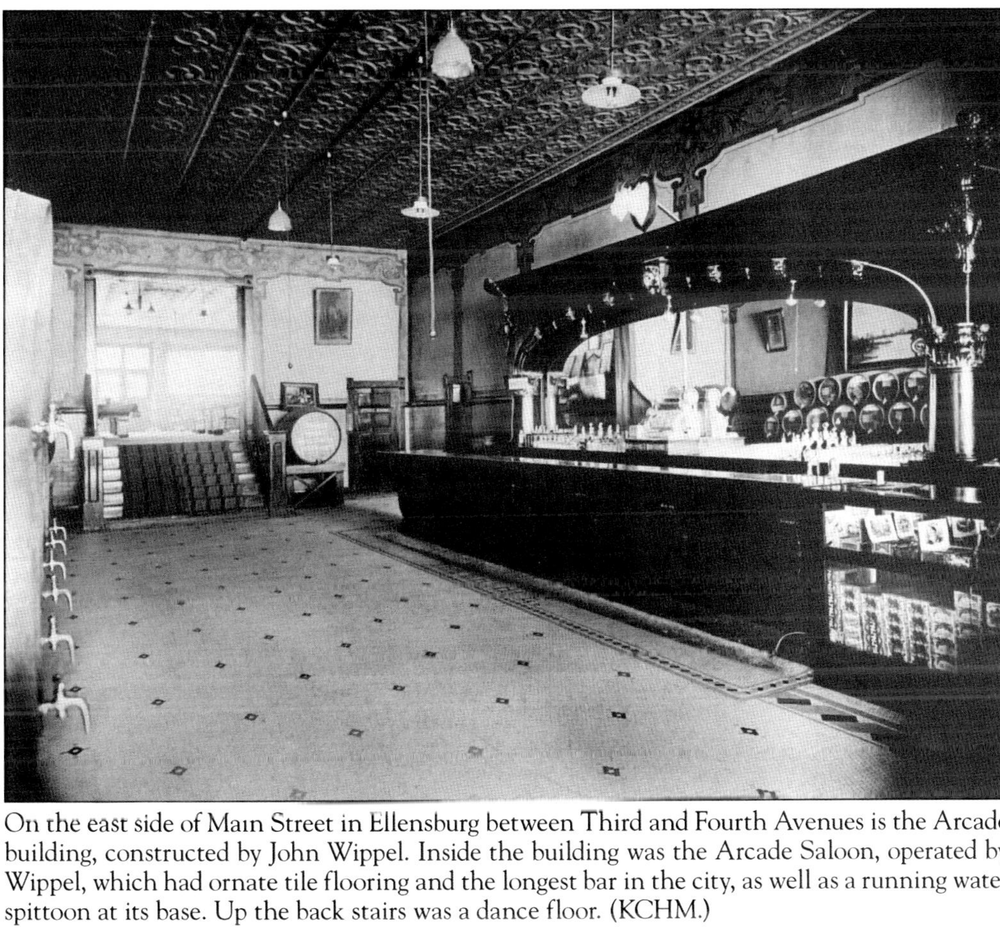

On the east side of Main Street in Ellensburg between Third and Fourth Avenues is the Arcade building, constructed by John Wippel. Inside the building was the Arcade Saloon, operated by Wippel, which had ornate tile flooring and the longest bar in the city, as well as a running water spittoon at its base. Up the back stairs was a dance floor. (KCHM.)

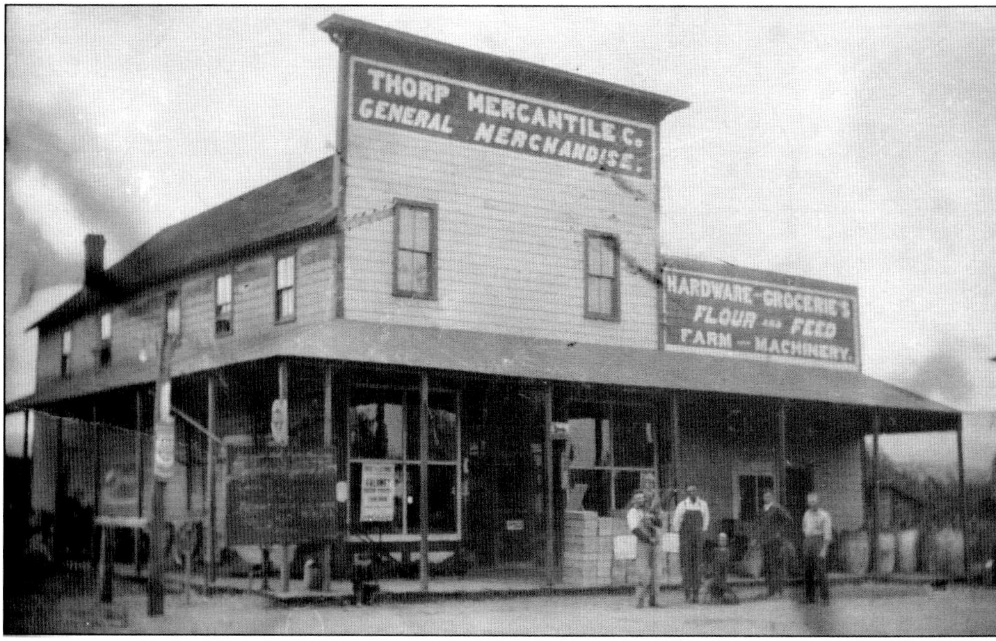

The Thorp Mercantile Company store in Thorp was owned by W.J. and K.E. McDonald in 1915. The store, which carried hardware, groceries, feed, merchandise, and more, was a conveniently located for residents of Thorp and the surrounding areas. In a 1915 business advertisement, the Thorp Mercantile Company boasted that it carried a full line of John Deere Machinery. (KCHM.)

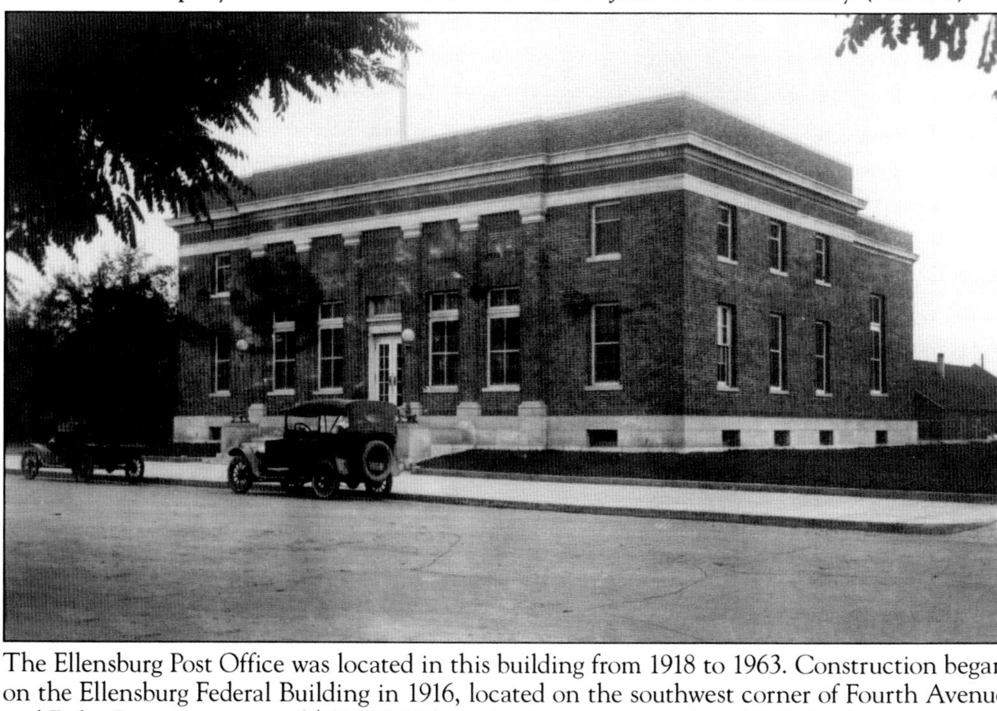

The Ellensburg Post Office was located in this building from 1918 to 1963. Construction began on the Ellensburg Federal Building in 1916, located on the southwest corner of Fourth Avenue and Ruby Street, at a cost of $53,915. When this location opened in 1918, the first postmaster was Robert A. Turner. The post office remained in this building until 1963, when the present-day post office opened. (EPL.)

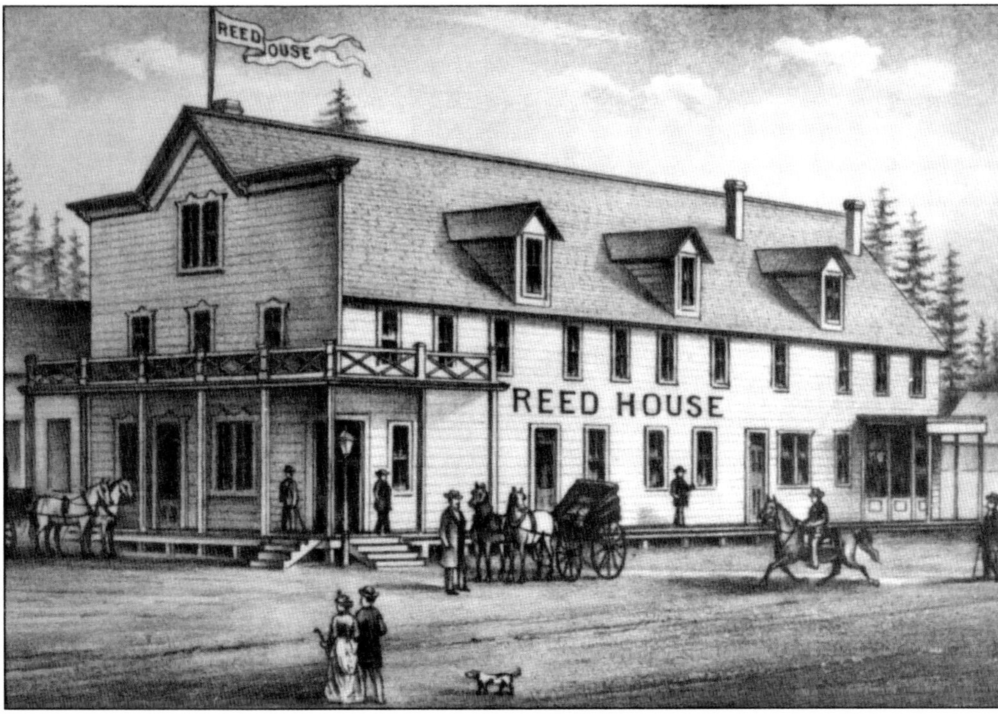

The Reed House Hotel, located on the northeast corner of Railroad and Pennsylvania Avenues in Cle Elum, was the first hotel in the area. When the Northern Pacific Railroad arrived in Cle Elum in 1886, Reed began construction of a hotel near the depot. Opened in 1887, it was the closest hotel to the train depot and offered rooms and meals for the weary rail travelers. (EPL.)

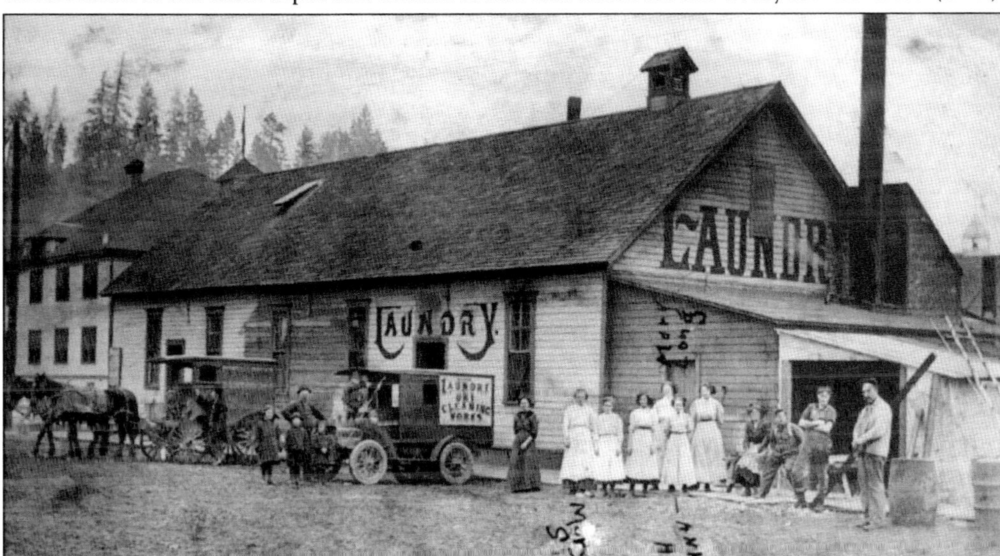

The Home Steam Laundry in Cle Elum, pictured around 1909, was located north of First Street on the east side of Harris Avenue. Since home washing was mainly done by hand, there was a big need for steam laundries that could wash sheets, drapes, and clothing, particularly miners' grimy clothes. The proprietor was Cornelius S. Enright, and three of the women identified here are Mary Sitko, Ann McKerman, and Mary Long. (EPL.)

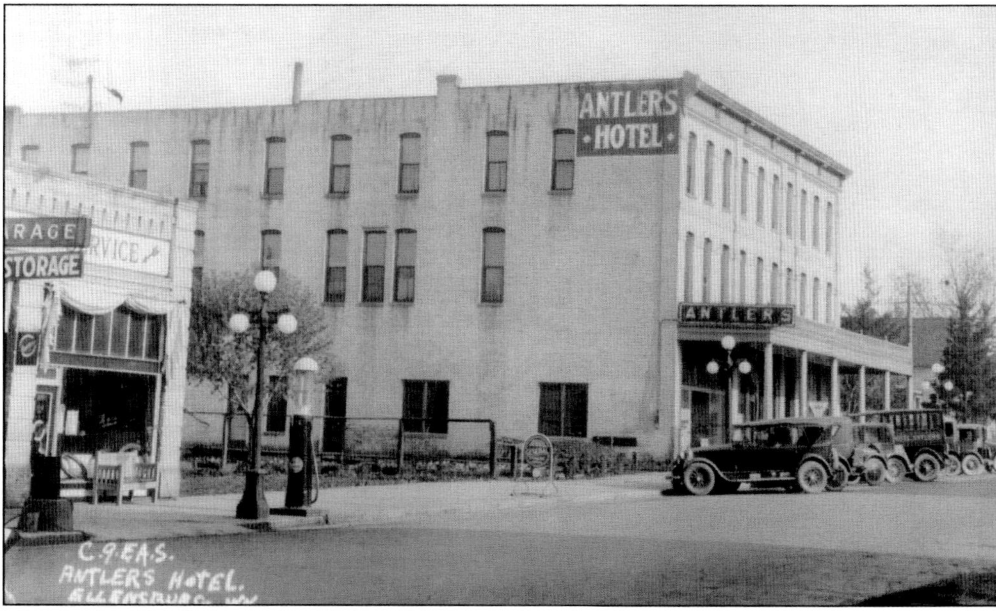

The Antlers Hotel, situated on the southwest corner of Sixth Avenue and Pearl Street, served the town of Ellensburg for many years. Originally opened as the Hotel Horton in 1890, the Antlers remained a prominent Ellensburg hotel until 1967, when a fire destroyed the building. On the left is Reynolds Garage, once operated by Alfred Reynolds, which is currently a Sears. (EPL.)

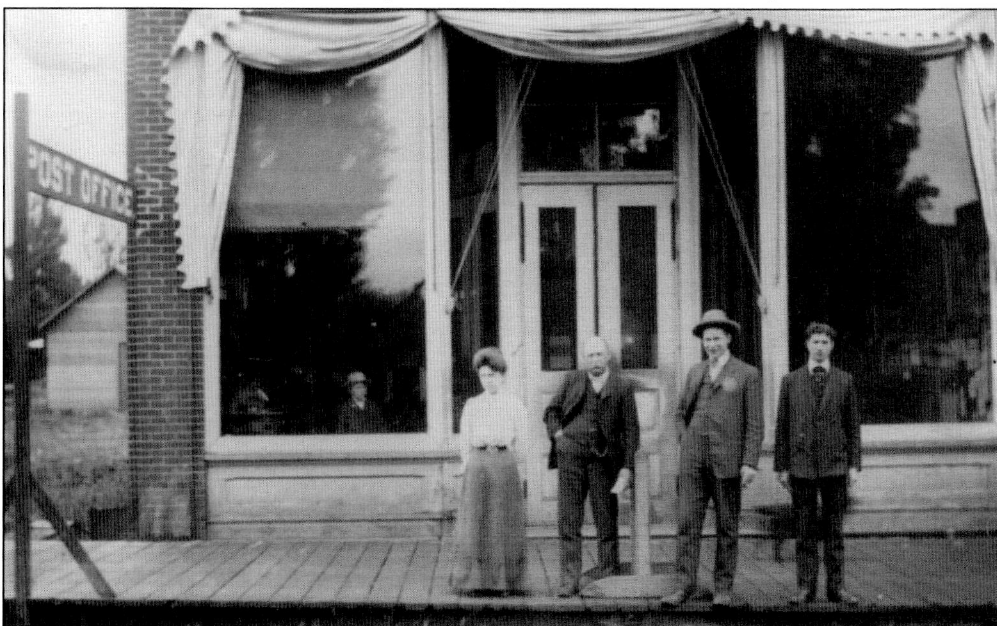

From 1902 to 1906, the Ellensburg Post Office was located in the Honolulu Building. Constructed by the McCandless brothers, the building was on the northeast corner of Fifth Avenue and Pearl Street. The physical address of this office was 506 North Pearl Street, which is now the location of a bank drive-through. Pictured from left to right are an unidentified boy in window, Hinman's daughter Elaine, postmaster Oliver Hinman, assistant postmaster Thompson, and an unidentified man. (EPL.)

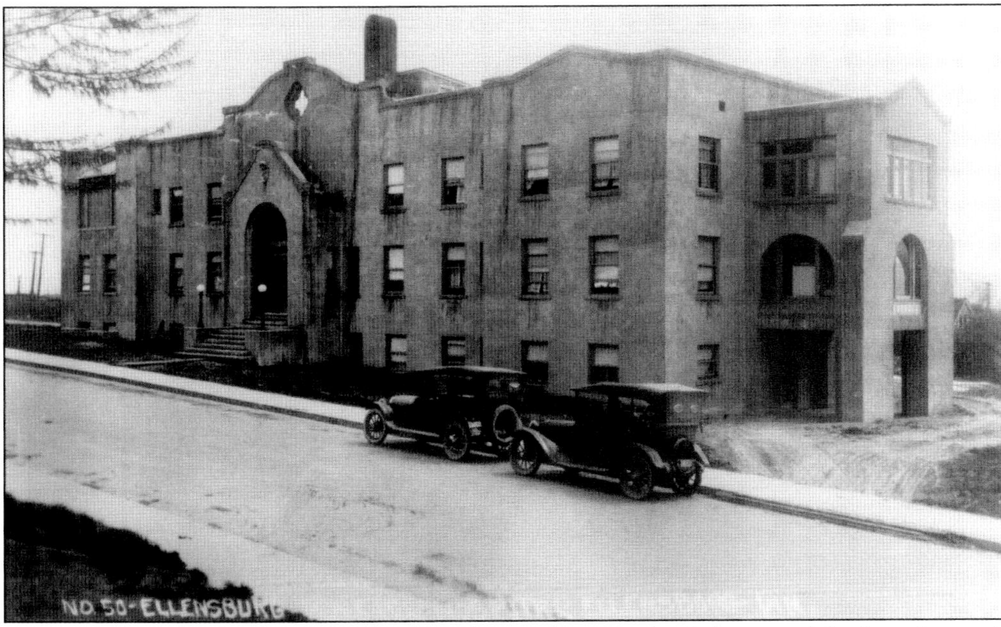

Built in 1918, the Ellensburg General Hospital opened in 1920, lauded as one of the finest hospitals in the Northwest. It boasted 21 patient rooms, two recovery sunrooms with large windows and views, rooms with private bathrooms, an elevator, a service kitchen, nurse's stations, a delivery room, an operating room with a skylight, and more. It closed as a hospital in 1964 when the newly built Kittitas County Memorial Hospital opened. (EPL.)

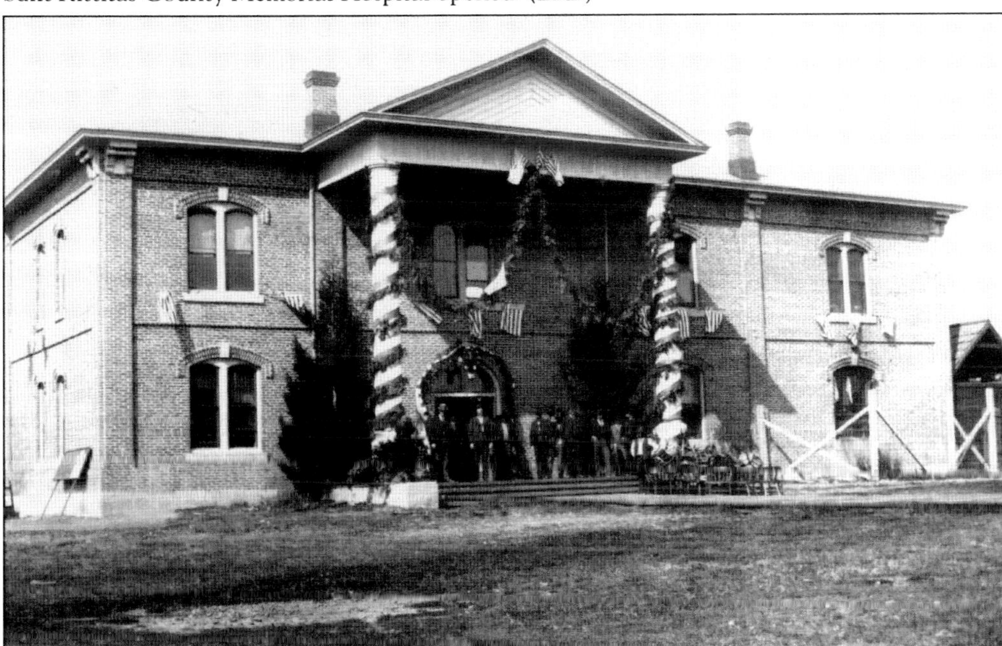

The Kittitas County Courthouse was completed in 1886 on the city block between Main and Water Streets and Fifth and Sixth Avenues. Here, it is decorated with American flags and garlands, possibly for the Fourth of July. This large brick building served the county for many years and was finally replaced with a modern courthouse on the same location in 1955. (EPL.)

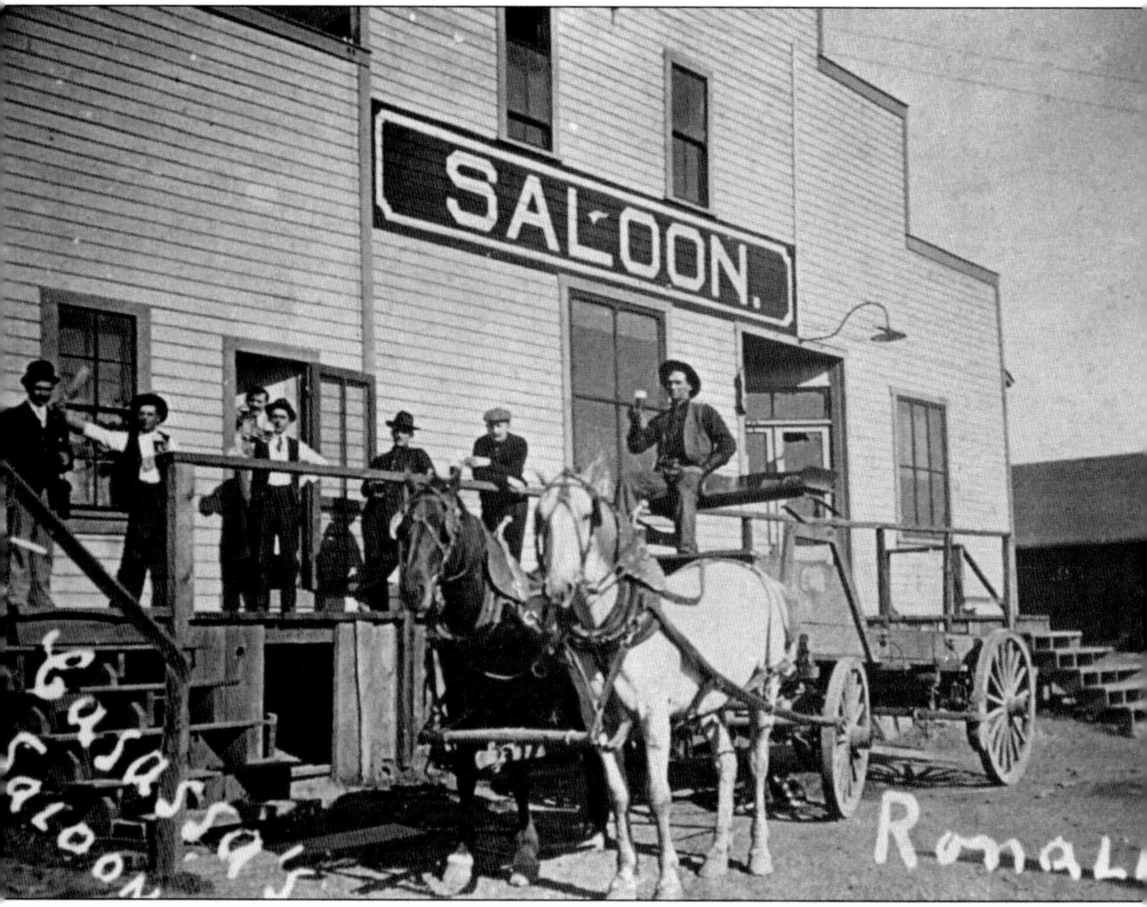

Peter Casassa was owner and operator of Casassa's Saloon, located in Ronald. Casassa was born in Casollo near Lenzo, Italy, in 1871. At 18, he left Italy to go to Coal City, Illinois, to work the coal mines there. From Illinois, he went to Colorado, then finally came to Roslyn in 1892 to work the mines. In 1901, Casassa married Louisa Avenatti, another Italian immigrant, in Roslyn. When the 1892 mine explosion occurred in Roslyn, Casassa became frightened and quit the mines, going into the saloon business with John Pistono in Ronald. He then bought half interest in the Ronald Saloon. Casassa operated both saloons until Prohibition came along, then sold out and opened a hardware and secondhand store in Roslyn. In 1932, when Prohibition ended, Casassa became one of first distributors of Rainier Beer. Casassa continued working in the wholesale beer business until his death in 1937. Louisa Casassa had passed away several years before in 1928. (EPL.)

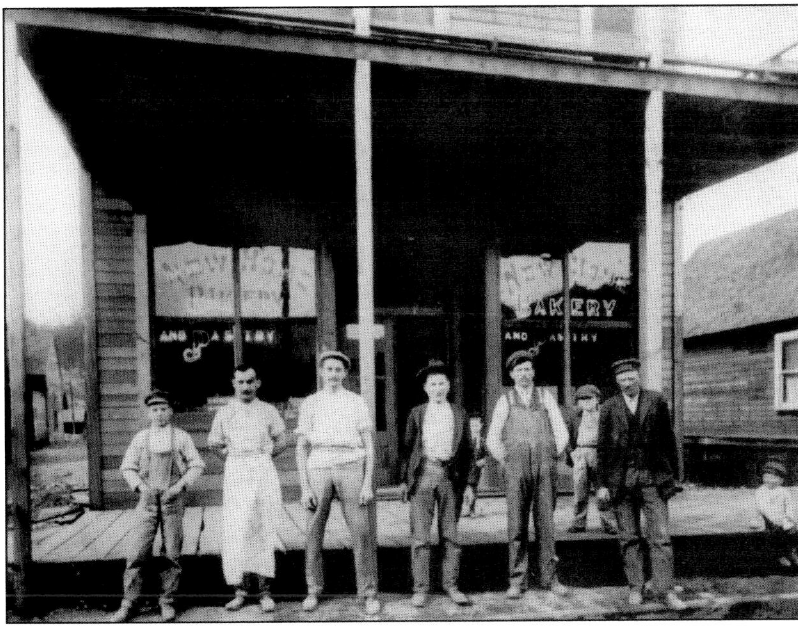

Some men and young boys stand in front of the New Home Bakery and Pastry in Roslyn around 1910. For those who did not have the time or resources to bake fresh items at home, they often relied on local bakeries like this one. This bakery was run by immigrants who had come to Roslyn. (EPL.)

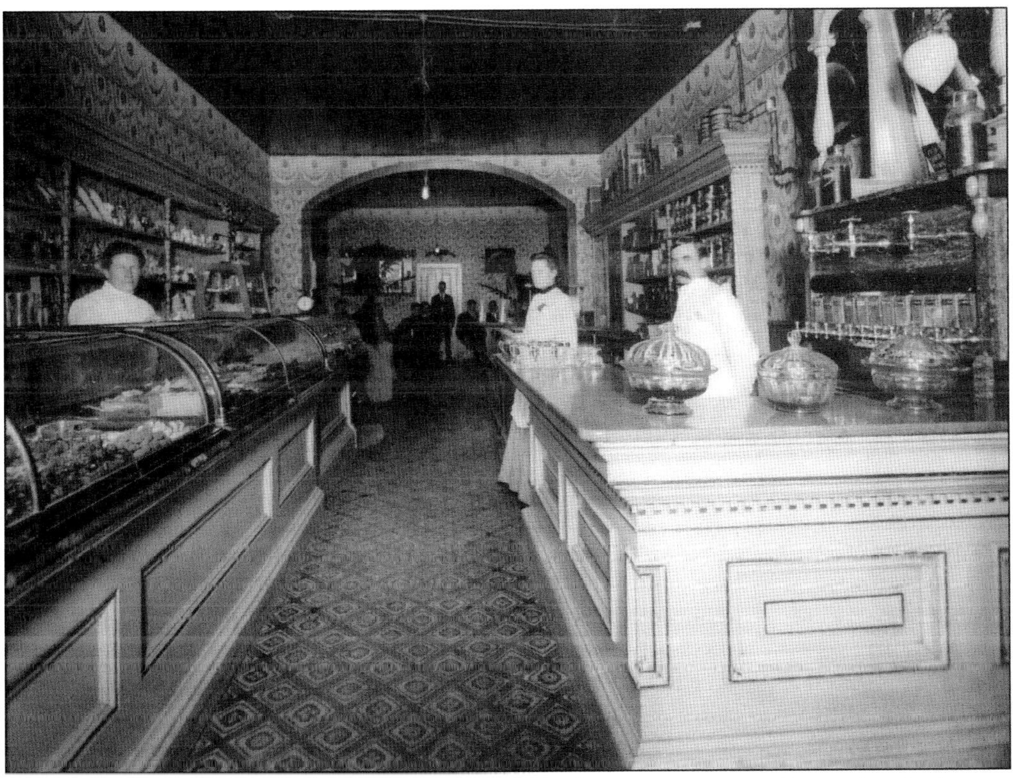

Robert Maxwell, owner of Maxwell's candy and confectionery store on Pennsylvania Avenue in Roslyn, waits for customers with his employees in 1909. Maxwell lived in Roslyn as early as 1904, but he did not open his store until after 1907. The location offered candies, cookies, and beverages and had seating in the back of the store. (EPL.)

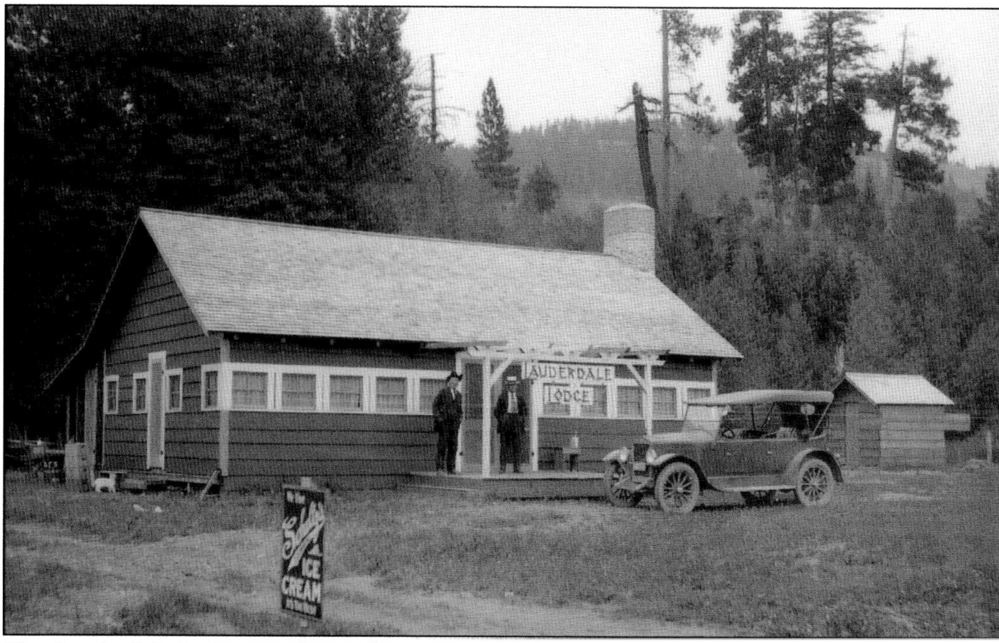

The Lauderdale Lodge was located in an area called Virden at the junction of Highways 970 and 97 between Ellensburg and Cle Elum along the Swauk Creek. Initially established as an old mining road, Highway 97 is the main thoroughfare over Blewett Pass between Kittitas County and Chelan County in the north. People traveling along Highway 97 passed by this lodge, which no longer stands. (EPL.)

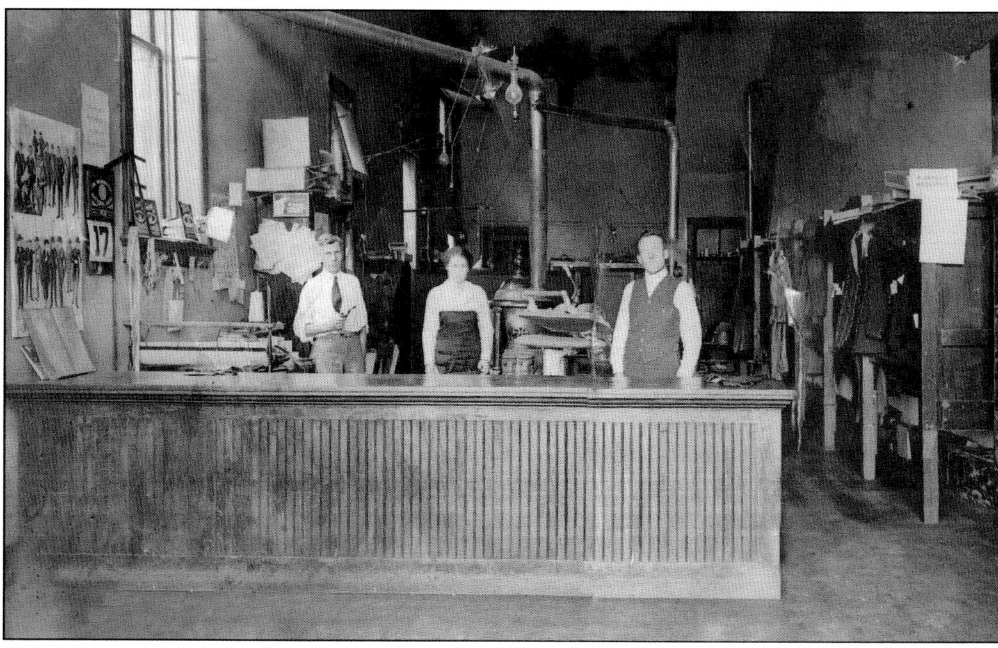

Tailors Horgen and Henderson were located in Ellensburg at 109 West Third Avenue in 1920. Edward C. Horgen (right), who lived four blocks away at 501 East Third Avenue, was the tailor and proprietor. E. Eugene Henderson (left), who lived at 714 East Second Avenue, was his business partner. Clara Correa, their employee, stands in the center. (EPL.)

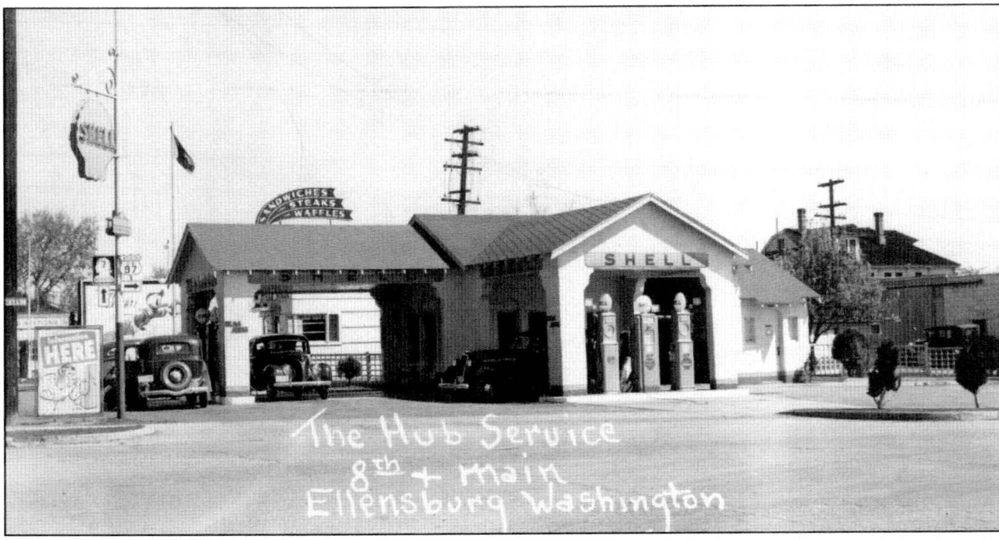

The Hub Service Station, located on the southeast corner of Eighth Avenue (currently University Way) and Main Street in Ellensburg. In 1937, Hubert S. Holmes was the manager. Before the interstate system came through Kittitas County, the main highway running east to west followed Eighth Avenue, passing right in front of this location. The Hub is long gone, but this location still serves as a gas station, currently as a 7-Eleven store. (EPL.)

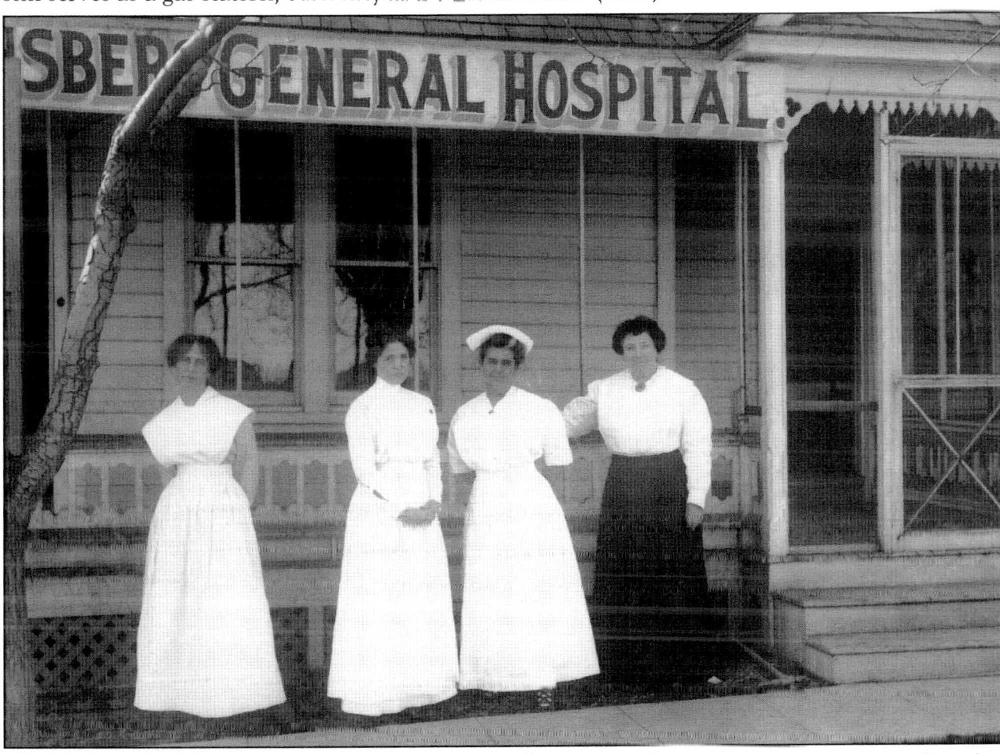

Early Ellensburg hospitals consisted of little more than a modified house and medical staff. Before an official hospital opened in 1918, there is a record of several houses-turned-hospitals around Ellensburg. The one pictured here was believed to have been located neat the intersection of Water Street and Tenth Avenue. (EPL.)

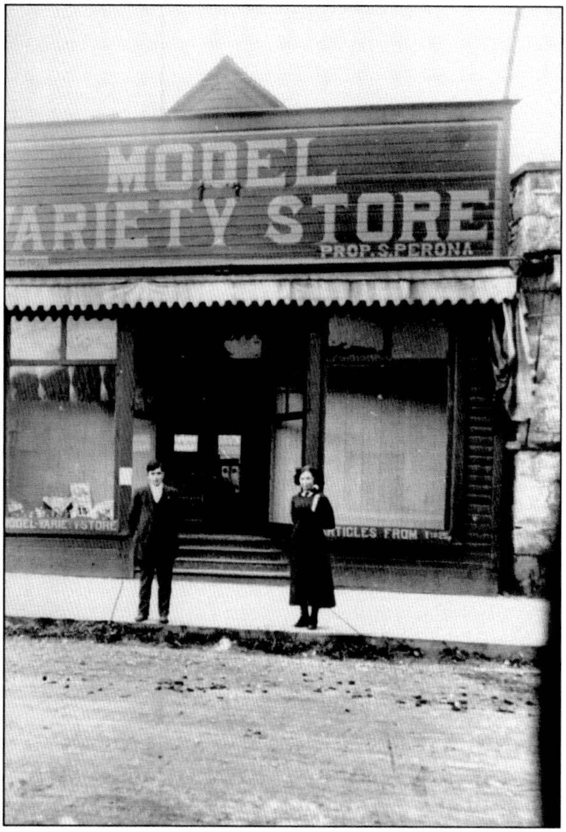

The Model Variety Store in Cle Elum, owned in 1914 by Theodore B. Lambson and his wife, Ella, was located at 119 East First Street. Carrying a little bit of everything, this store sold items that cost 1¢ to 25¢. The fire of 1918 gutted this building, but the brick storefront was saved and still stands today. (EPL.)

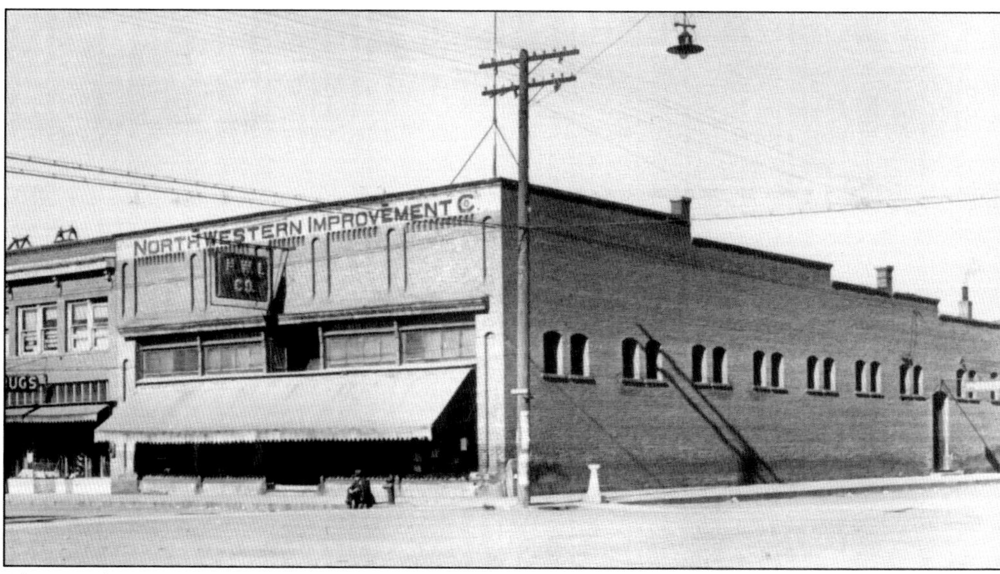

The Northwestern Improvement Company store in Cle Elum was located on the southwest corner of First Street and Pennsylvania Avenue. The company-owned stores, located in Roslyn, Ronald, and Cle Elum, carried many home and clothing items, especially work pants, shirts, and boots for the miners. Today, the Cle Elum store location is an empty lot, and the drugstore next door is now Pioneer Coffee. (EPL.)

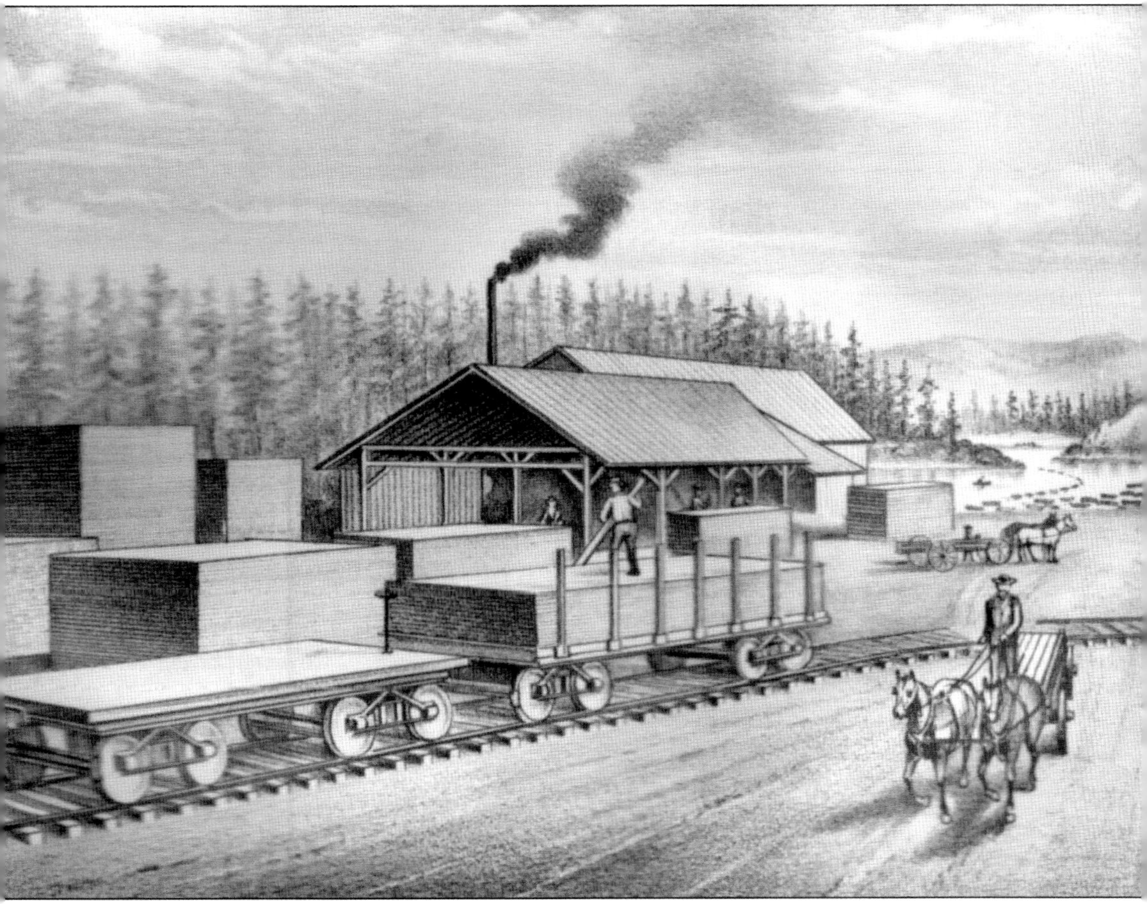

Pictured here is Thomas Johnson's sawmill near Cle Elum as it looked around 1889. Johnson operated a ferry, farmed, raised cattle, and started the town of Goldendale, Washington—all before coming to Kittitas County. Johnson came to Ellensburg in the early 1880s, opened a sawmill and a mercantile, and began the Johnson House Hotel. Not long after, he opened a sawmill at Sunday Creek and the one seen here in Cle Elum. Johnson moved to Cle Elum by 1890 and oversaw this Cle Elum mill, which could produce 60,000 board feet of lumber per day. Logs arrived at the mill via the Yakima River and were cut in the steam-powered mill, which also got its water from the river. Johnson sold much of his lumber to the railroad for trusses, as well as cribbing and support in the Stampede Pass tunnel. (EPL.)

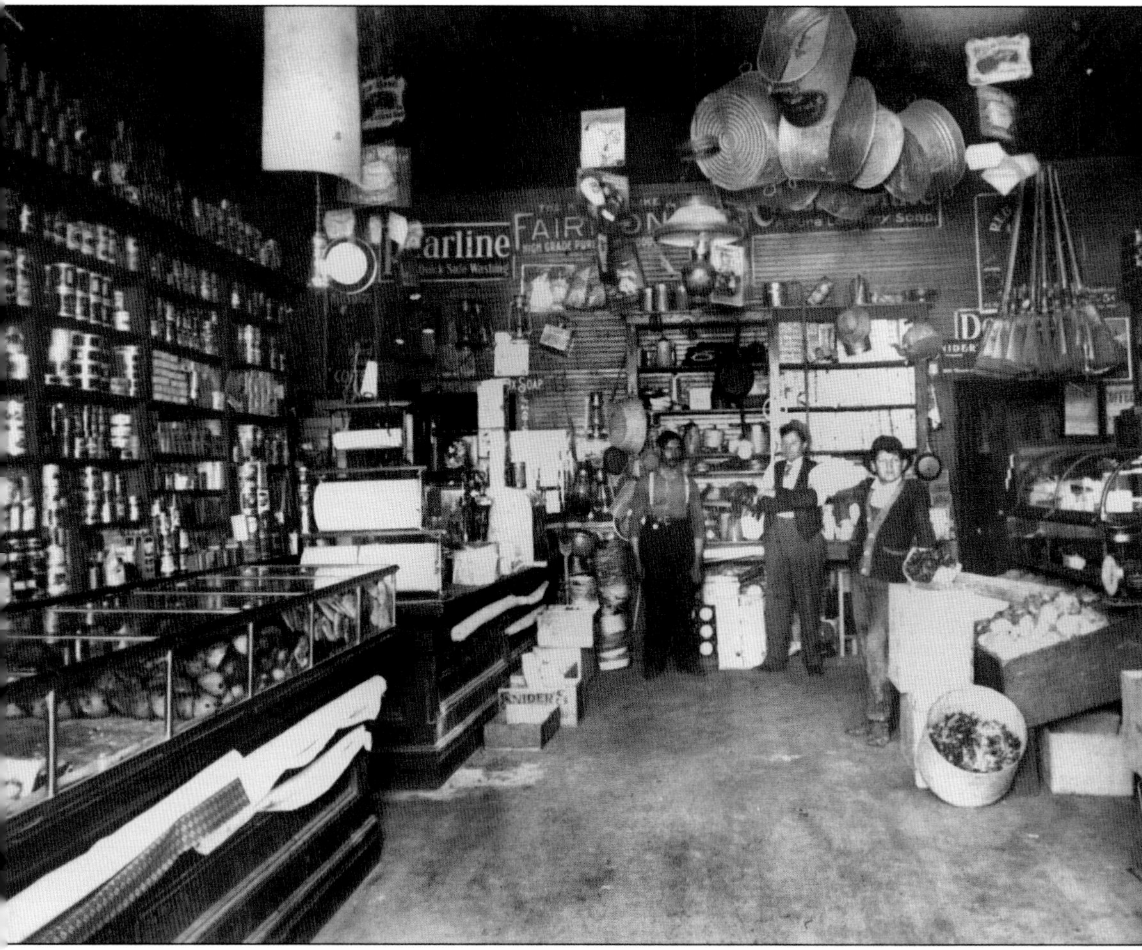

The interior of the Hazelwood Grocery and Bakery store in Cle Elum is pictured here. The store was run by Joe Schober, who came to the United States from Austria in 1890. He mined coal in Alabama for nine years, where he learned much about American society and learned the English language. After a few other ventures, Schober came to Cle Elum between 1904 and 1907, where he formed a partnership with John Giacomine, operating a grocery and bakery firm. The Hazelwood Bakery turned out over 400 loaves of bread daily, as well as many other baked goods, and delivered them via wagon to surrounding houses. In this picture, groceries line the shelves, and some of the baked goods produced by the store are on display in the glass case on the left. This store was located at 428 East First Street. (EPL.)

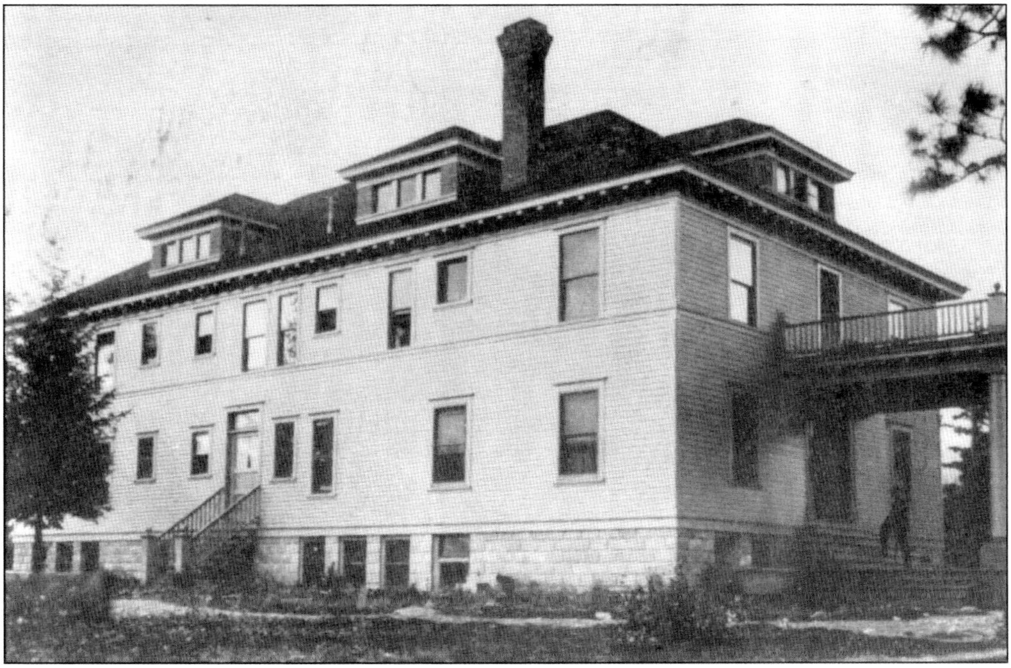

This impressive hospital sat on the hill, once dubbed Hospital Hill, situated to the west of Cle Elum from the early 1900s into the 1970s. The Roslyn-Cle Elum Hospital served many people over the years, but with a declining population in the area, along with a more modern hospital in Ellensburg, it was no longer needed. (EPL.)

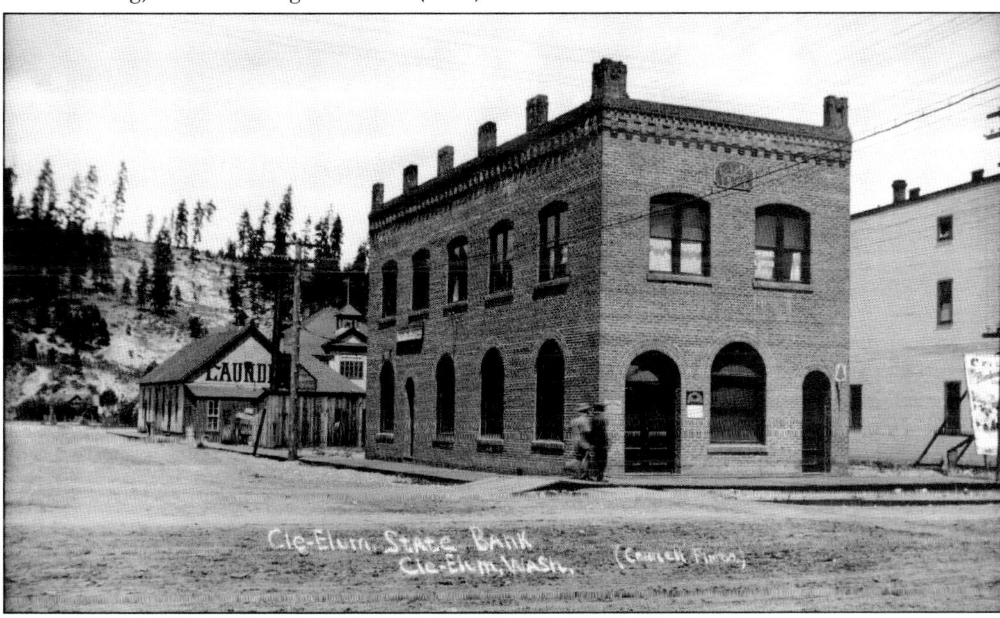

The Cle Elum State Bank was built in 1906 on the northeast corner of First Street and Harris Avenue. In 1918, a large fire broke out in Cle Elum, burning most of the downtown district and displacing many businesses and residents. The bank burned in the fire, but being made of brick, it was mostly intact and rebuilt afterwards. It still stands today and houses a bank on the first floor. (EPL.)

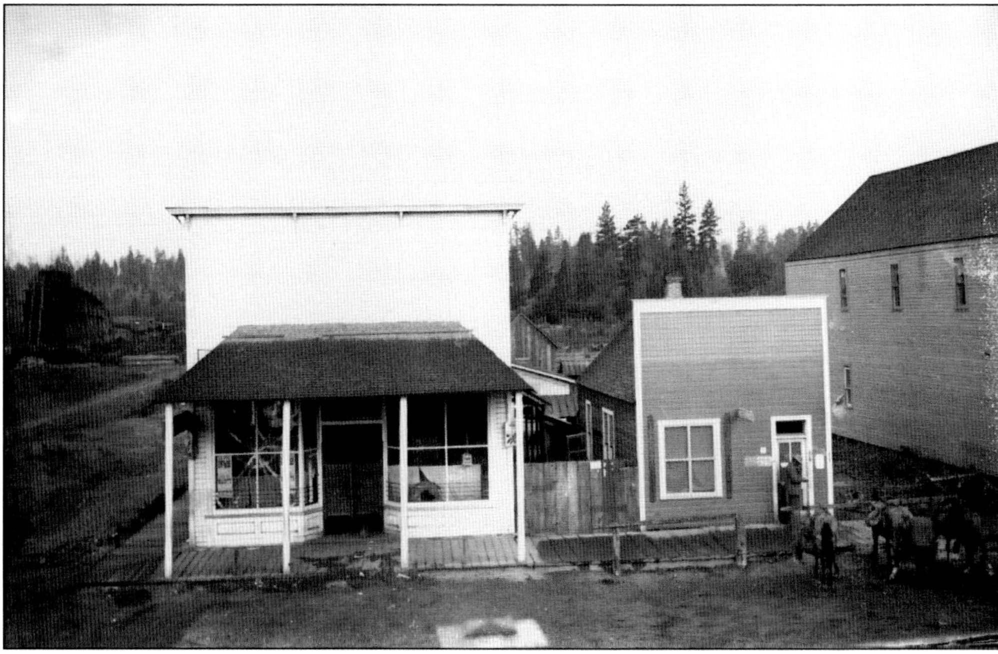

This early view of the west side of Pennsylvania Avenue in Cle Elum was taken from the second-floor balcony of the Reed House Hotel. The building on the left is a saloon, and the smaller one on the right was the post office, which also sold cigarettes, tobacco, fruits, and candies. On the far left is the coal-loading ramp along the Northern Pacific Railroad. (EPL.)

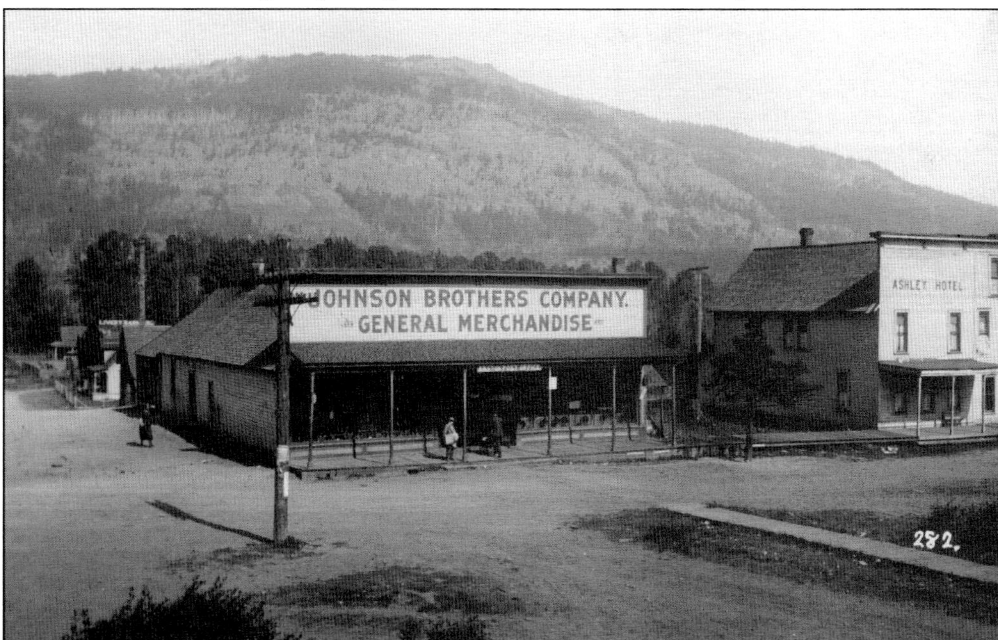

The Johnson Brothers Company, a general merchandise store in Easton, was also the post office and the Ashley Hotel. The Johnson brothers platted Easton in 1902 and named it Easton because it was the first town east of the Cascade divide. One of the brothers, W.W. Johnson, was the Easton postmaster in the 1920s. (CWU.)

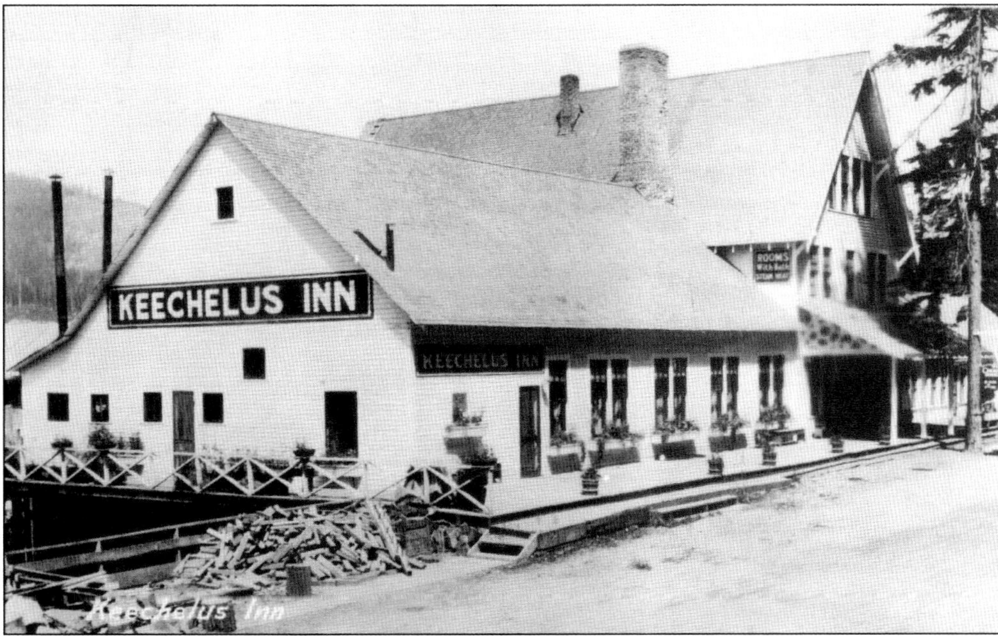

As soon as roads were navigable over Snoqualmie Pass and road traffic began to grow, many people along the route saw a business opportunity. Camping spots and inns opened along the highway, especially between North Bend and Ellensburg. The Keechelus Inn was along the shores of Lake Keechelus and offered rooms with baths, steam heat, and gasoline, as well as a hot meal. (CWU.)

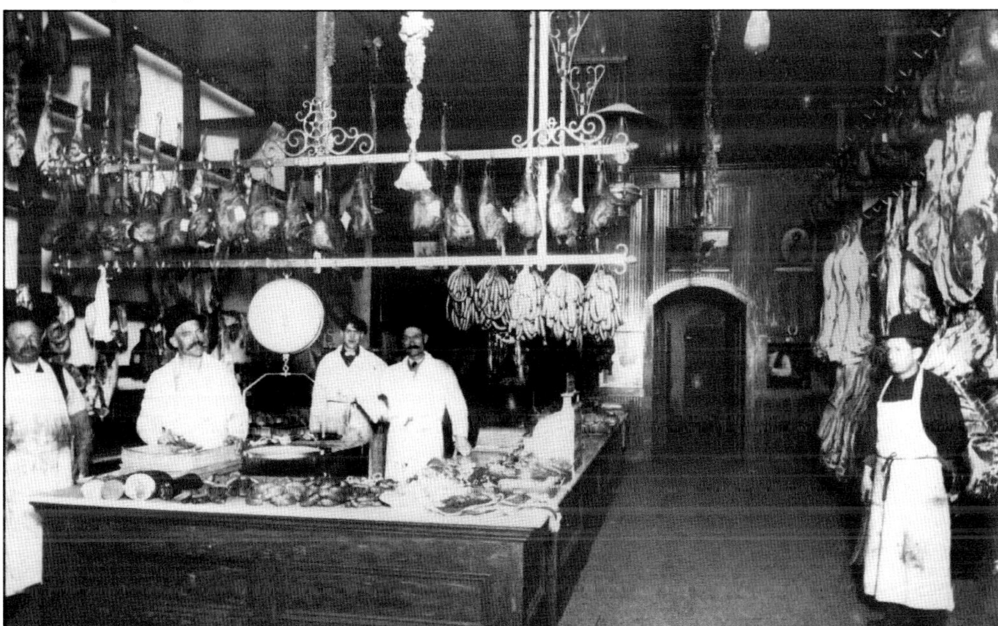

The interior of the Butcher's Market butcher shop on Pennsylvania Avenue in Roslyn is seen here around 1895. Before grocery stores had refrigeration, the main ways to get meat were to harvest it or go to the local butcher. This location changed hands over the years, and in 1978, it became the Roslyn Café, a popular spot in Roslyn to this day. (CWU.)

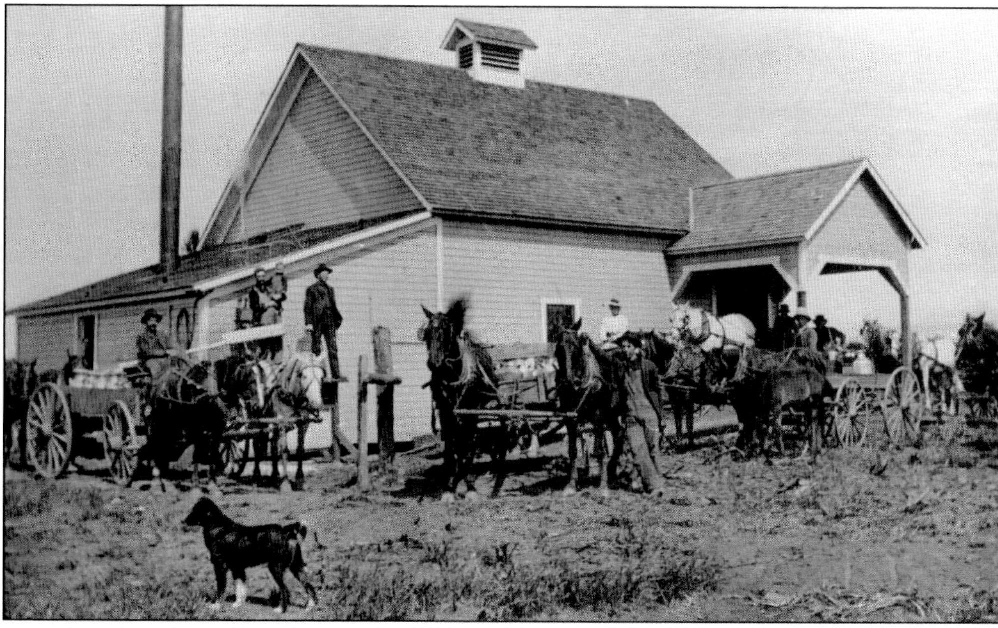

Of all the creameries in Kittitas County, the Alberto Cooperative Creamery Company in Ellensburg was the largest in the early 1900s. The creamery had an office in downtown Ellensburg with Charles Bull as the secretary and manager in 1904. The company supplied feed to farmers. It would collect the milk into cans like the ones in these wagons and process it into cheese or butter. (EPL.)

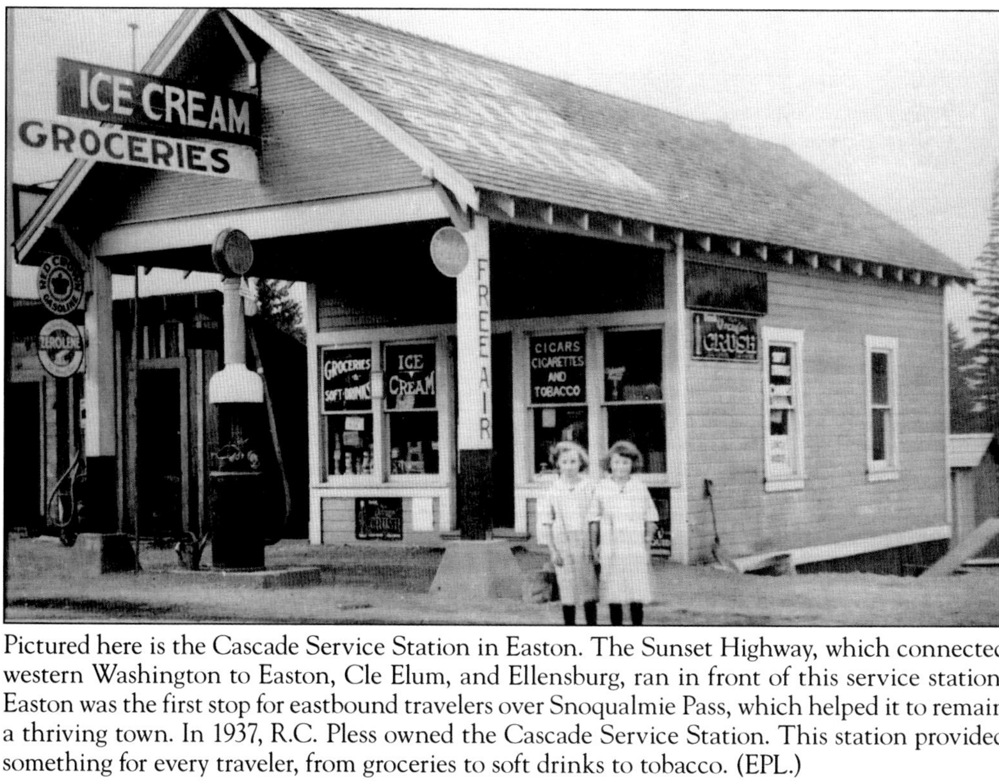

Pictured here is the Cascade Service Station in Easton. The Sunset Highway, which connected western Washington to Easton, Cle Elum, and Ellensburg, ran in front of this service station. Easton was the first stop for eastbound travelers over Snoqualmie Pass, which helped it to remain a thriving town. In 1937, R.C. Pless owned the Cascade Service Station. This station provided something for every traveler, from groceries to soft drinks to tobacco. (EPL.)

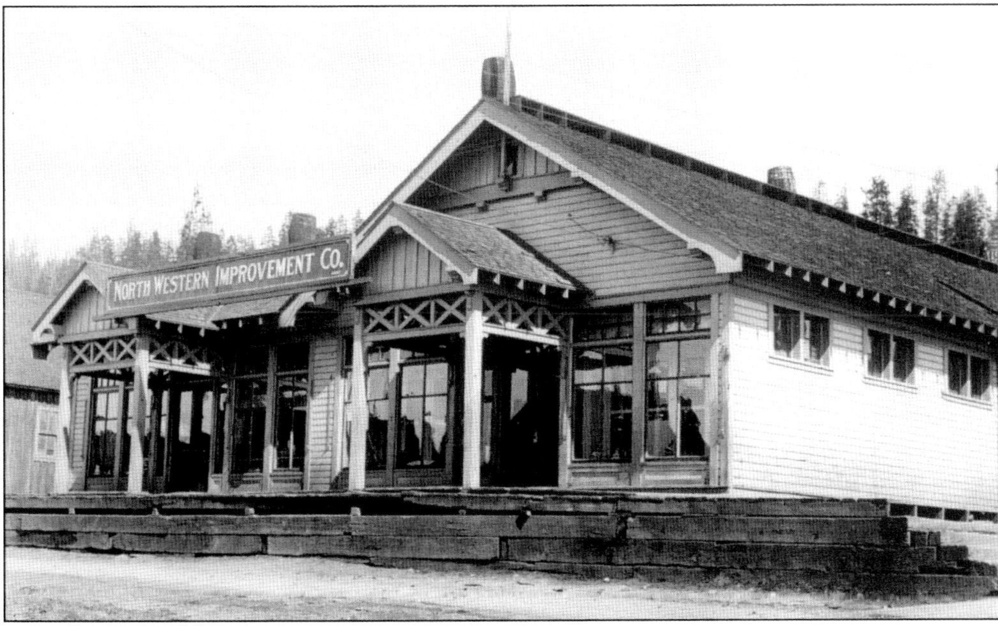

The Northwestern Improvement Company store in Ronald served the many miners who worked in and around Ronald. The smallest of the three company stores in the county, it filled a niche market in Ronald since the Roslyn store was about two miles away and many of the miners did not own horses. (EPL.)

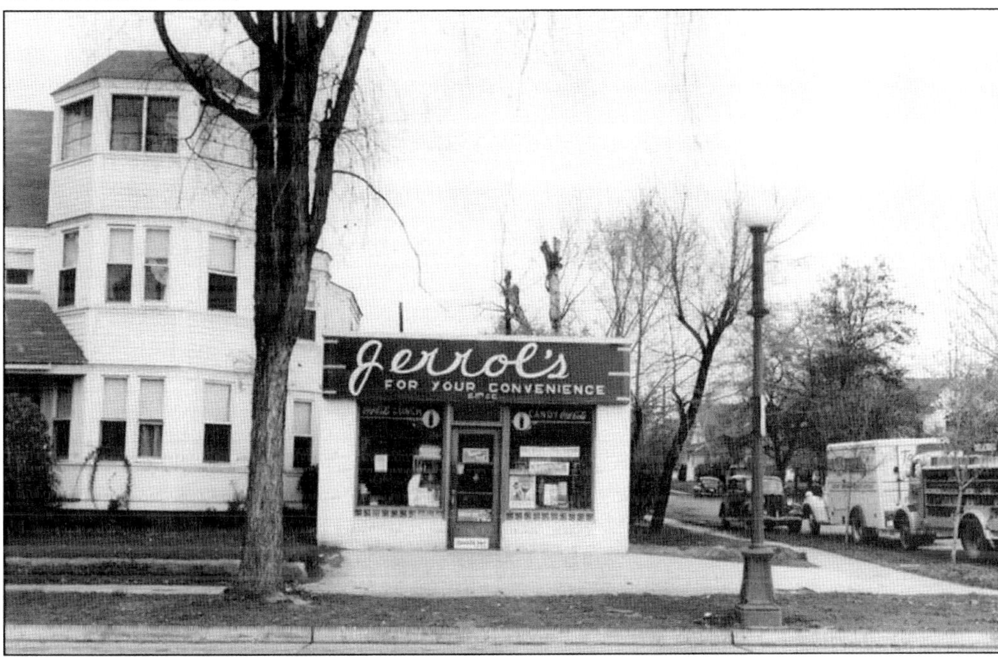

Jerrol's Book and Office Supply, located in Ellensburg, has been in the same location since 1947, although this original building is long gone. Don and Irene Williams owned the house next door and started the store, initially selling tobacco, books, school supplies, and other sundries. The store also had a soda fountain and snack bar. They built the current store in the 1950s, which has since undergone a few remodels. (Pat Stanton.)

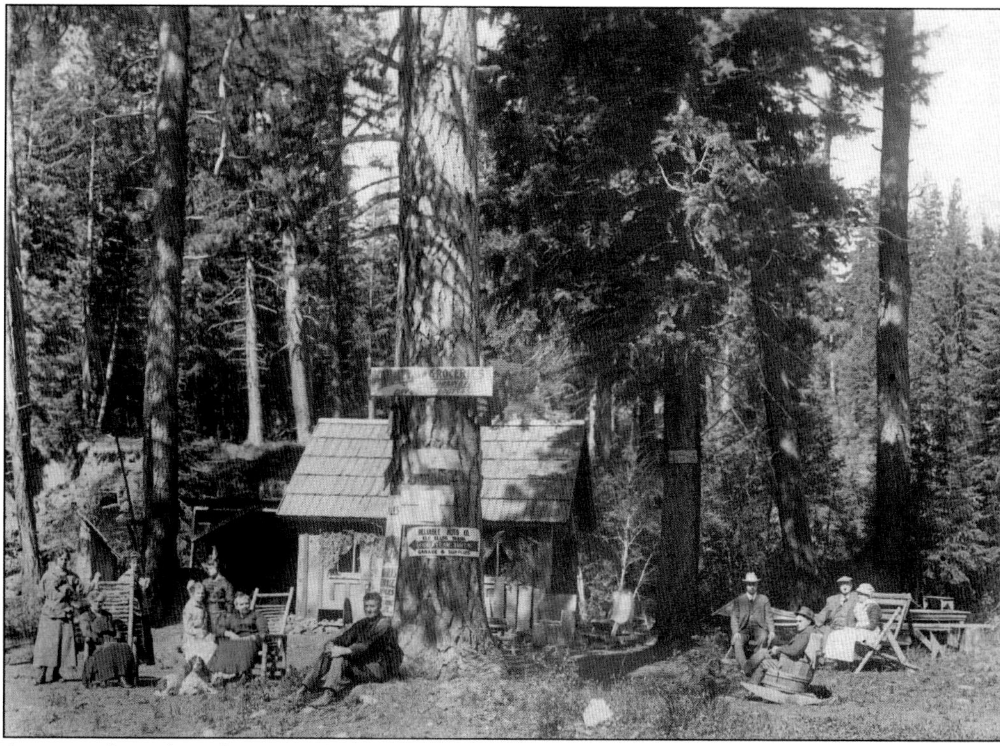

A group of people gathers outside Kinney's Groceries, located along the road towards Blewett Pass, in this early-1900s photograph. The sign on the tree advertises hay, grain, feed, dry goods, boots, and shoes. The arrow is an advertisement for Reliable Auto in Cle Elum. Though not a large store, Kinney's Groceries likely filled a need among both travelers and miners in the area. (EPL.)

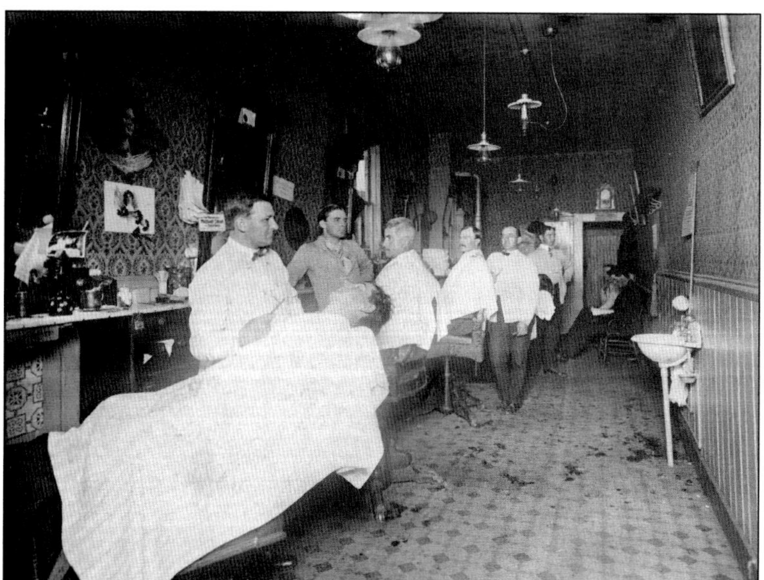

As important then as it is now, the barbershop was one of the earliest businesses in frontier towns. This photograph shows the interior of Frank Meyer's barbershop at 315 North Main Street in Ellensburg. At the far left, Meyer shaves a customer with a straight razor. (KCHM.)

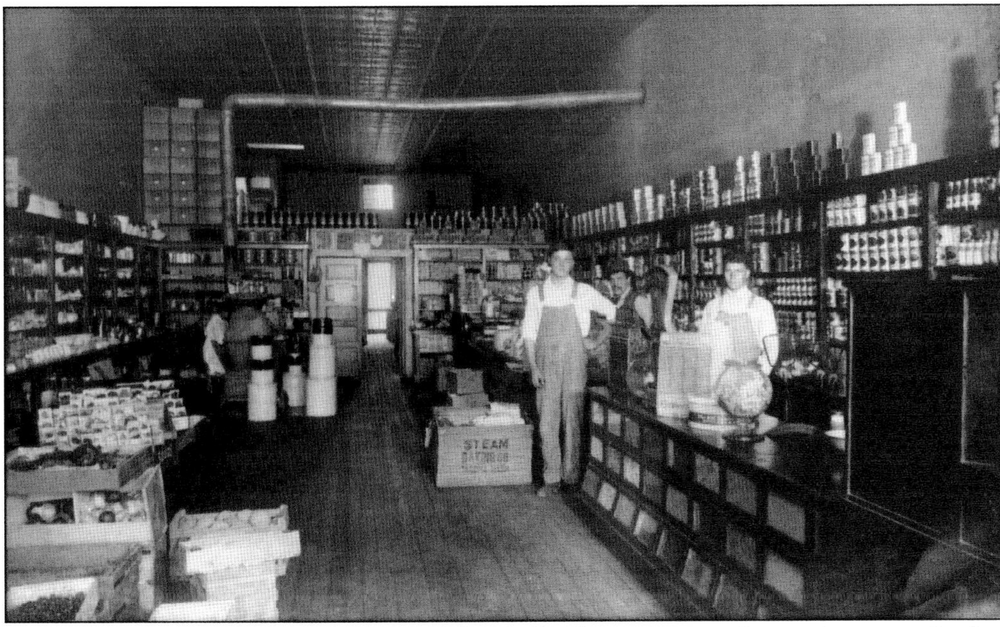

The Pioneer Grocery, located just west of the Brick saloon on Pennsylvania Avenue in Roslyn, was a popular store with locals. Next to the stove is Edna Kuchin, and beside the counter is Fabian Kuchin. The men behind the counter are store owner Steve Kuchin (wearing a hat) and Frank Juanick, one of the early employees. (RM.)

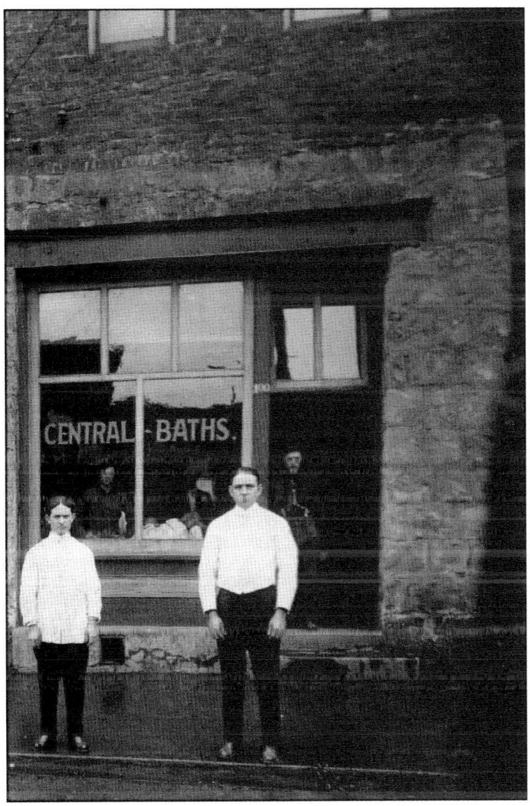

Ludwig Hallberg and Stephen Oversby stand in front of their Cle Elum business around 1909. In keeping with the times, the two barbers wear white shirts and are clean cut. Along with a shave and a haircut, patrons could also take a hot bath, which was something of a luxury to most people. The shop was located on the southeast corner of Pennsylvania Avenue and First Street. (RM.)

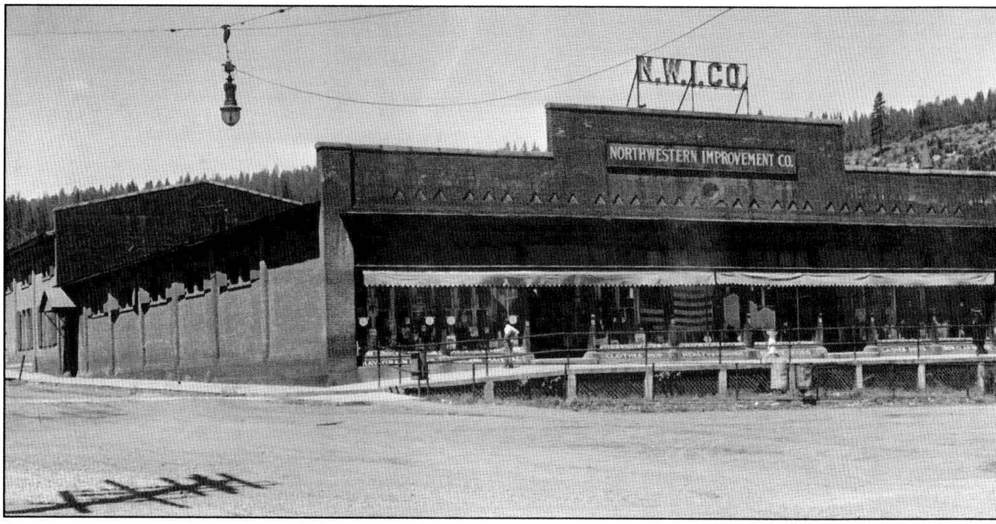

The Northwestern Improvement Company store in Roslyn was the biggest and busiest of its three locations in the Upper County. This store, situated on the northeast corner of Pennsylvania Avenue and First Street, was a popular location with many of the miners and their families. The building still stands, and during the 1990s, it was one of the settings for the television show *Northern Exposure*. (RM.)

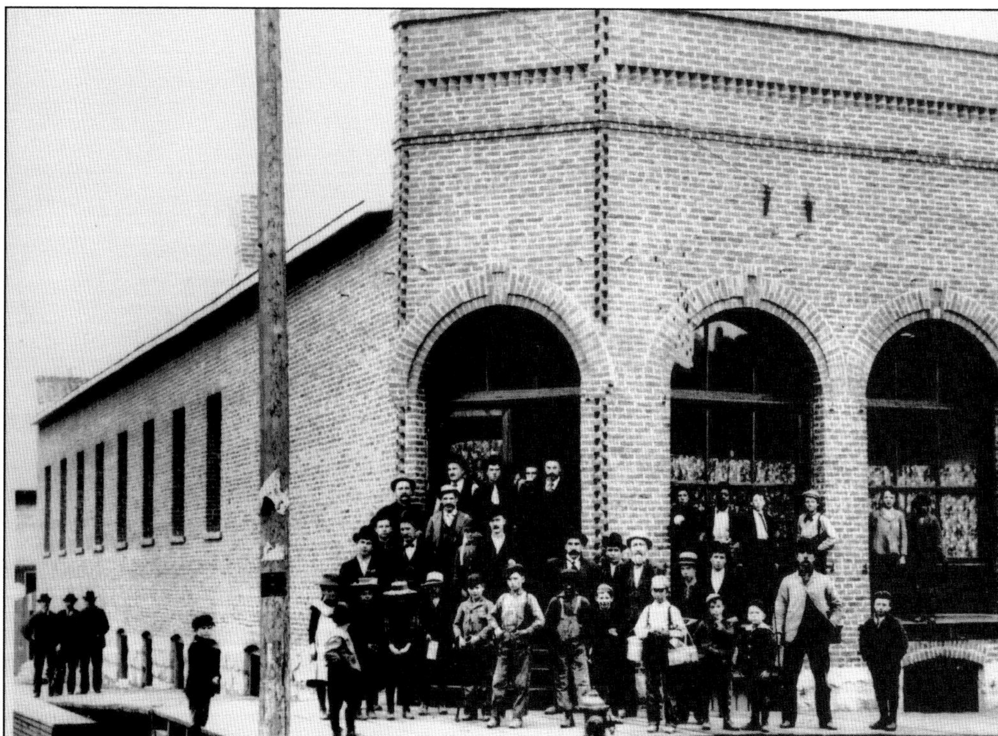

The Brick saloon in Roslyn, built with over 40,000 Roslyn-made bricks, was constructed by Peter Giovanini. The Brick opened in 1898 and was a popular watering hole for the miners and citizens of Roslyn. Still in operation, it is the oldest continually operating tavern in the state and is just as popular today as it was then. (EPL.)

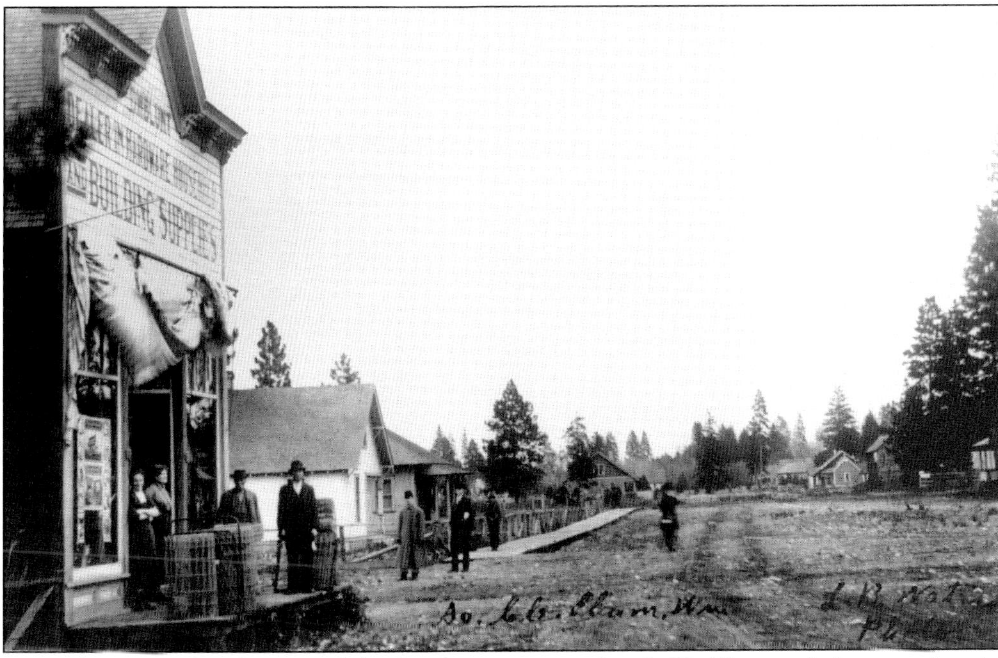

D.W. Blunt owned and operated this hardware store in South Cle Elum and also served as the local postmaster. When South Cle Elum was platted in 1905, Blunt began construction of the first store and opened it in 1906. The Chicago, Milwaukee & St. Paul Railroad was under construction, and Blunt saw an opportunity to open a business for the budding town. (EPL.)

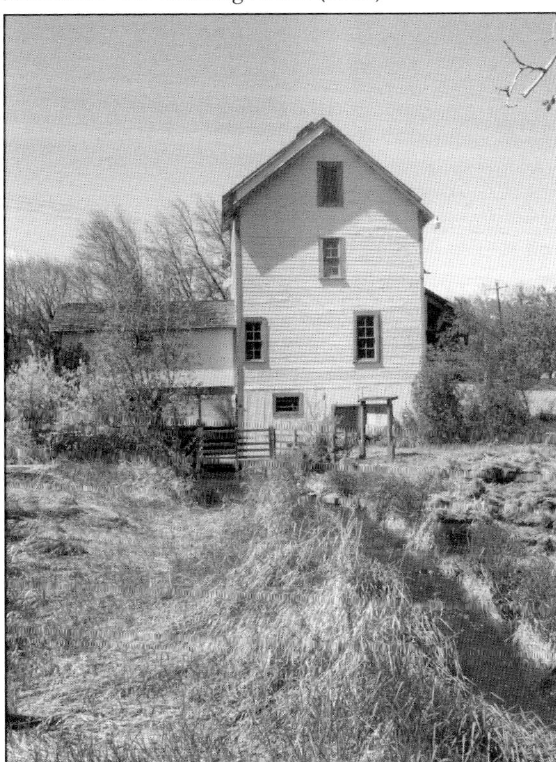

In 1879, James Mills diverted water from the Yakima River to his property near present-day Thorp. In 1880, he built a sawmill. In 1883, a gristmill was built by Oren Hutchinson, and both the sawmill and gristmill utilized the water Mills diverted to his property. The lumber used to build the gristmill came from the sawmill, and the mill was in use until 1946. In 1988, it was restored and opened as a museum, which is still a popular attraction today. (Author's collection.)

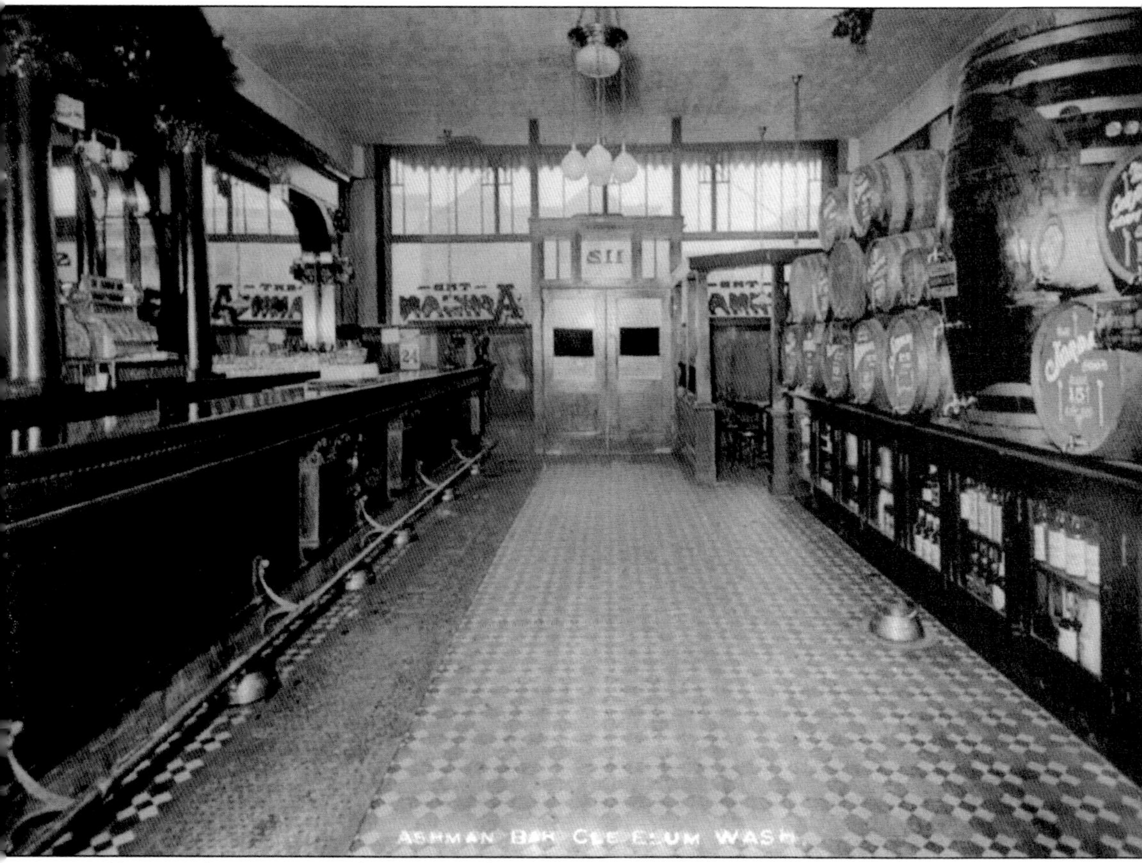

Bruce Ashman operated a variety of Cle Elum businesses between 1907 and 1948; the Ashman Bar was a popular one. The Ashman Bar was located at 112 First Street in Cle Elum and had an ornate imported bar, which survived the fire of 1918. The Ashman Bar served beer and spirits and charged 10¢ to 15¢ per drink. (EPL.)

Four

EDUCATION AND RELIGION

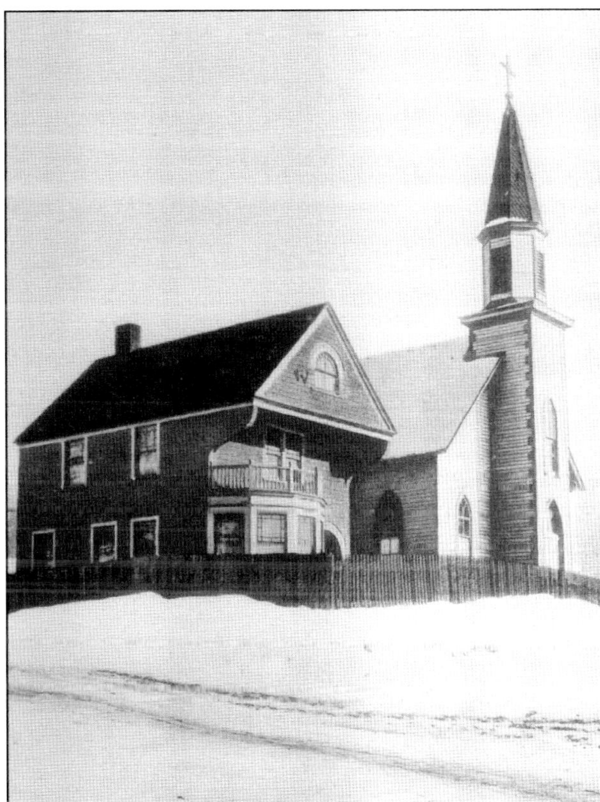

Built in 1887, the Immaculate Conception Catholic Church sits on the hill overlooking Roslyn. The parish itself was formed in August 1889 as a branch of the Nisqually Dioceses. Reverend Kusters, the first priest, lived in the rectory, which was built in the 1890s next to the church. This magnificent church has undergone a few cosmetic changes but remains a focal point in Roslyn. (EPL.)

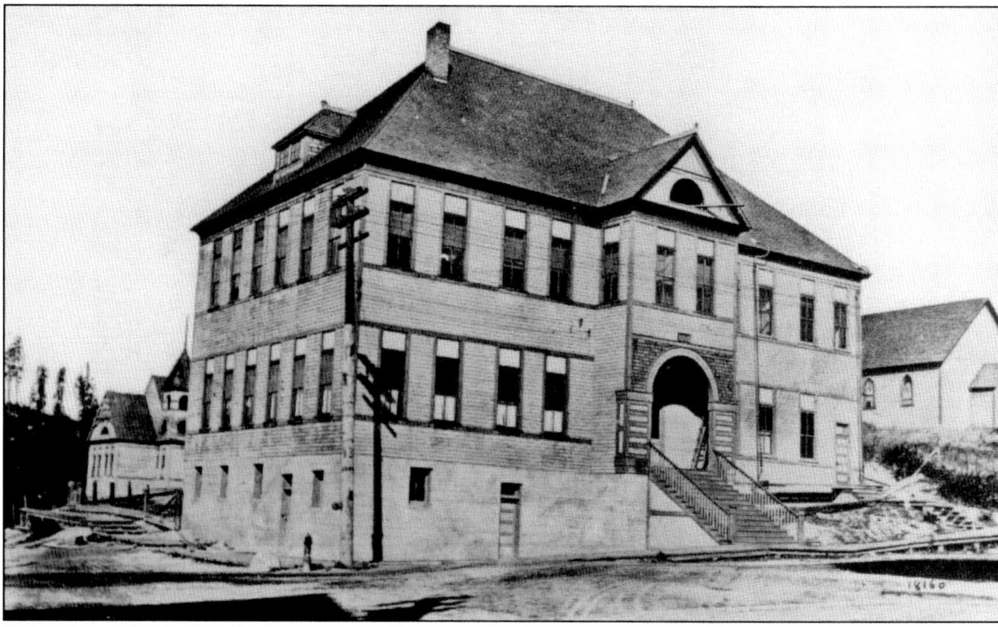

When the Roslyn Public School, which housed all primary and secondary grades, became overcrowded, this high school building was constructed in 1910 for the older students. The last graduating class enrolled in this school attended during the spring of 1931. After sitting vacant for six years, it was torn down in 1937. (EPL.)

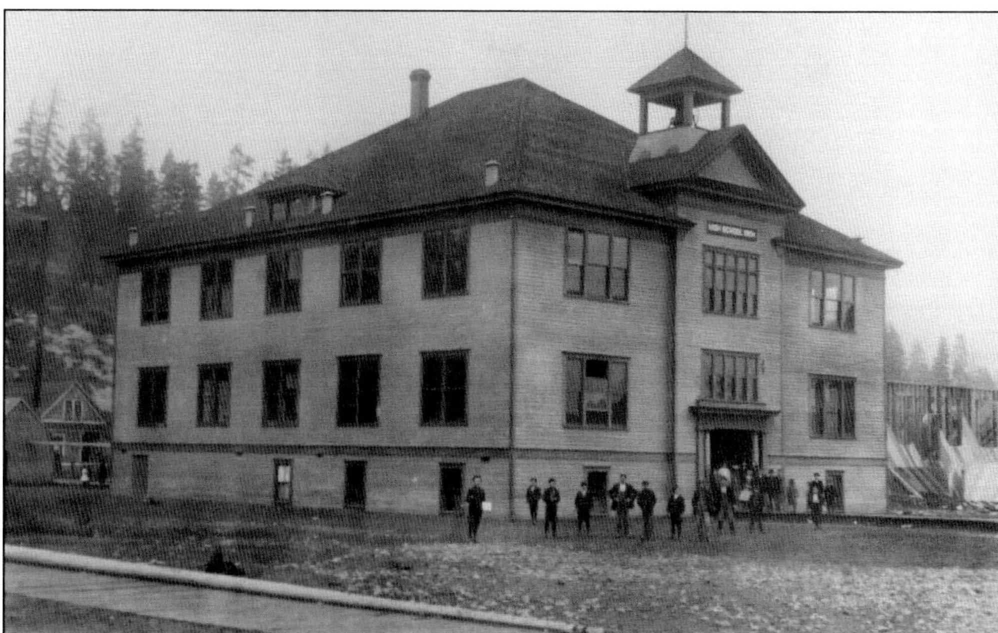

Cle Elum High School, built in 1904 on East Second Street, initially had eight rooms with four on each floor. James Thomas was principal of the high school, which offered students three years of schooling. After this building was gone, a new brick school was erected at this location and housed the high school until 1968. (EPL.)

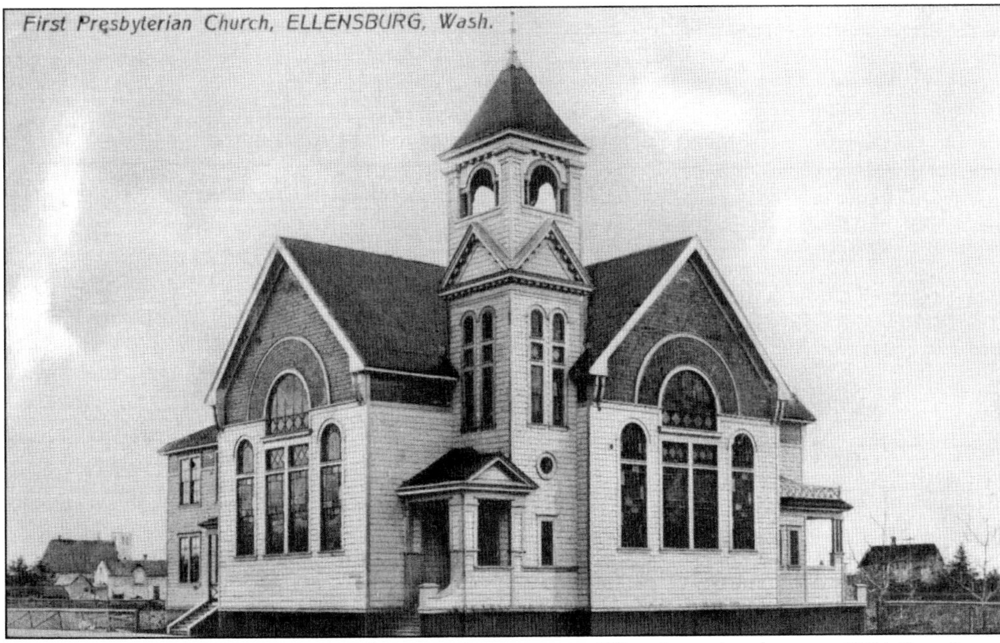

The First Presbyterian Church in Ellensburg began as the Ellensburg Academy in 1884. Rev. James Laurie started the academy, which was mainly used as a school. When the public school was built in 1891, the Presbyterian academy was moved across the street, modified, and became the church. The church was torn down in 1958 to make way for the Safeway grocery store. (EPL.)

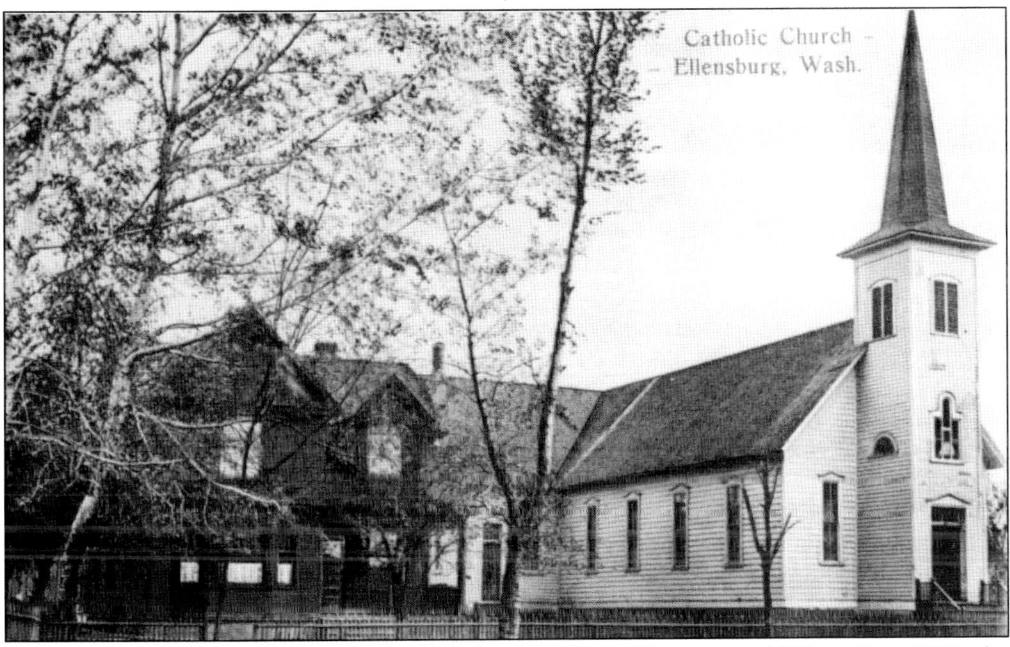

Pictured are Ellensburg's St. Andrews Catholic Church and Rectory in 1910. Built in 1884, the church structure was originally located on Water Street. It was moved to Pine Street in 1904 when the rectory was added. These buildings, along with neighboring Lourde's Academy School, were used until 1966, when they were torn down to make room for a new grocery store that still stands today. (EPL.)

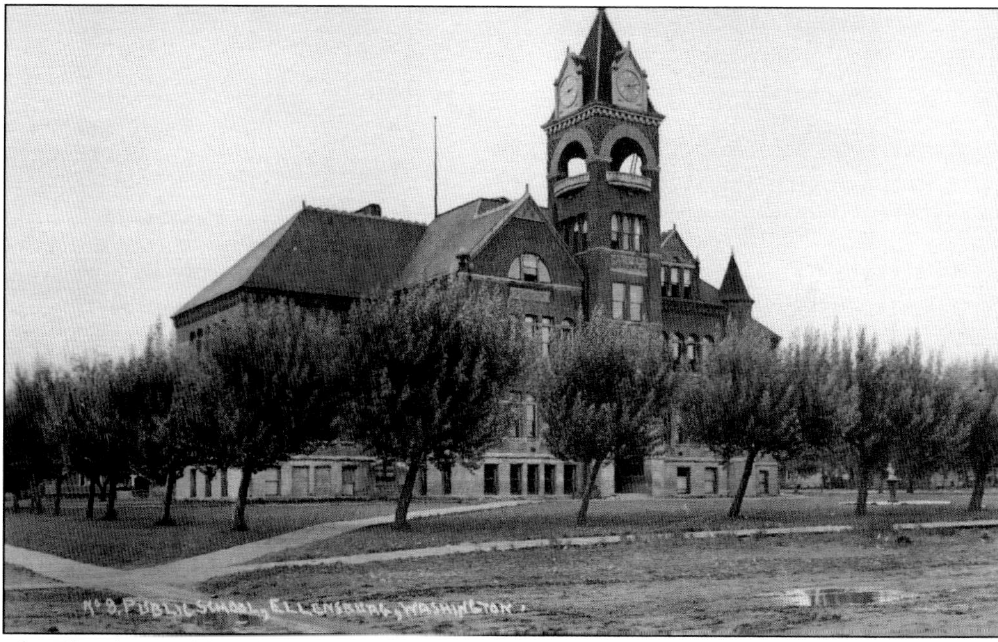

The Ellensburg Public School was built in 1890 and opened for classes in 1891. The first two floors were the primary and secondary classes, and from 1891 to 1894, the third floor was home to the newly created Washington State Normal School. The impressive bell tower had a clock face on all four sides and was visible from most parts of town. A fire in 1924 destroyed the school. (EPL.)

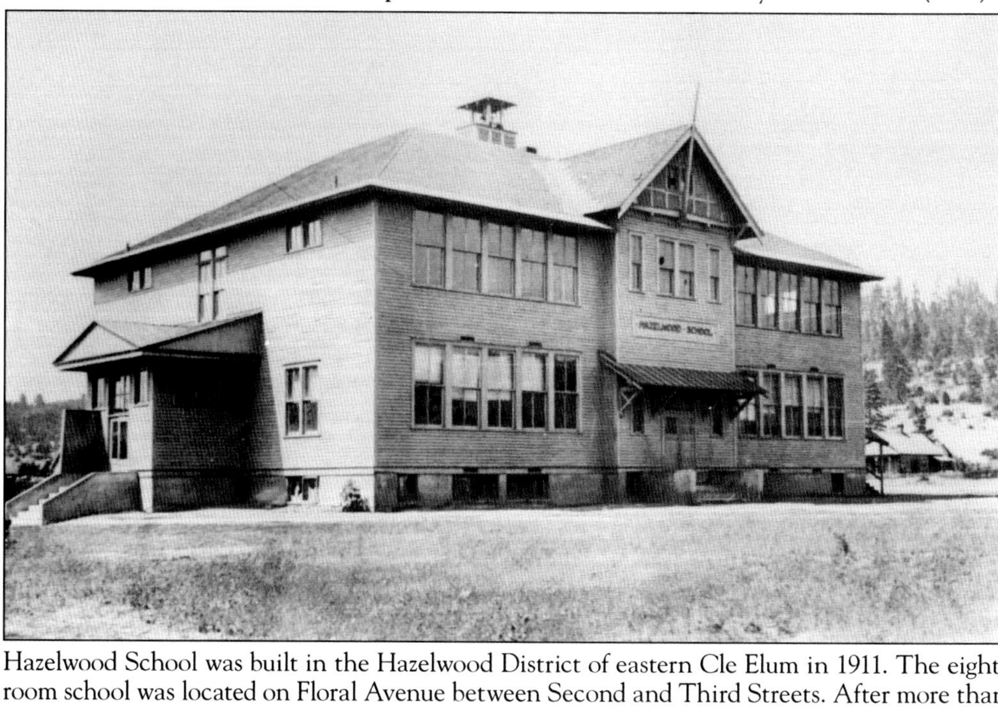

Hazelwood School was built in the Hazelwood District of eastern Cle Elum in 1911. The eight-room school was located on Floral Avenue between Second and Third Streets. After more than 20 years of service, this district decided to consolidate with the Cle Elum School District. The school closed in the 1930s, and the students that lived in the area began attending school in Cle Elum. (EPL.)

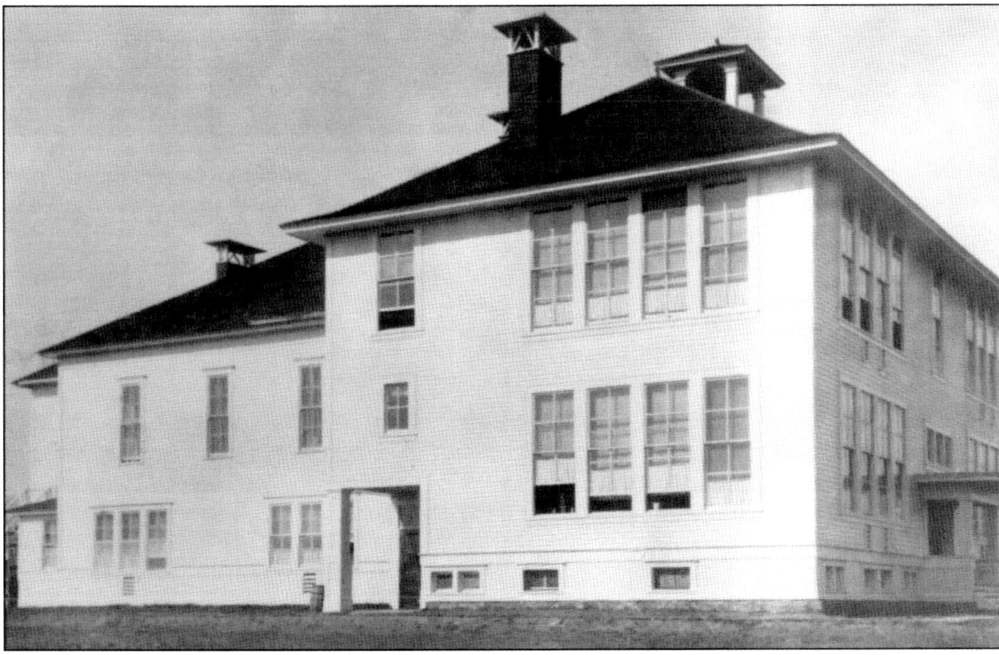

The Thorp School is shown as it looked in 1916. The large building housed all the grades in Thorp until 1935 when a brick elementary school was constructed; it was then used for secondary students. By the 1950s, the building was aging and in need of replacement. It was torn down in 1957, and a modern high school was built in 1958. (EPL.)

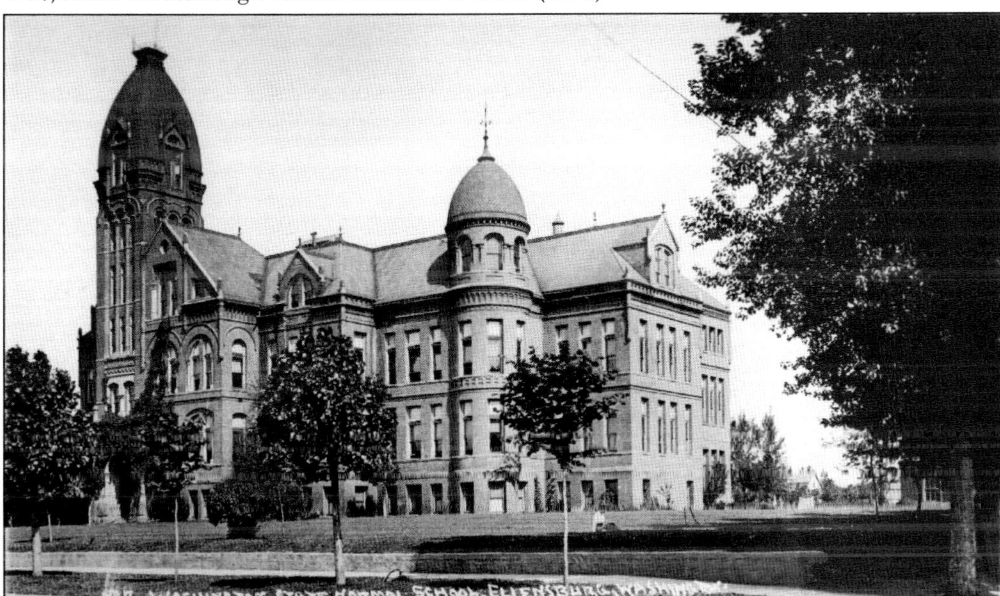

Barge Hall, the first building constructed for the Washington State Normal School in Ellensburg, was completed in 1894. It was the only building on the campus for 14 years and housed all of the classrooms, an auditorium, a library, and the administrative offices for the college. The bricks were made in the Fowler Brick Yard in Ellensburg, and the sandstone blocks were brought in from Tenino, Washington. (EPL.)

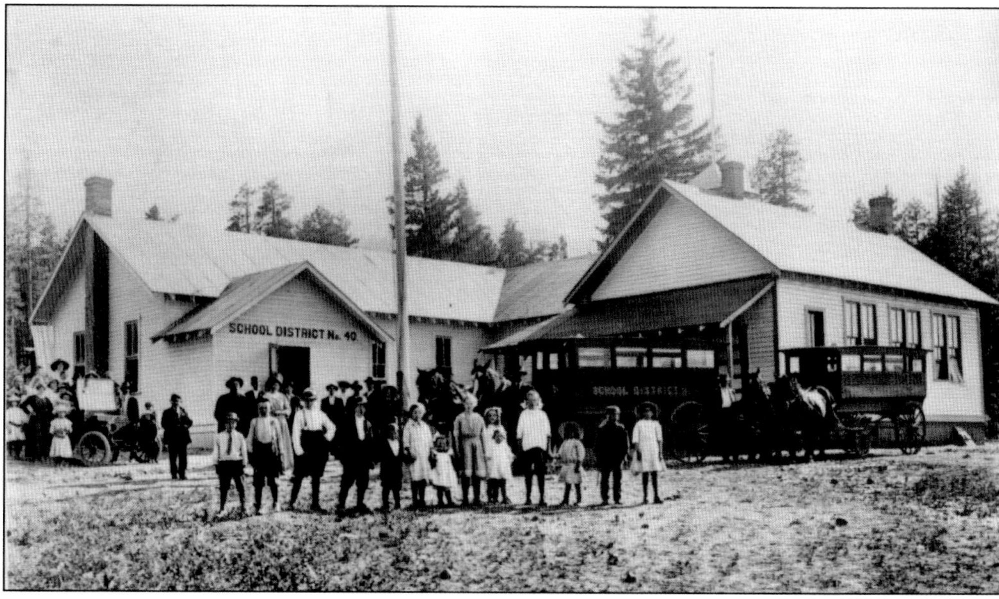

Peoh Point School was located across the Yakima River from Cle Elum, in South Cle Elum. As seen in this photograph, the school's busses were pulled by horses in 1915. Peoh Point School District merged with the Cle Elum School District in 1917, and the school building became the Peoh Point Grange. (EPL.)

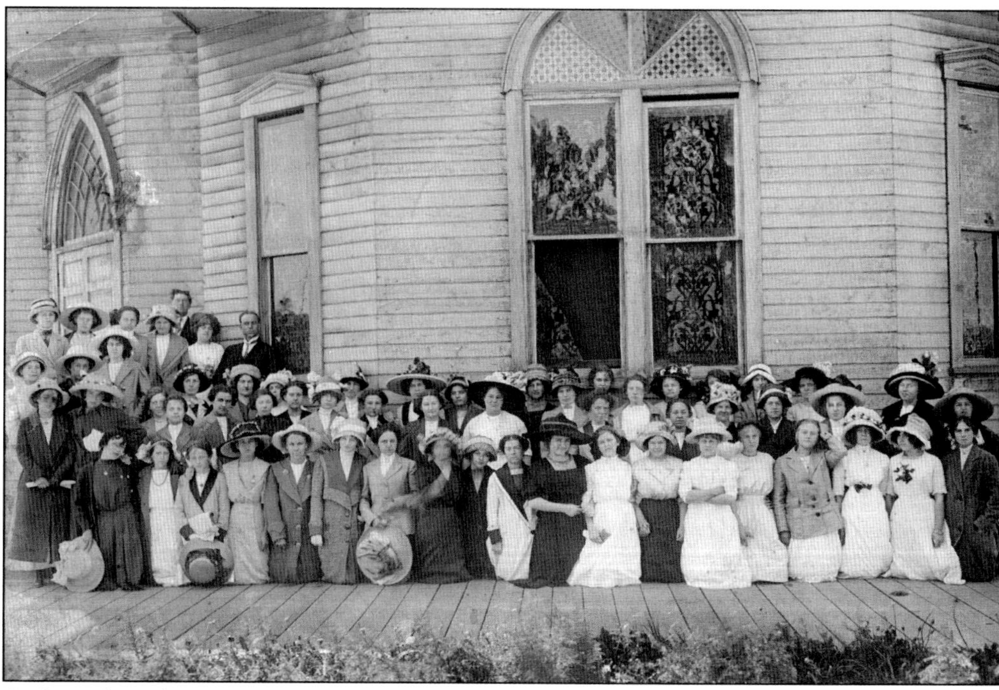

A class of Washington State Normal School students taught by Max E. Wilson poses by the First Christian Church in Ellensburg in this 1910 photograph. This church was located on the southwest corner of Fourth Avenue and Ruby Street where the old post office now sits across from Safeway. The church behind the students was built in 1886 and moved to this location on log rollers by church volunteers and horses. (EPL.)

Pictured is St. John the Baptist Catholic Church in Cle Elum around 1912. The church was built in 1902 near the corner of East Second Street and Bullitt Avenue on land donated by town founder Walter J. Reed. In the photograph below, a procession of altar boys and other parish members pose near the decorated entrance with Bishop Edward O'Dea of the Seattle Diocese, who was visiting to confirm the Sacrament of Confirmation for the first time. Six short years after this picture was taken, this beautiful church burned to the ground in the 1918 Cle Elum fire. After the fire, the parishioners temporarily met at public school buildings until a new location could be purchased. The new church and rectory opened in 1921 and are still in use today. (Right, CWU; below, EPL.)

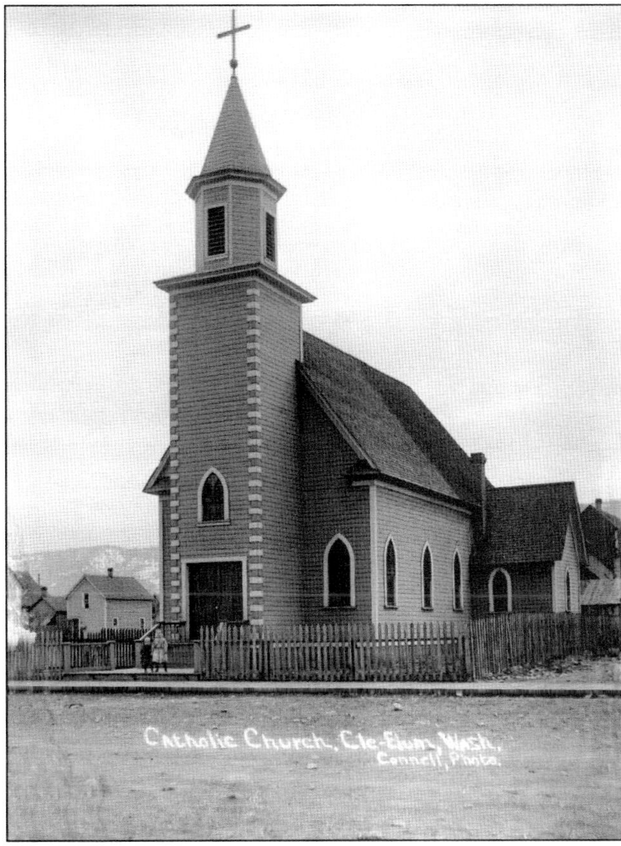

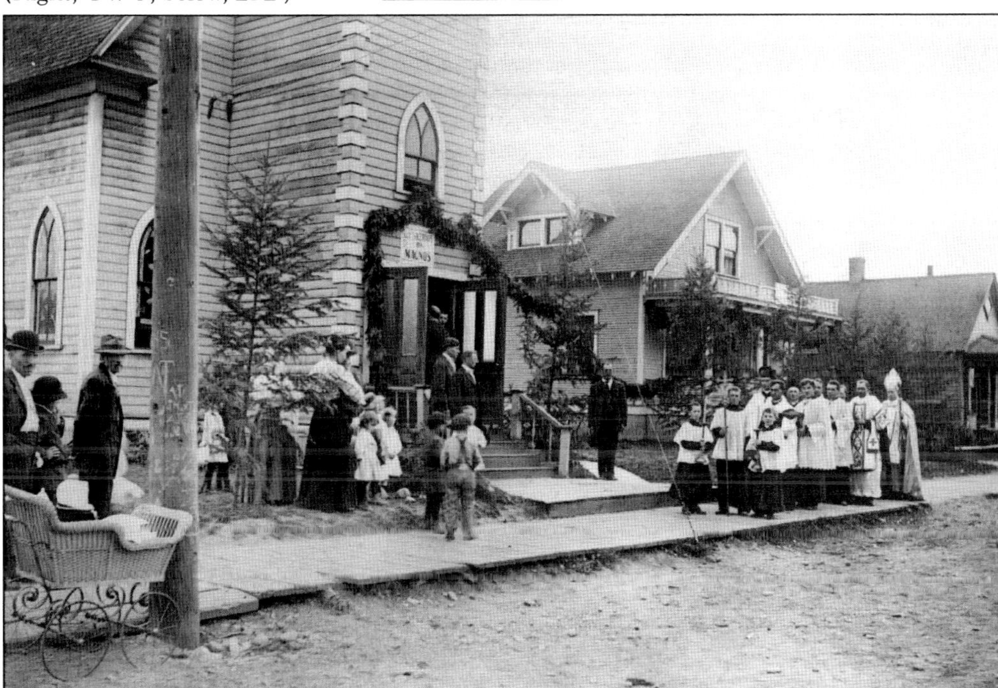

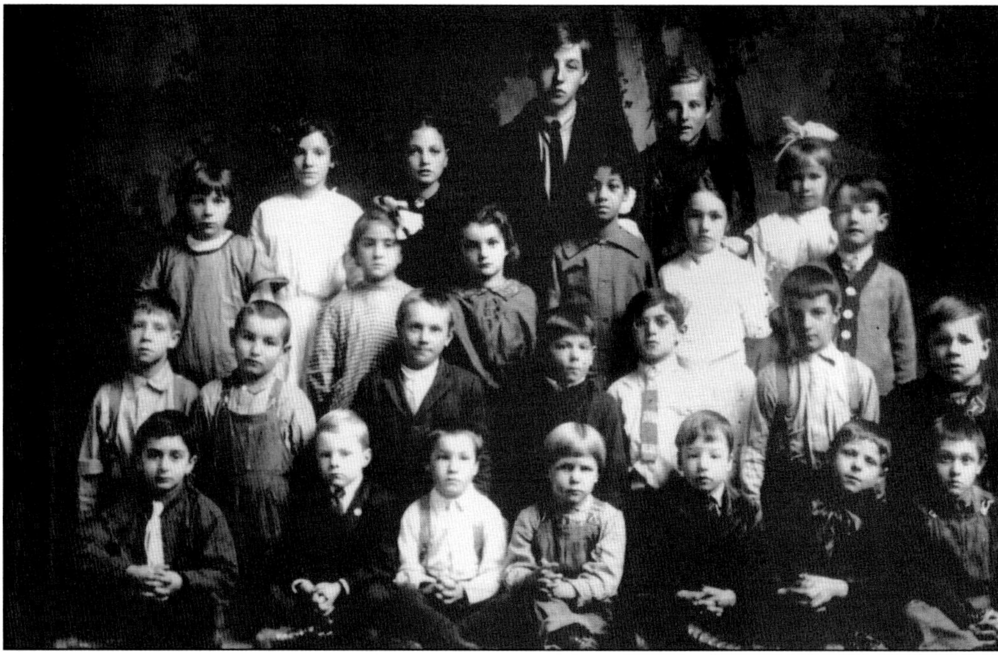

Taken in 1913, this picture shows children representing at least 25 of the different nationalities living in Roslyn at this time. Miners and their families came from all over the world, many times not speaking English, to work in the coal mines around Roslyn and Ronald. Their legacy can be seen in the cemeteries near Roslyn, which are divided ethnically and fraternally. (EPL.)

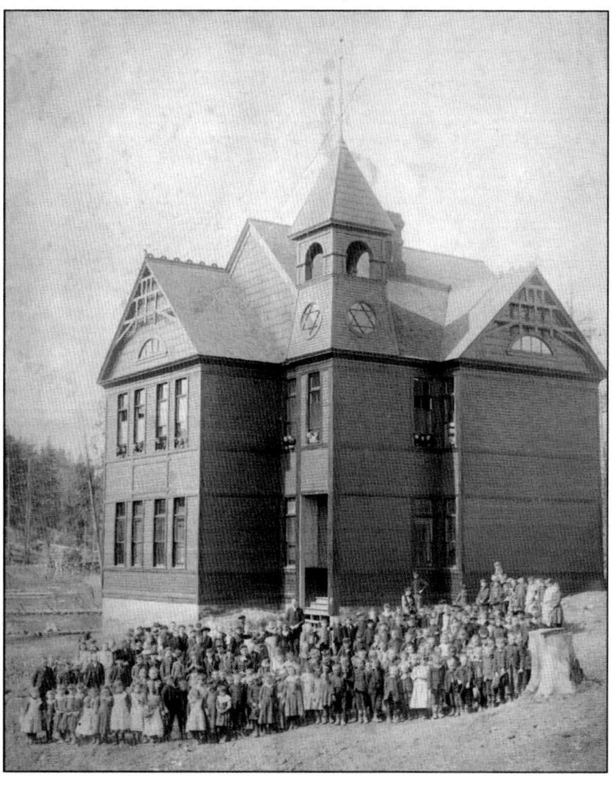

The student body and teachers of the Roslyn Public School gather in front of the school in 1893. The school was built in 1890 after a $5,000 bond was approved to buy the land. All grades were taught in this building until 1900, when a primary structure was added. In 1910, a high school was built. (RM.)

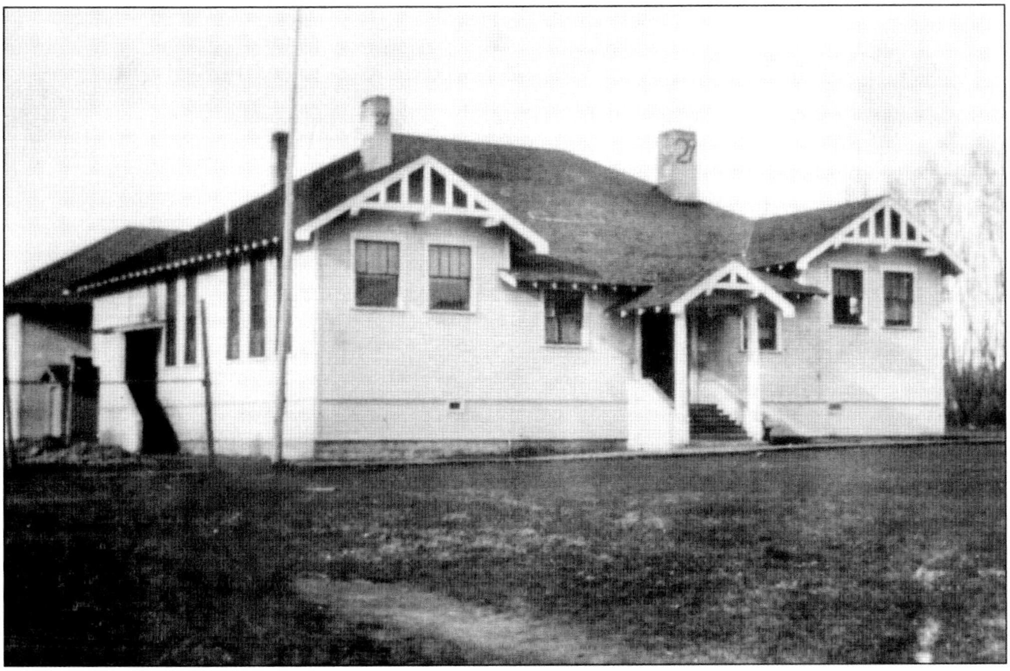

Kittitas Union High School was formed in 1912, taking in students from the Fairview, Denmark, Kittitas, and Lyons Districts. The first principal was Amos Foster, and the first class graduated in 1913 with three graduates. The building was used until 1950, when a new high school was completed. Other structures on this campus were a gymnasium, a science and history classroom building, and a barn for horses. (EPL.)

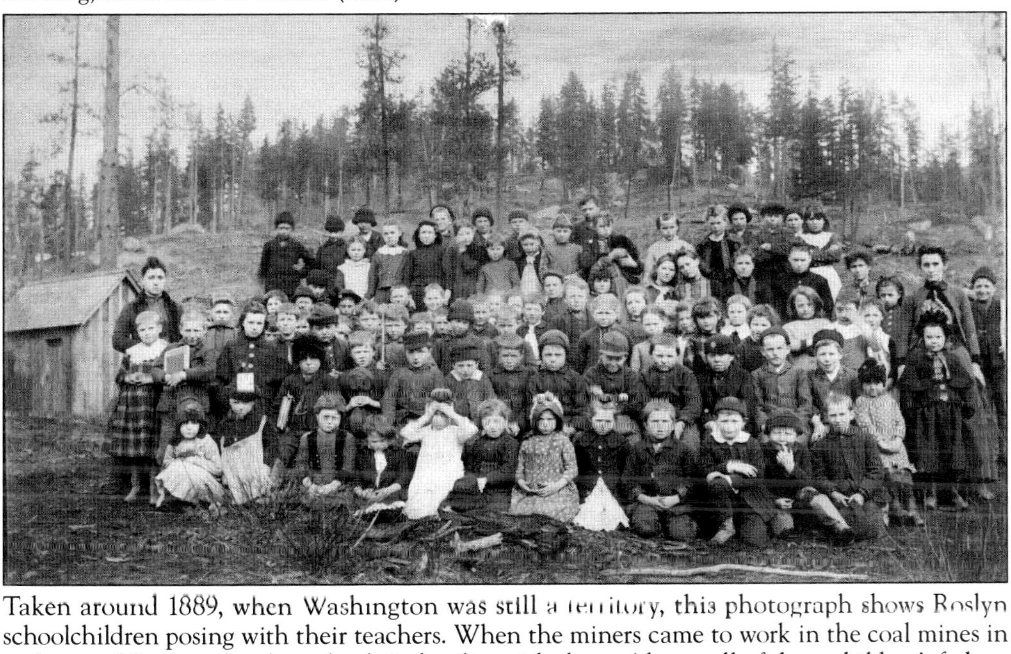

Taken around 1889, when Washington was still a territory, this photograph shows Roslyn schoolchildren posing with their teachers. When the miners came to work in the coal mines in and around Roslyn, they brought their families with them. Almost all of these children's fathers worked in the coal industry. As can be seen by the number of children, the need for a larger school building was eminent. (RM.)

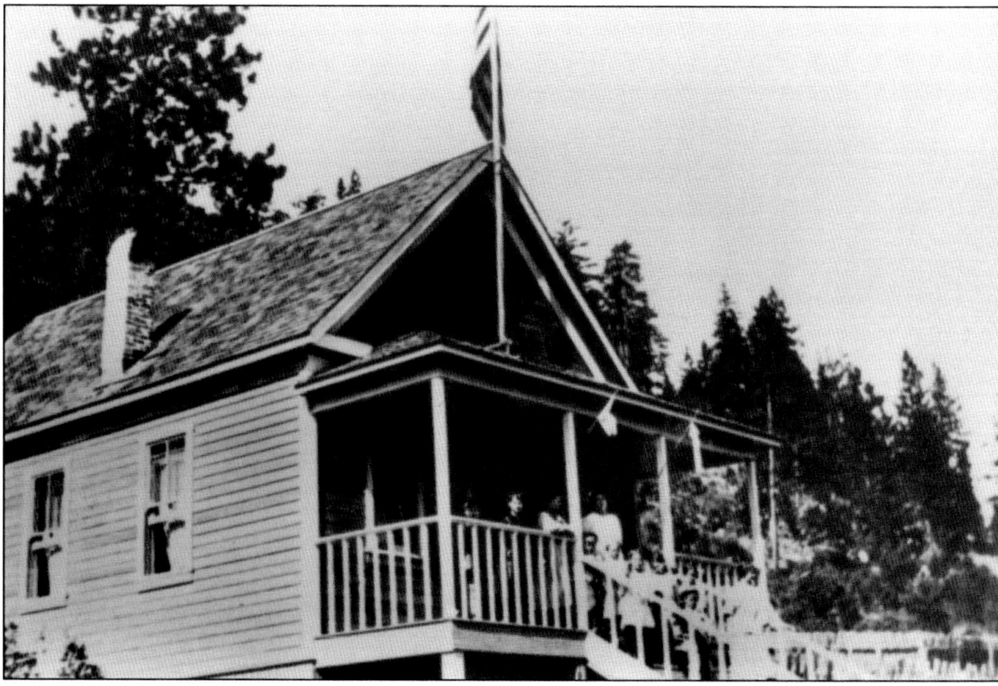

The school building of the Liberty and Meaghersville District was organized in 1895. When it began, there were 13 families that had school-age children, with 21 children attending this school. Liberty and Meaghersville—separate towns at the time—were located in the Swauk Mining District, and most families that came to the area came in search of gold. (EPL.)

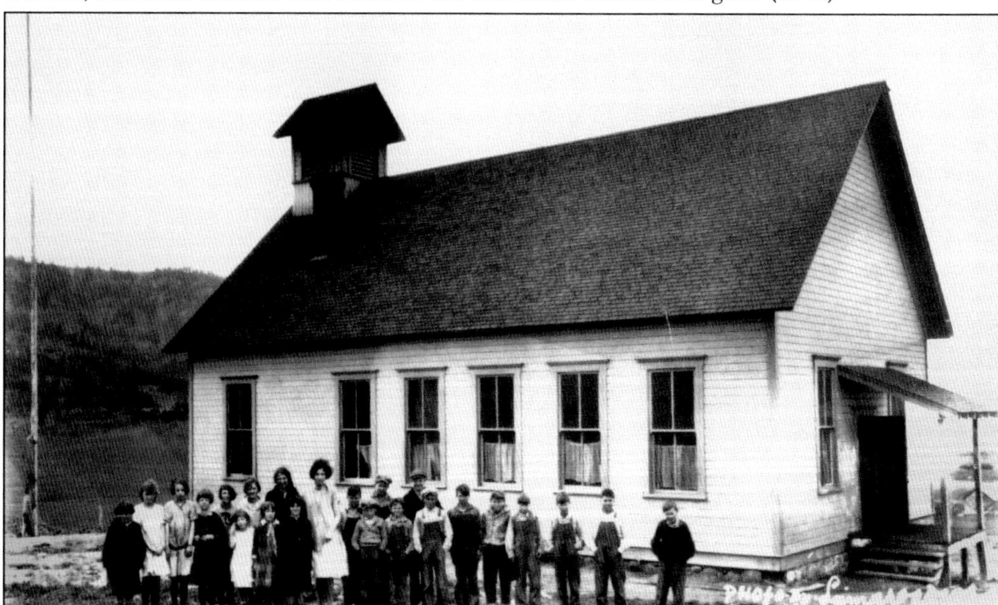

The Ballard School was located on Ballard Hill Road near the Teanaway Valley and Swauk Prairie in 1927. Built in 1904, the school was in use until 1937, when it consolidated with the Cle Elum School District and area children were bused into Cle Elum. The building then served as the Swauk Teanaway Grange until it was destroyed by fire in 2005. (EPL.)

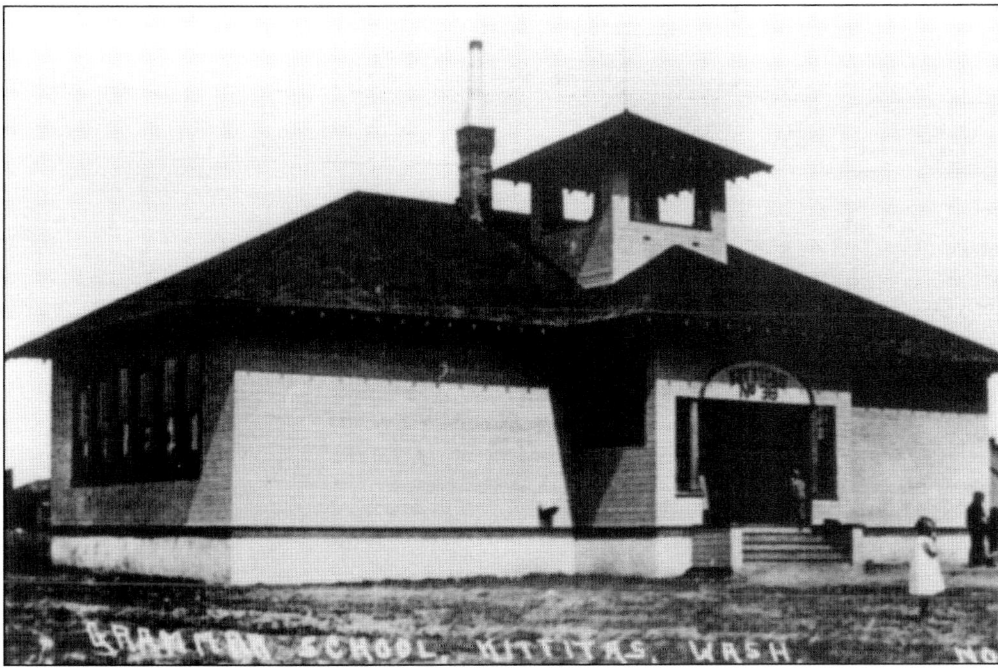

Kittitas Grade School, or Kittitas Grammar School, is shown as it looked in the late 19th century. The first grade school in Kittitas was established in 1893, but lack of students closed it from 1899 to 1909. In 1909, the school reopened in this building and continued here until 1936. Later, this structure became the Kittitas City Hall and Library. (EPL.)

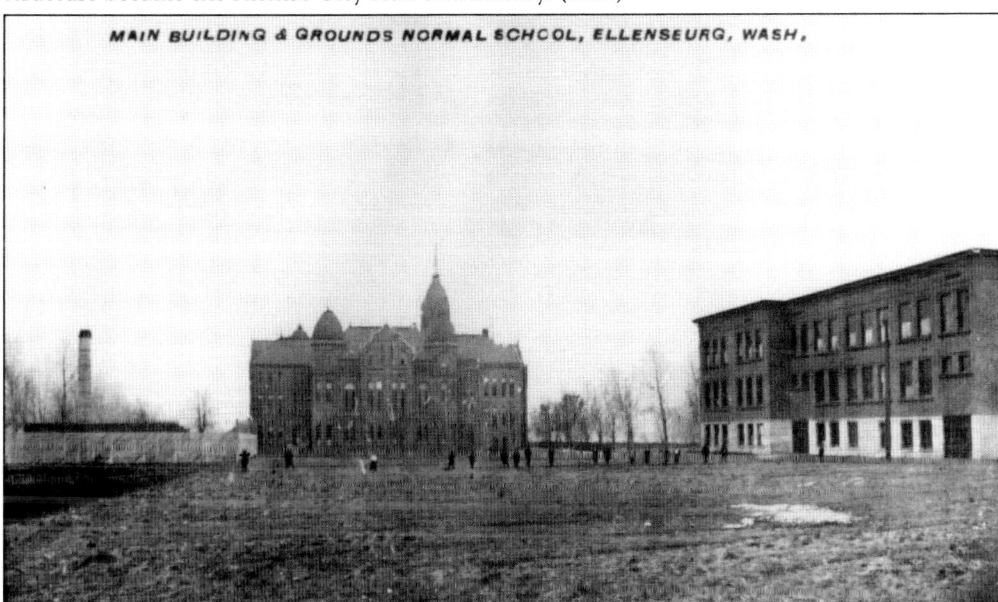

This early-1900s view looking south shows the Central Washington University campus. Barge Hall is at center, and on the right is Edison Hall, built in 1908 for teacher training with classrooms and an on-campus elementary school. On the left, the smokestack from the heat plant can be seen. Not long after this picture was taken, the heat plant was rebuilt into a three-story science structure. (EPL.)

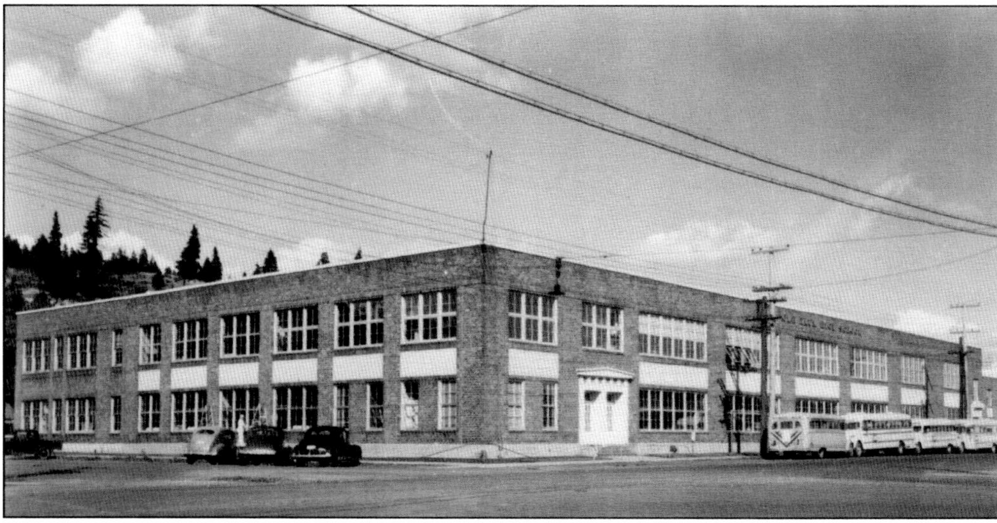

Cle Elum High School, which occupied the block between Second and Third Streets and Wright and Harris Avenues, housed not only the high school, but also all grades of the Cle Elum School District. When Cle Elum consolidated districts with Roslyn, this building became the elementary school, middle school students went to school in Roslyn, and a new high school was constructed between Cle Elum and Roslyn in 1968. (EPL.)

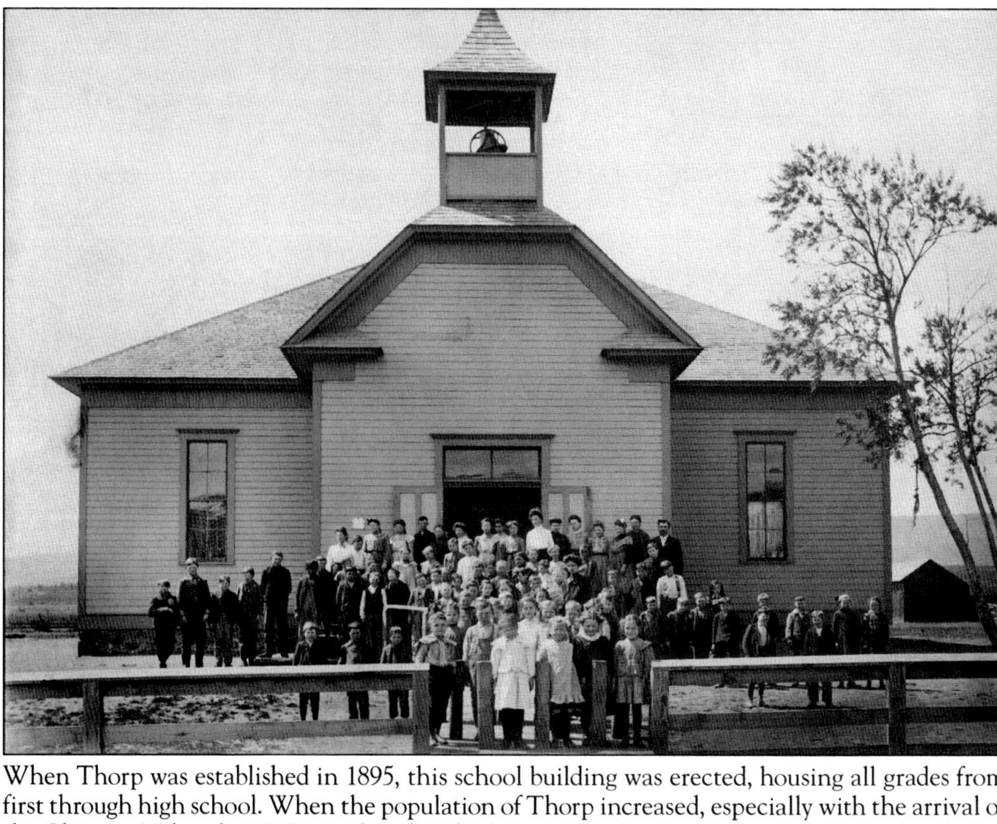

When Thorp was established in 1895, this school building was erected, housing all grades from first through high school. When the population of Thorp increased, especially with the arrival of the Chicago, Milwaukee & St. Paul Railroad, a bigger schoolhouse was needed. This schoolhouse was used until a larger school was built in 1912. (KCHM.)

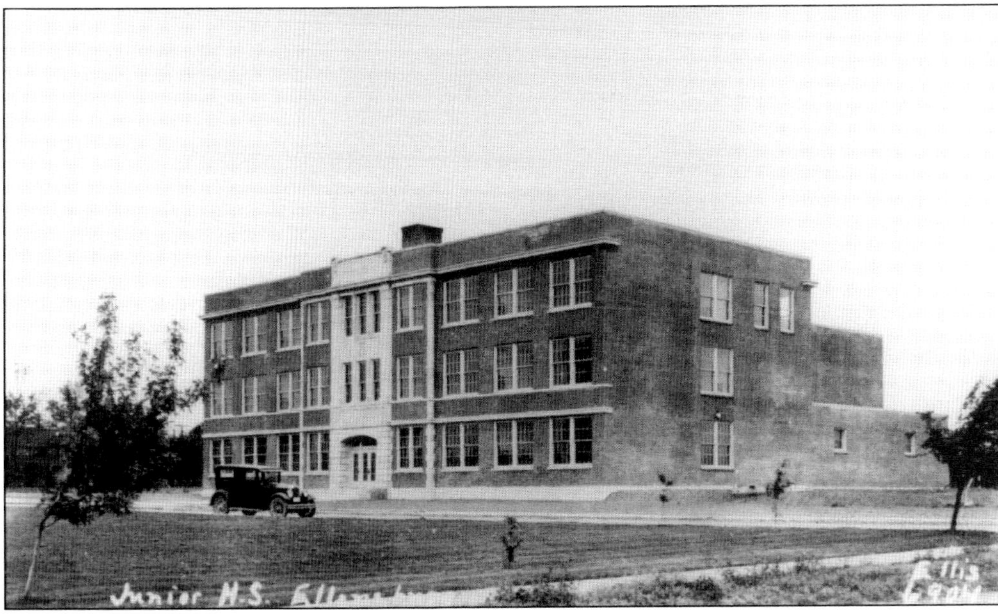

Morgan Middle School was built in 1929 to house the junior high students that had been displaced by the public school building fire. Morgan was erected facing the Ellensburg High School structure, and the two schools shared facilities. The high school used the Morgan Auditorium, and the junior high used the cafeteria in the high school. Morgan still stands, but it has been deemed unsafe, and the decision to either remodel it or demolish it is undetermined. (EPL.)

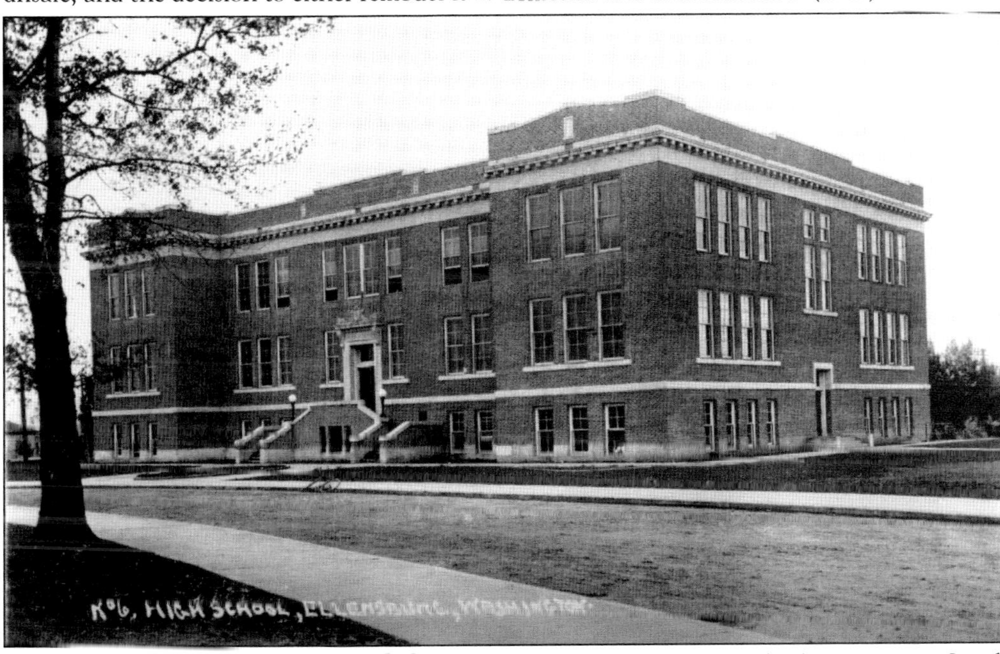

The main entrance of Ellensburg High School, which faced east, was built in 1912 on South Sprague Street. The structure was last used as a high school during the 1955–1956 school year. For a few years, the building remained empty except for use by staff and students of Morgan Junior High. The old school was eventually used as a school storage facility until it was demolished in 1991. (EPL.)

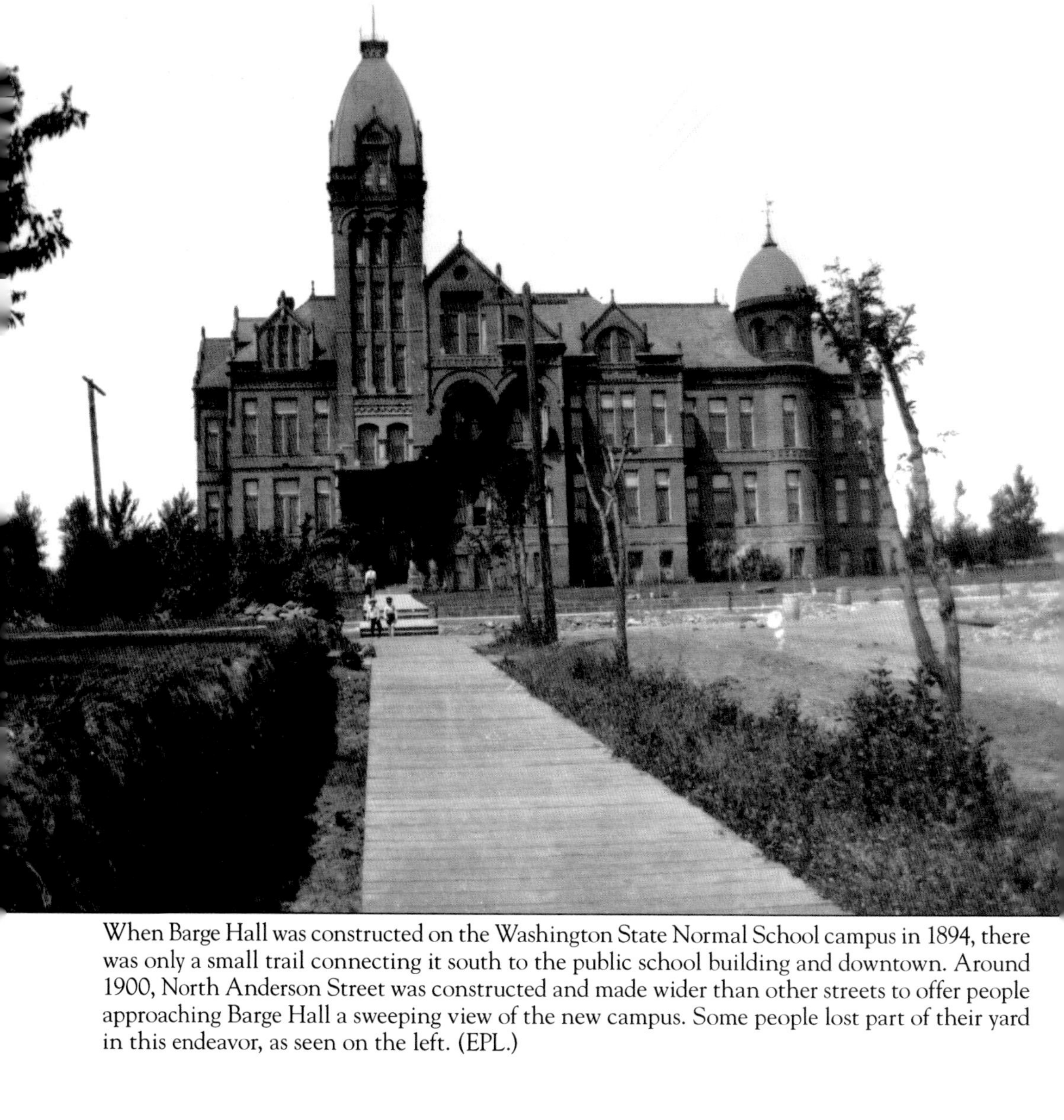

When Barge Hall was constructed on the Washington State Normal School campus in 1894, there was only a small trail connecting it south to the public school building and downtown. Around 1900, North Anderson Street was constructed and made wider than other streets to offer people approaching Barge Hall a sweeping view of the new campus. Some people lost part of their yard in this endeavor, as seen on the left. (EPL.)

Five

INDUSTRY

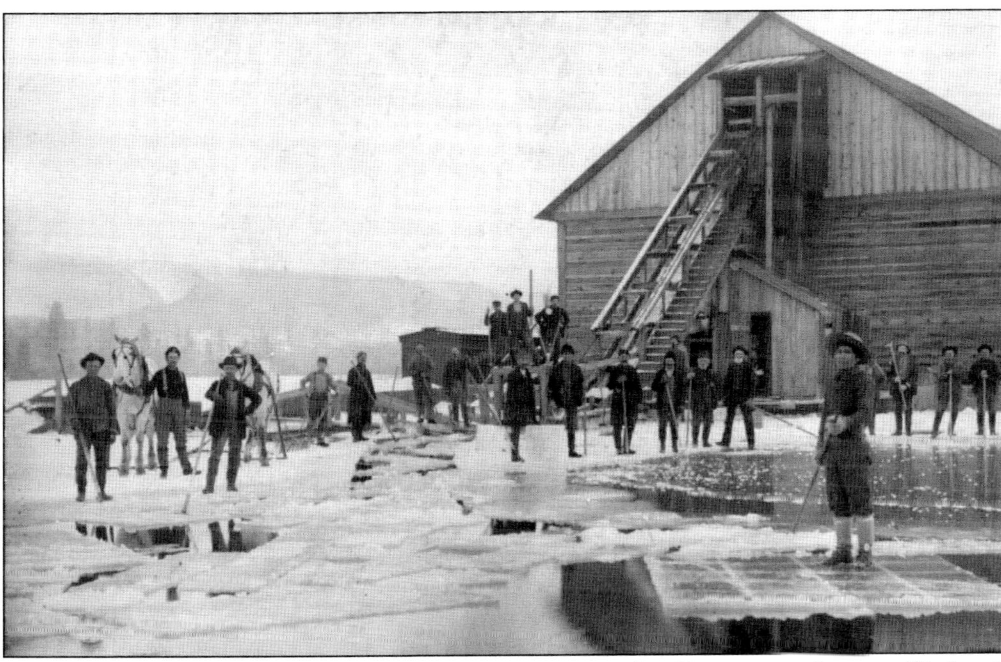

Next to the sawmill and gristmill in Thorp was an ice pond, a 22-acre area that was filled with water from the mill ditch. The shallow pond was filled to capacity and left to freeze in the cold winter months. Then ice blocks were cut out and stored in icehouses to either be used locally or shipped out on the Northern Pacific Railroad. (KCHM.)

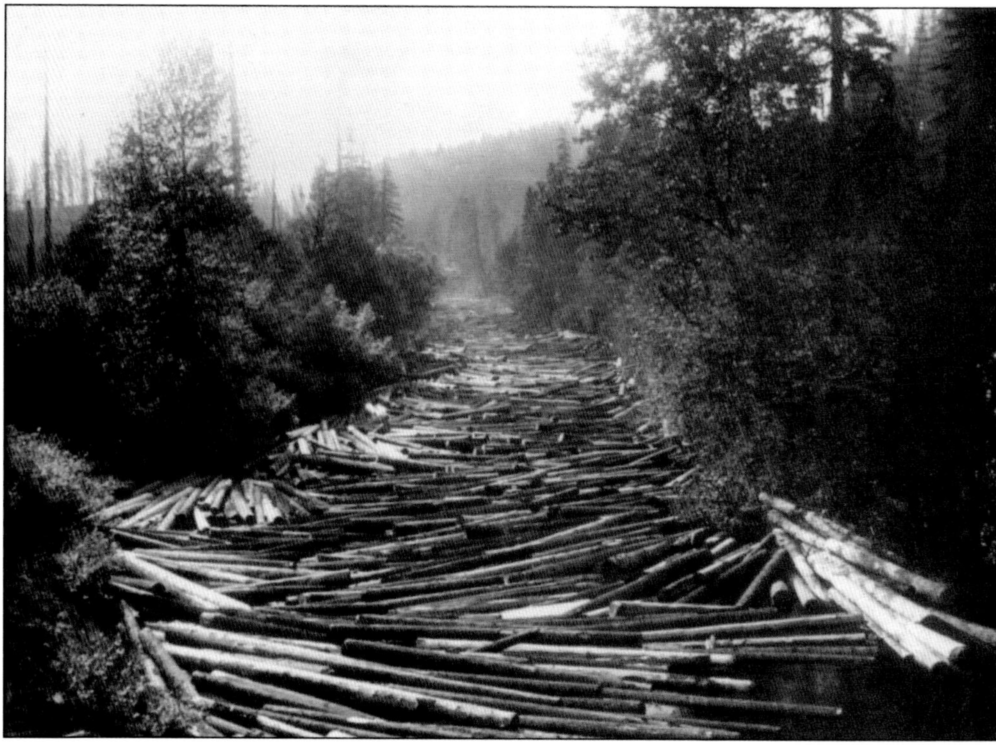

During the spring, when the river was at its highest, loggers would float their harvest down the Teanaway and Yakima Rivers to the sawmills. Taken in 1909, this view shows the immense amount of logs that were sent down the Teanaway River, just outside of Cle Elum. Logging began in the area around 1891, and logjams like this one were commonplace until the logging railroad lines reached the area in 1912. To clear up such a jam, "river rats" or "river pigs," as the men were called, would carry out the dangerous task of walking on the logs and using peavey poles to clear the jam. It took six weeks for logs to float from Easton to Yakima. These logs were mainly used at the Cascade Lumber mill in Yakima. (Above, EPL; below, KCHM.)

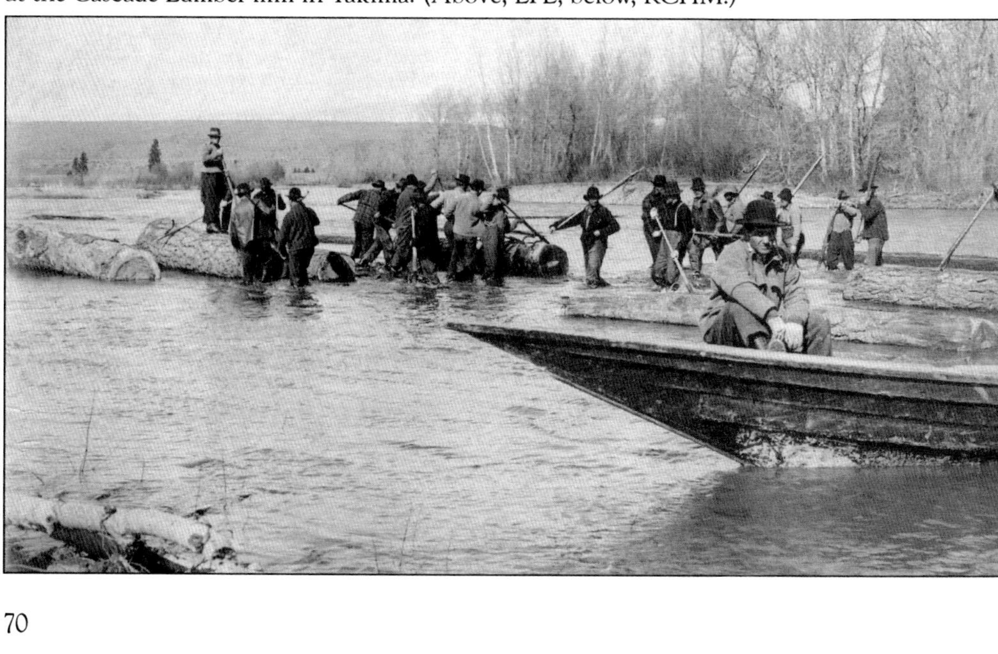

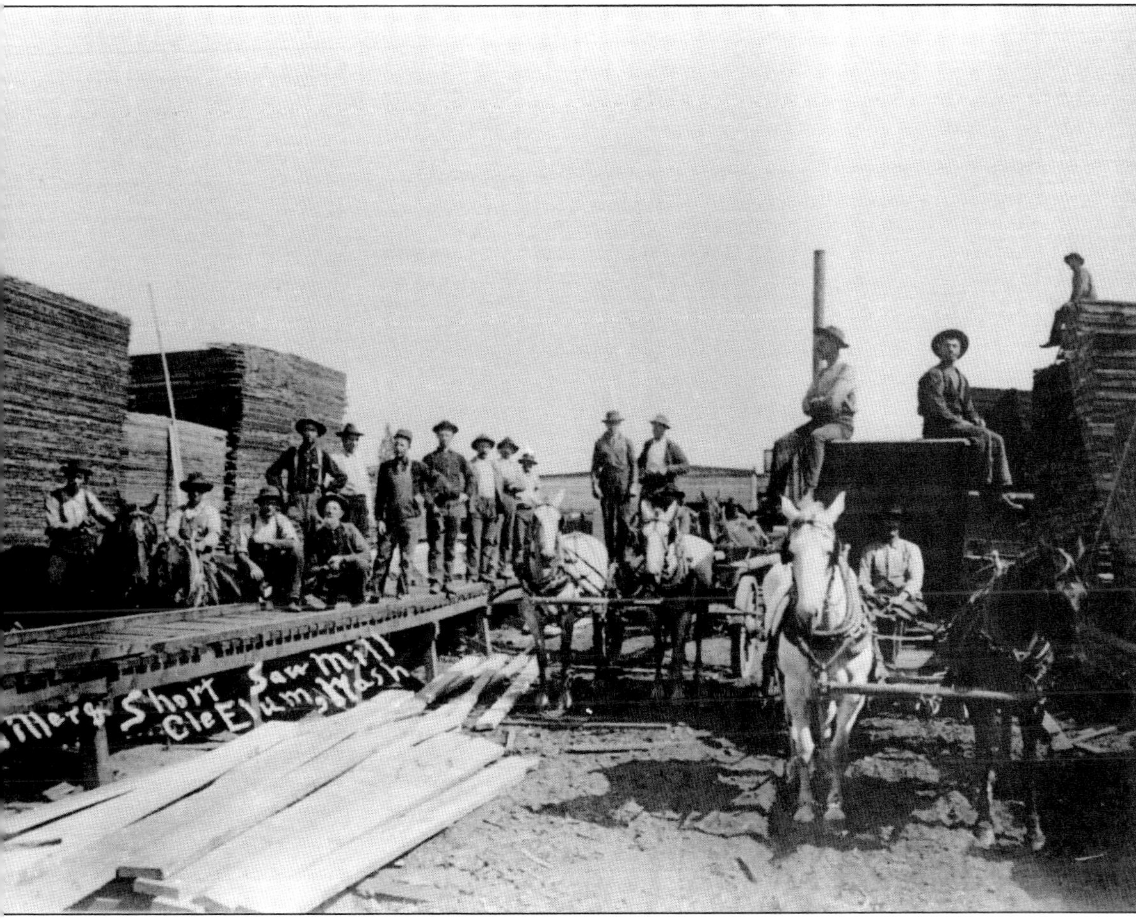

Michael Miller and his partner, a Mr. Short, established Miller and Short Sawmill in South Cle Elum in 1891; it was later called the M.C. Miller Lumber Company. At first, it was a hand sawmill, but by 1903, Miller had upgraded to machinery that increased production drastically. The mill was producing between 12,000 and 15,000 board feet of lumber per day. Most of their logs came from logging camps around Lake Cle Elum, Lake Kachess, and Lake Keechelus and were floated down the river to Cle Elum. The lumber was used for many buildings in Cle Elum, Roslyn, Ronald, and surrounding areas, as well as for ties for the Chicago, Milwaukee, & St. Paul Railroad when it came through the area. Lumber from this mill was also used in the mines around Cle Elum and Roslyn. (EPL.)

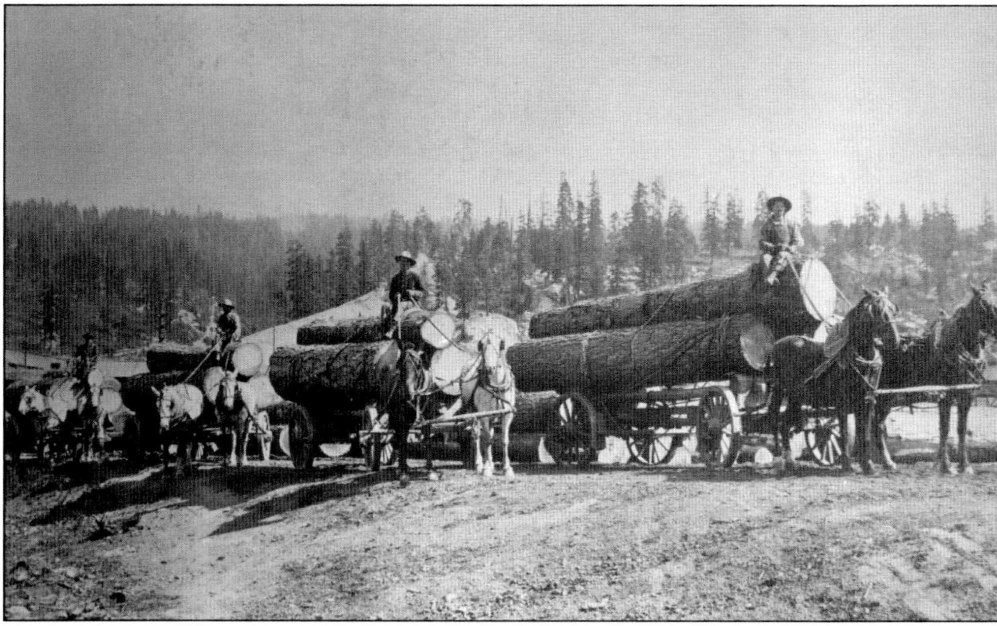

When rivers were not available, horse and wagon were used to haul the logs from the hills to the river or directly to the mill. This picture, taken around 1900, shows the immense size of the trees in the Kittitas Valley. Nearly every house, building, railroad line, or mine shaft needed lumber, which was one of the biggest industries in early Kittitas County. (EPL.)

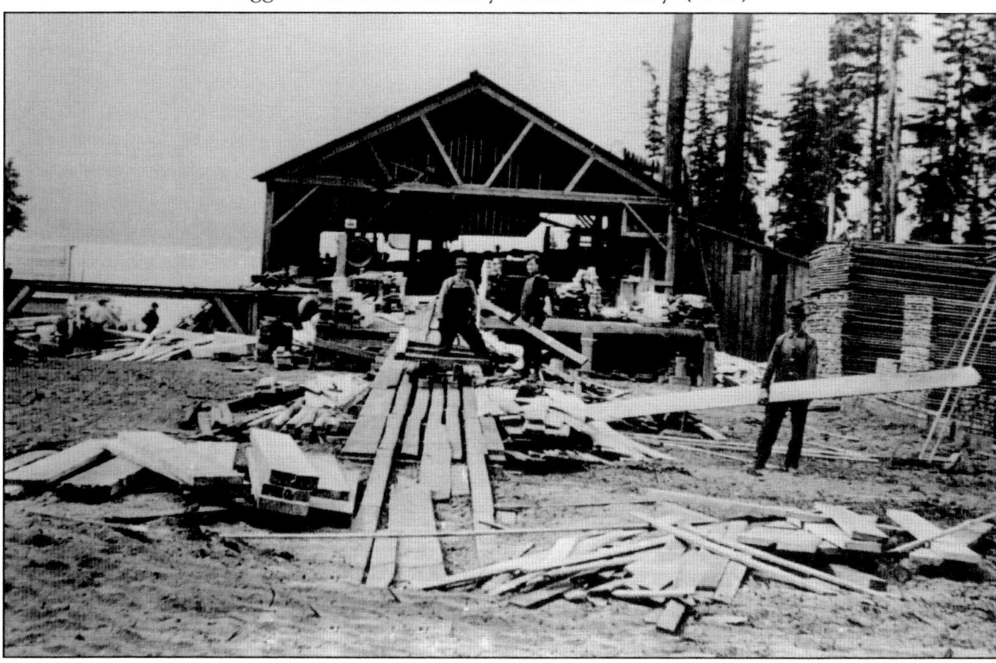

The Roslyn Lumber Company, which began in 1909 on the shores of Lake Cle Elum, was operated by Joseph T. Walsh and his sons. Logs were brought to the mill by tugboat, and the lumber was used mostly in the mines around Roslyn and Ronald. The mill owned a company store, where workers bought supplies, and offered boardinghouses for their employees, which came with all-you-can-eat food. (EPL.)

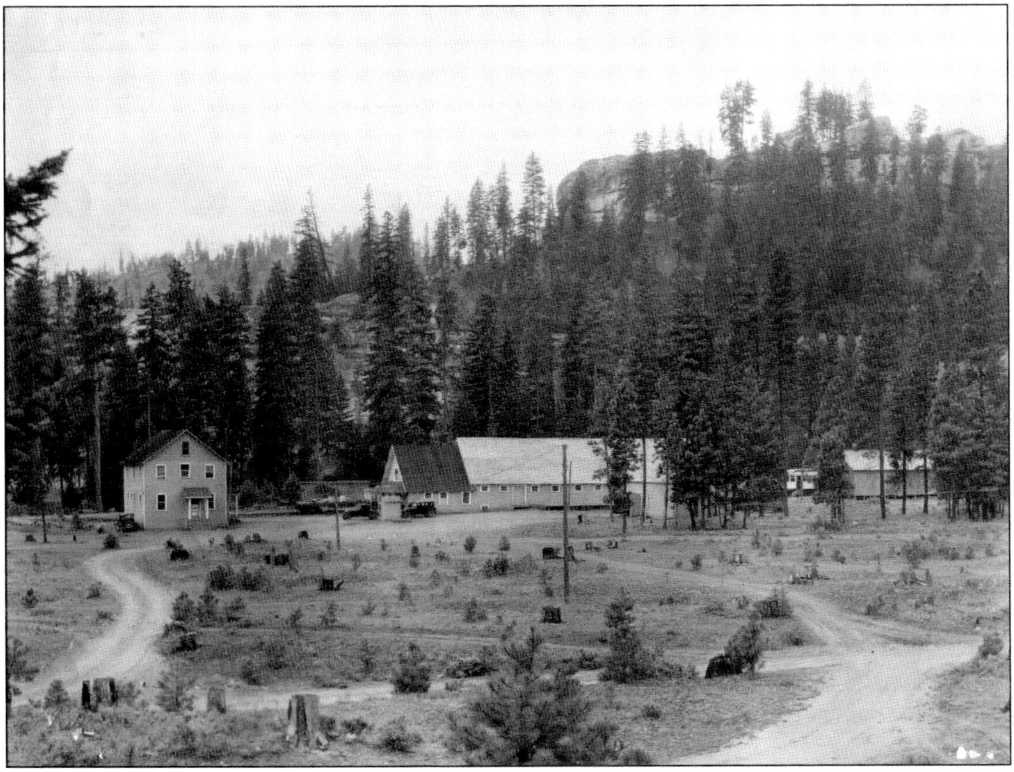

The Cascade Lumber Company's operations in the Teanaway Valley were so extensive that a semipermanent town sprang up. Casland, situated at the junction of the North, Middle, and West Forks of the Teanway River, had a commissary, a school, houses, a dance hall, and a machine shop for the locomotives. The office was located in the house on the left, and the store and warehouse are on the right. (EPL.)

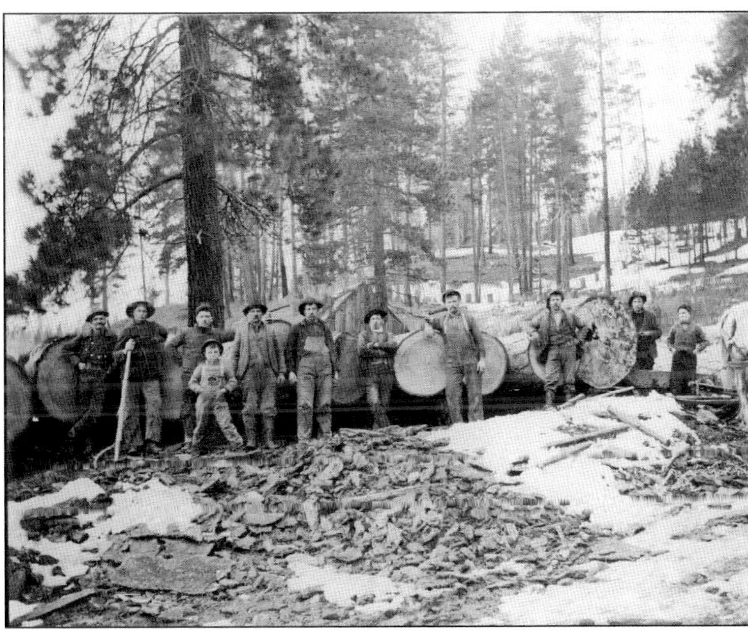

Several men and a boy pose in front of some large logs cut in the Teanaway area. The Teanaway was one of the biggest logging operations in Kittitas County, and hundreds of men were employed with the Cascade Lumber Company or other contracted lumber companies. These logs were rolled onto a sled and pulled by a horse down to staging areas by the Teanaway River. (KCHM.)

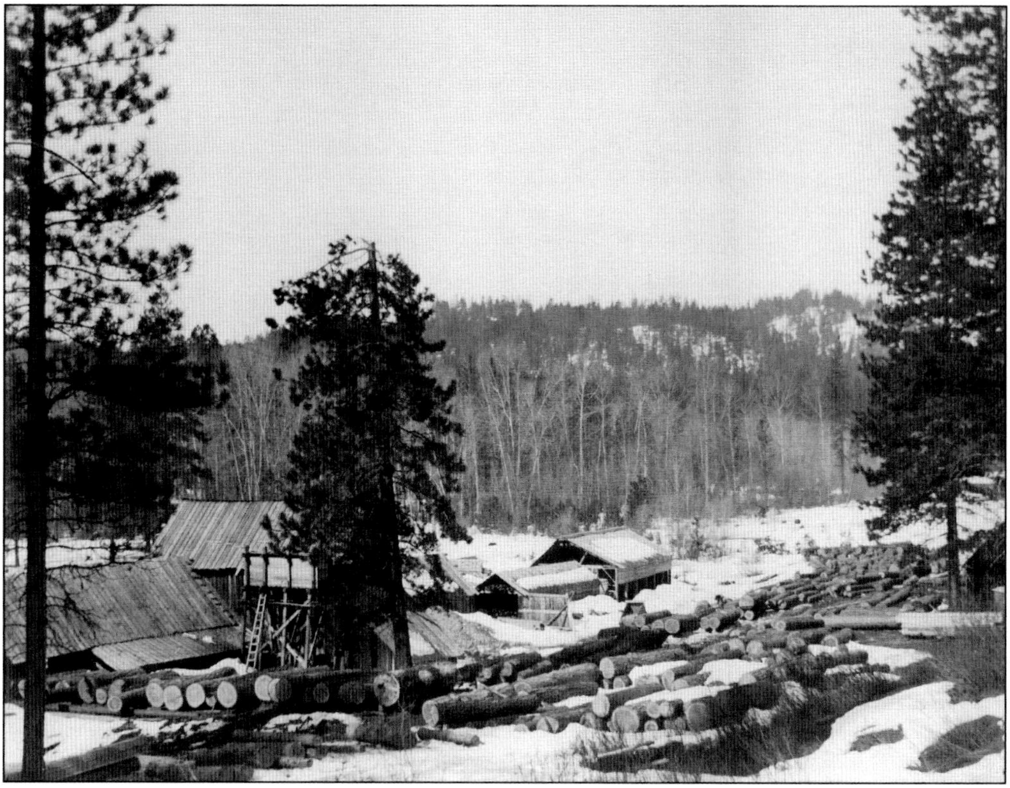

While most of the trees felled in the Teanaway area were sent downriver to Yakima and used in the Cascade Mill, there were smaller operations that cut lumber in the Teanaway Valley. Most of the lumber cut in the Teanaway was used either for houses, mine shaft cribbing, or for railroad ties when the Cascade built logging rail lines into the valley. (KCHM.)

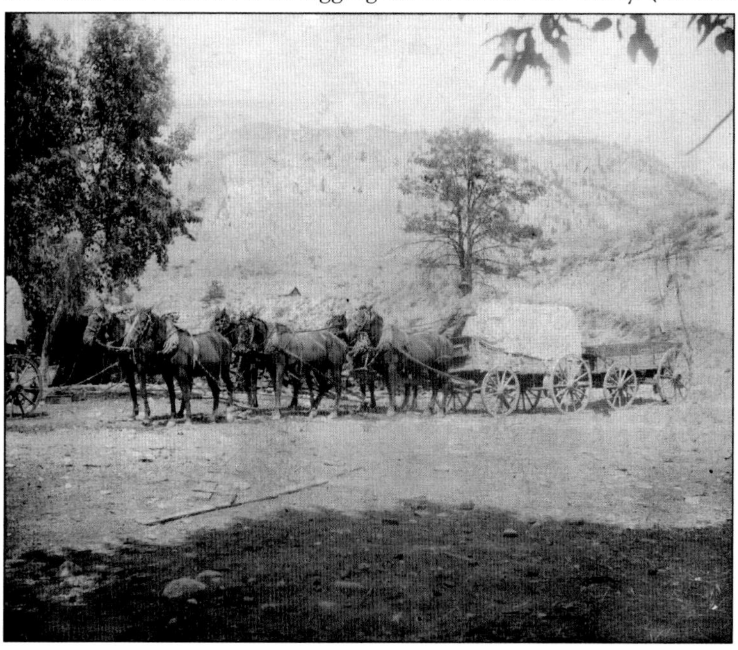

Jim Curtis was a Kittitas Valley pioneer, arriving in the area around 1873. Before roads and rail lines carried supplies around the county, dry goods and other items were freighted in from The Dalles on the Columbia River. Curtis hauled goods with this team of horses from The Dalles to Goldendale, over Satus Pass to Yakima, and then into Kittitas Valley over the Squaw Creek trail. (KCHM.)

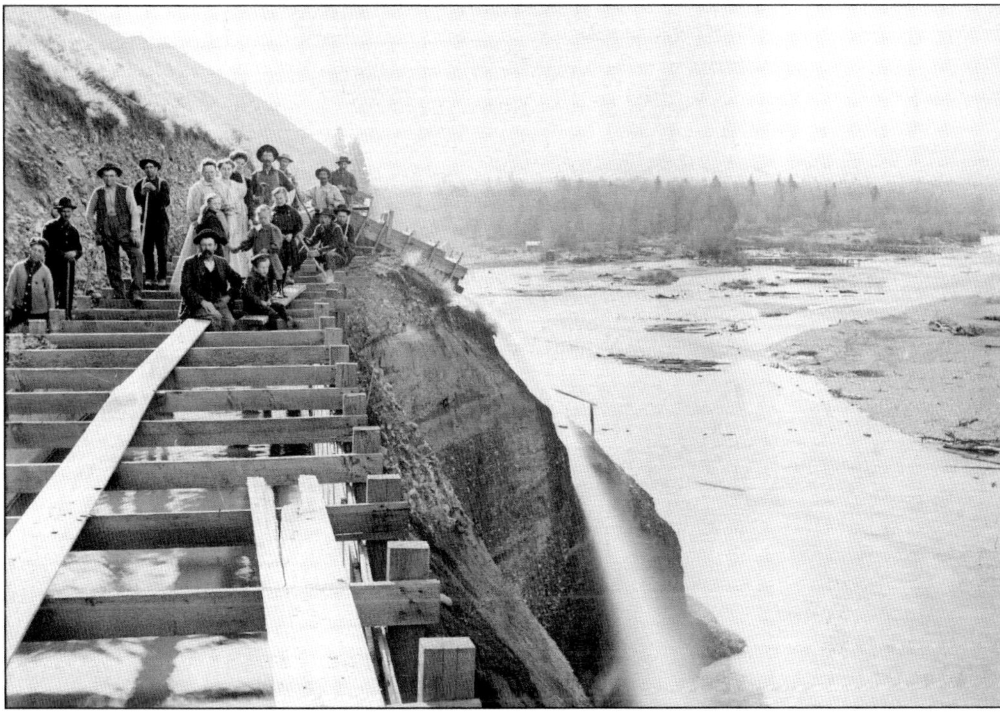

The crew working on the Cascade Irrigation Canal pauses for the camera in this early-20th-century photograph. Below the canal is the Yakima River, making its way towards Ellensburg and then on to Yakima. Note the logs in the river, likely caught on sandbars during a log drive from the Upper County logging operations in Teanaway. (KCHM.)

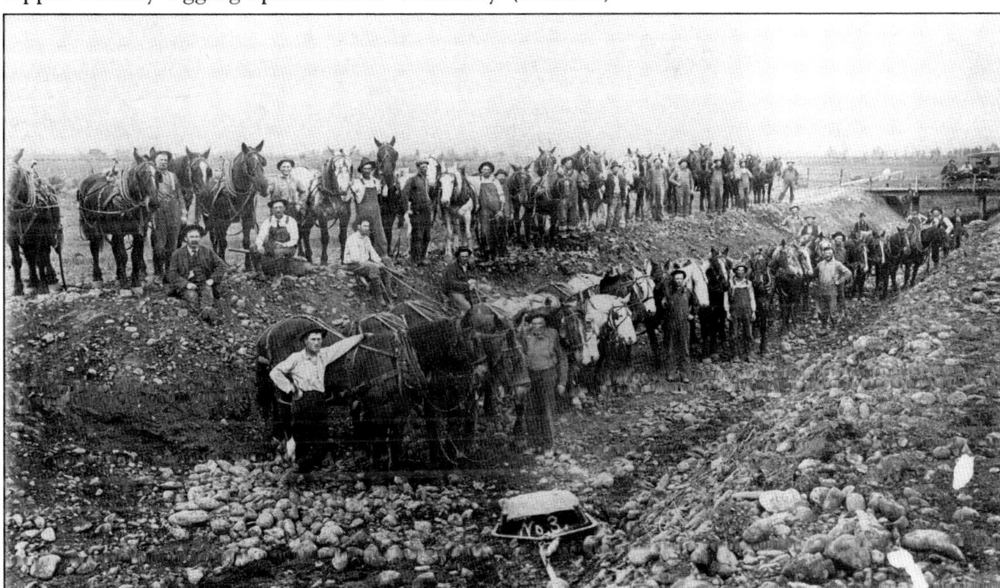

The Kittitas Valley is intertwined with creeks and irrigation canals that were initially dug by hand by many farmers. Pictured here is an irrigation ditch-digging crew utilizing horsepower to haul away the dirt and many rocks that are in the soil. Most of the irrigation water in the Kittitas Valley comes from Upper County lakes, a distance of about 50 miles. (KCHM.)

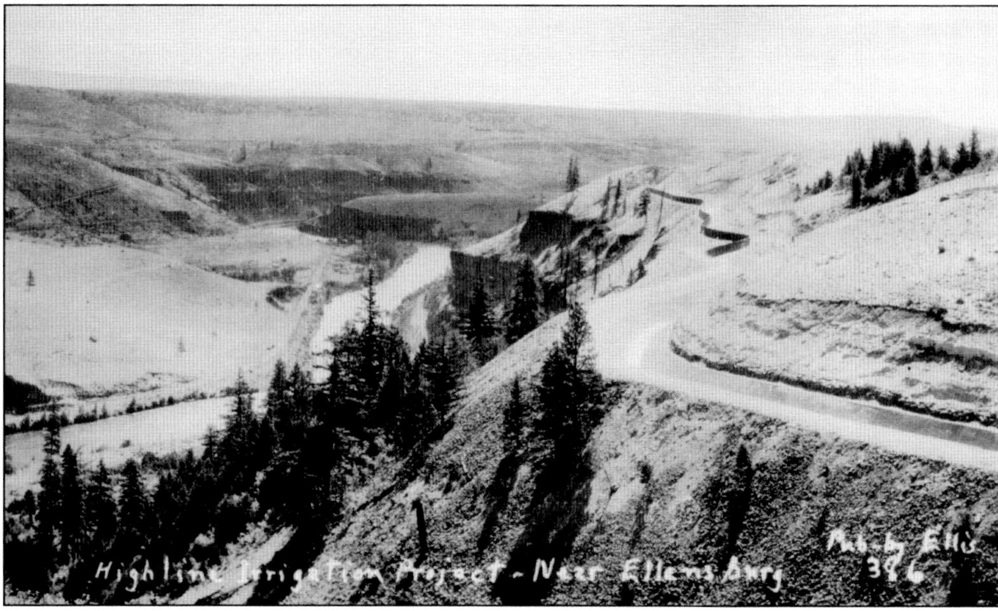

This view is looking east along the Highline Canal between Cle Elum and Ellensburg with the Yakima River in the canyon below. When construction began on this canal in 1926, there were already a few canals serving the Kittitas Valley. However, those canals only serviced about half of the Kittitas Valley. The Highline Canal was needed to irrigate the other half, and it was completed in 1932. (EPL.)

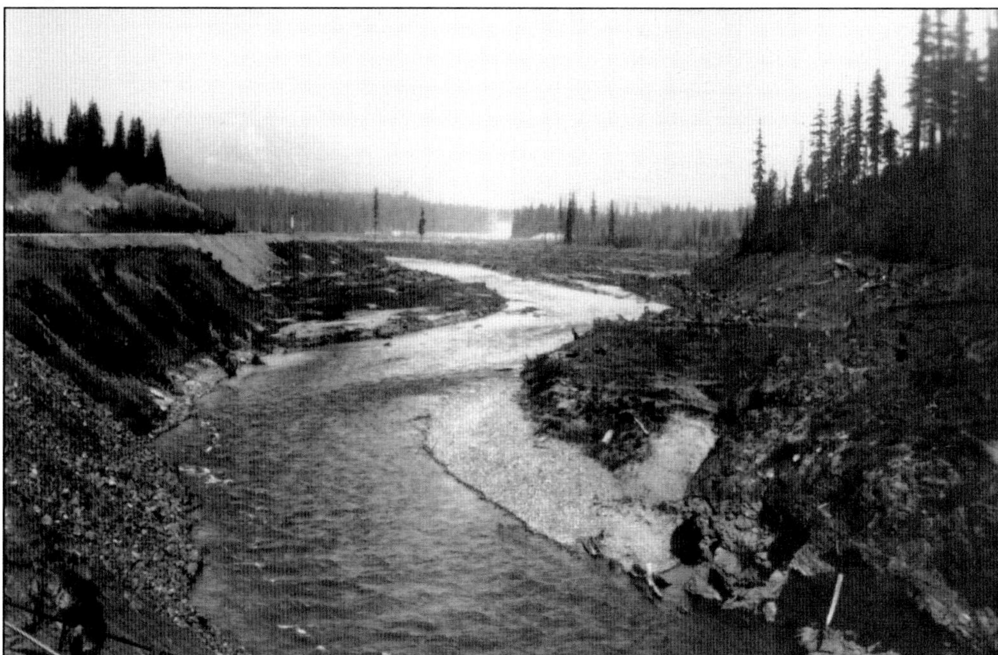

Lake Easton, on the east side of Snoqualmie Pass, is one of the major sources of irrigation water for the county. A dam was built at the outlet of Lake Easton with a diversion to funnel water to the canal system. This view is looking towards Snoqualmie Pass across what would become Lake Easton once the dam was built. See page 120 for an "after" picture. (EPL.)

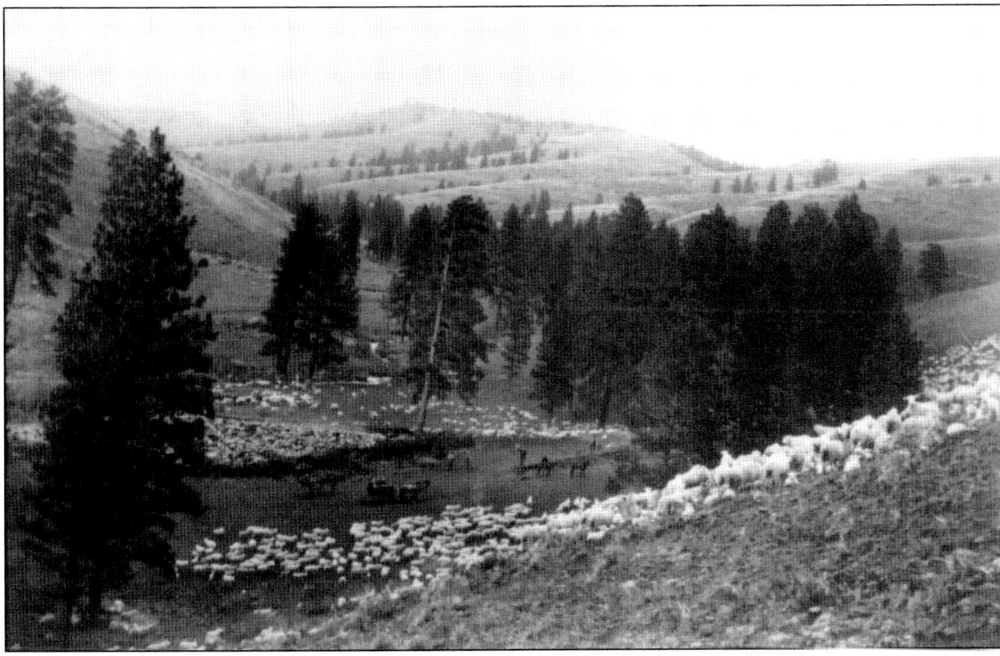

Sheep have roamed the valley since the 1870s, raised for their wool and meat. The demand was not great at first, but when the railroad arrived in the county, it opened up export markets and increased demand. Sheep roamed all over the county, wintering on the Columbia River near Vantage and summering in the Cascade foothills near Salmon la Sac, Cooper Lake, Teanaway, Taneum, Easton, and other locations. Along the way, they were sheared, and the wool was bagged and taken to shipping points. In the fall, after the last cutting of hay, the sheep would come into the Kittitas Valley and graze. Lambs were harvested, and the rest of the sheep were off to winter pasturage. Pictured below is the Hamilton sheep company crew. (EPL.)

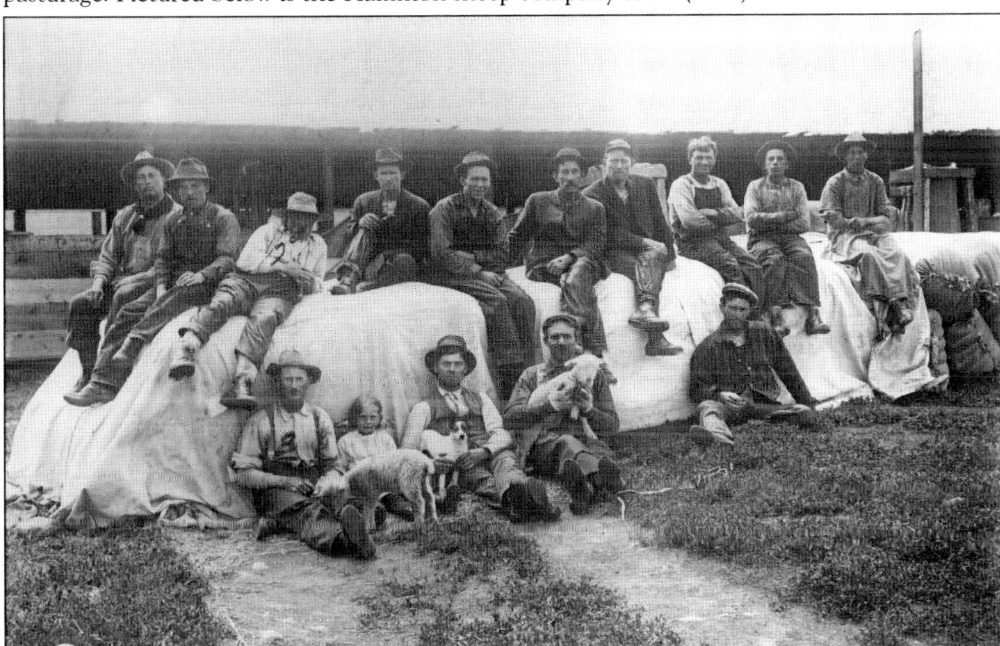

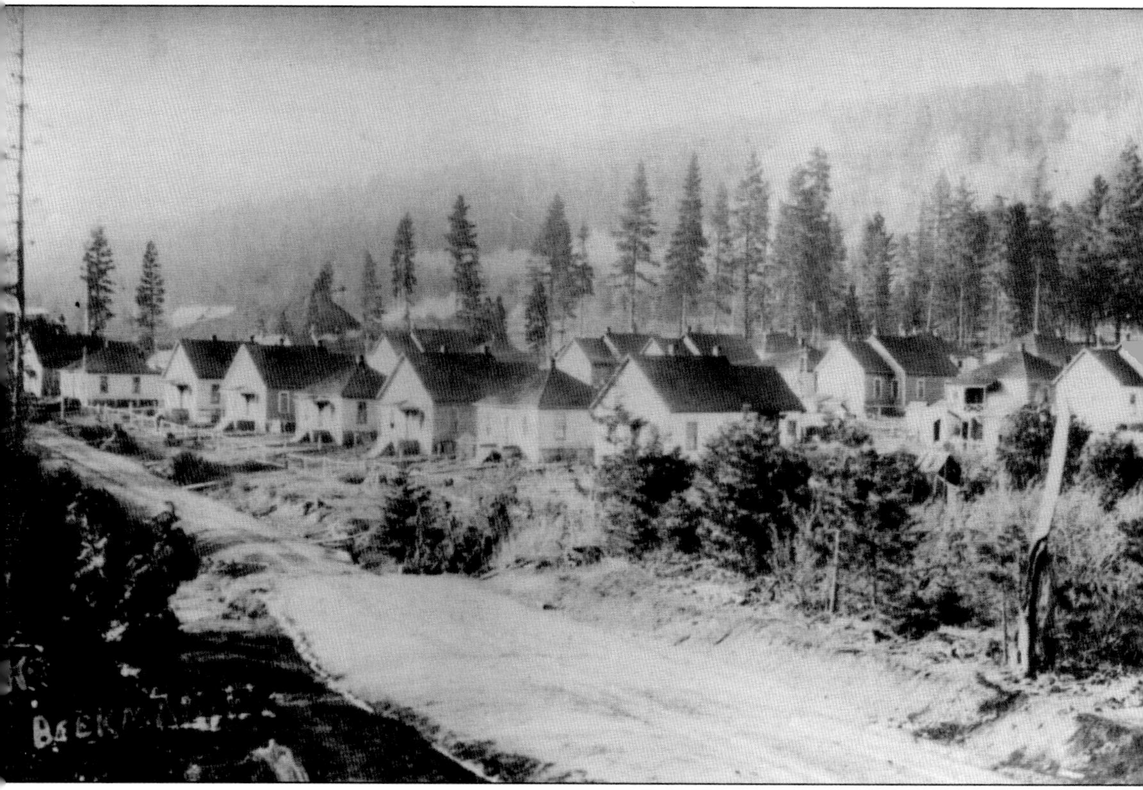

Officially called Beekman but known as Jonesville for mine superintendent Charley Jones, Jonesville was a small community located between Ronald and Lake Cle Elum at the Jonesville Mine. About 300 people lived in the community at its largest size; most all worked in the coal mine nearby. There were two double rows of company houses for employees, a large washhouse with tin tubs to bathe in, and two boardinghouses with beds for 40 men. There was a doctor's office, where Dr. E.C. Heston served for several years. The highlight of the week for families was the Saturday night dance, held in the Jonesville community hall. Many people walked the tracks from Ronald and Roslyn to come to the dance, bringing food and drink, and everyone had a good time. When the mine closed, this community was abandoned, and some of the houses were moved out of the area. (EPL.)

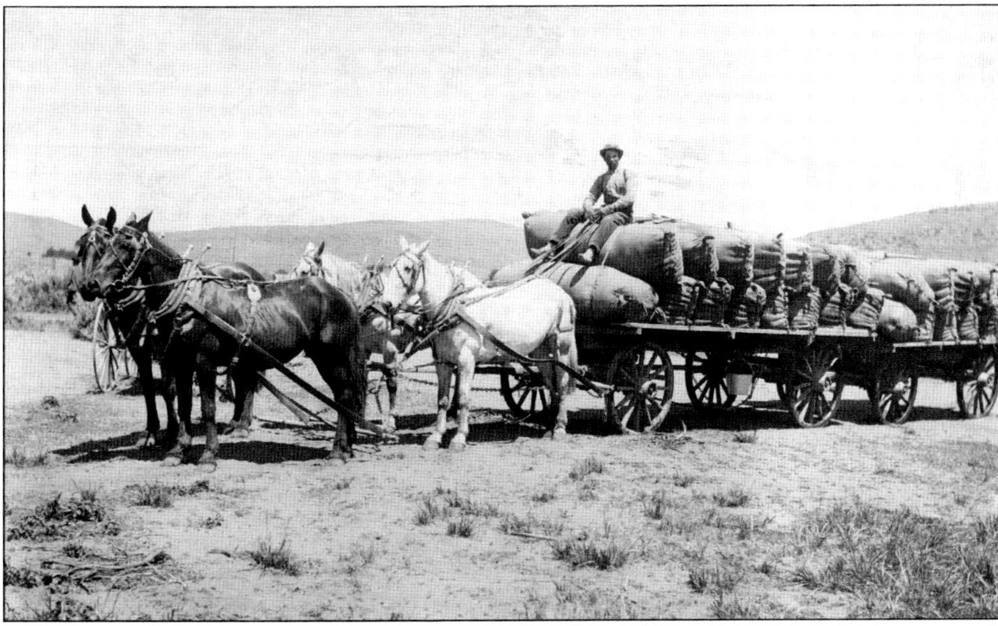

A team of horses pulls a wagon loaded with bags of sheared wool from one of the many early sheep ranches that dotted Kittitas County. The sheep were herded into shearing stations, and the wool was harvested and bagged. It was then loaded onto wagons and taken to shipping points or to the woolen mill in Ellensburg. (KCHM.)

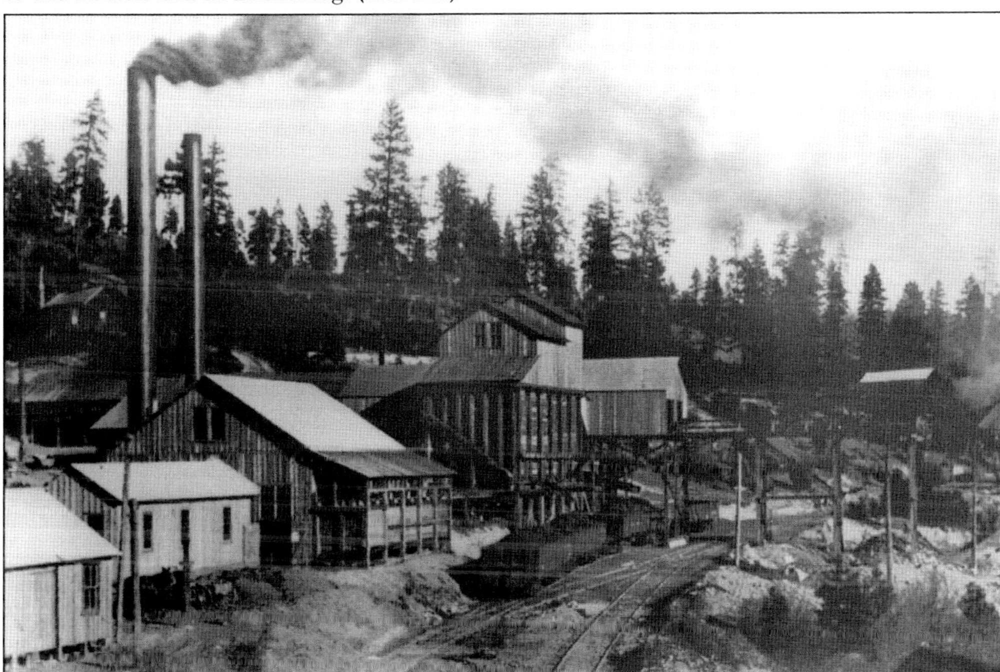

The Independent Mine, located at the east end of Cle Elum, was in operation from 1900 to 1927. The mine was located on the homestead of Thomas Gamble, cofounder of Cle Elum. Gamble leased the land to the mine company and made a percentage of the mine income, which made him a lot of money. (EPL.)

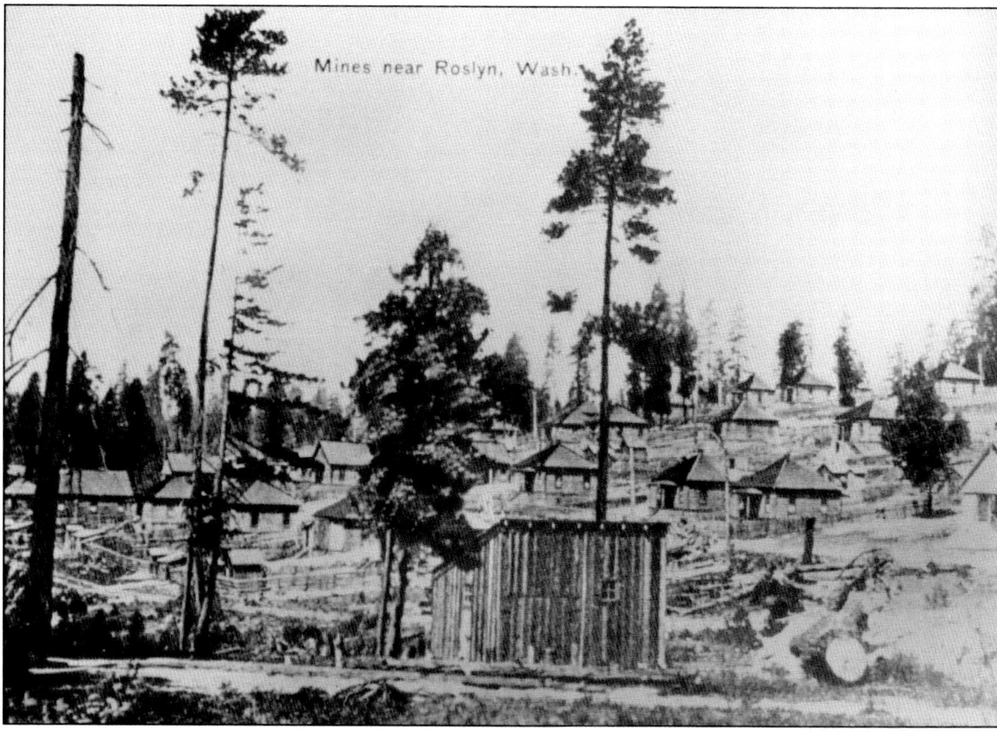

A small community of houses dots the hillside near the No. 5 Mine, situated about halfway between Cle Elum and Roslyn. For the mine company, it was easier to build and provide houses for the miners and their families at the mine. After the mine closed, some of these houses were moved to West Second Street in Cle Elum and are still used today. (CWU.)

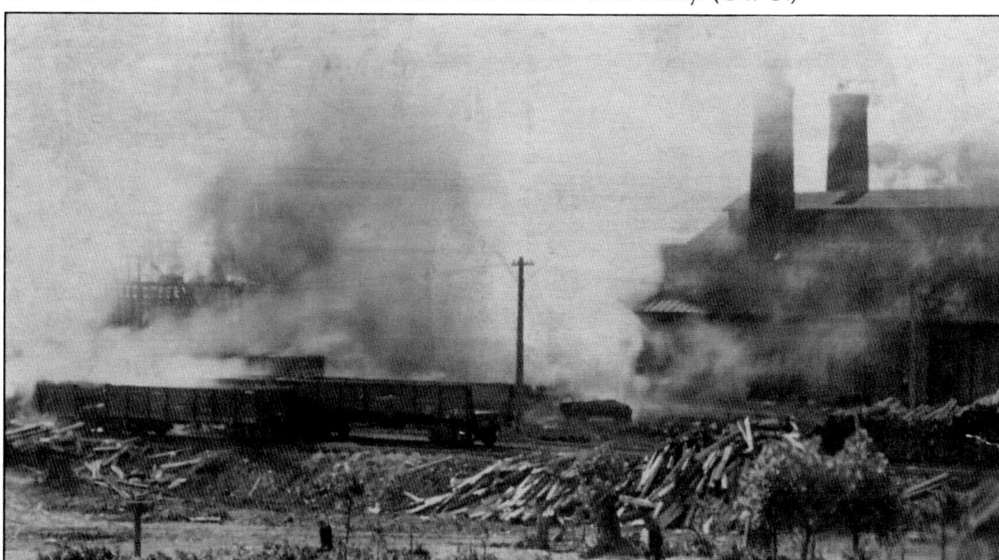

On October 3, 1909, the No. 4 Mine near Roslyn exploded in a ball of fire, killing 10 men and setting fire to the buildings at the entrance of the mine. The explosion was so great that it heavily damaged the mine, making it hard for rescue crews to search for survivors or bodies. The last body was not recovered until six months later, and three bodies were never found. (CWU.)

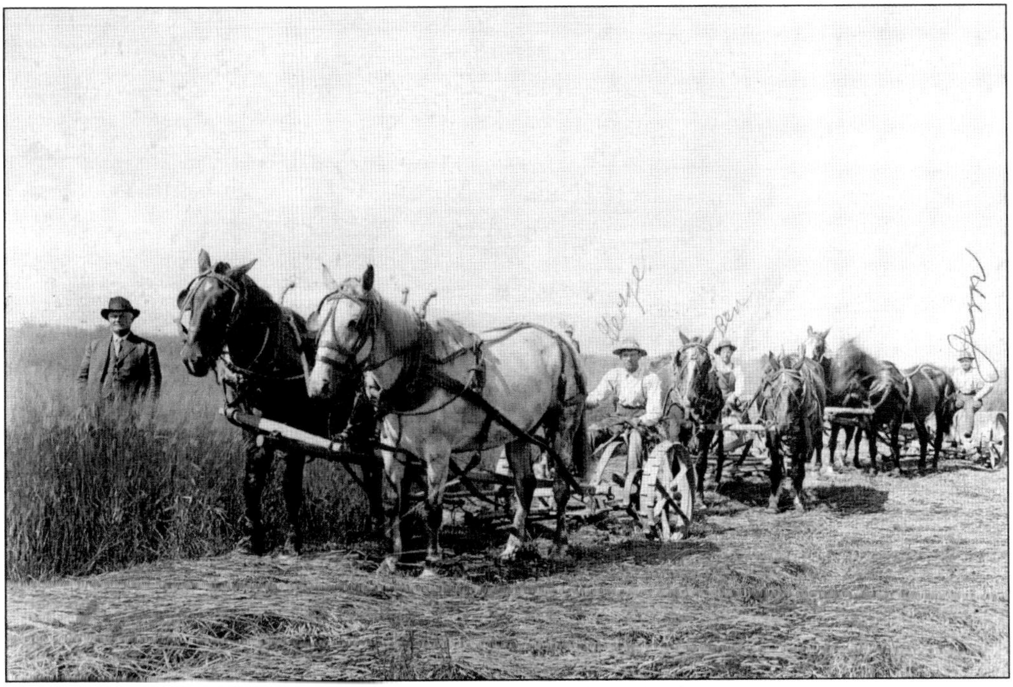

Farmers harvest their crop of grains in the Kittitas Valley. The horses pulled a combine, which cut the grains, usually wheat or oats, into bundles or piles. Once the grains were cut and ready, a thresher separated the grain from the stalk, bagging the grain and discarding the chaff. Much of the harvested wheat was taken to the local gristmills and ground into flour. (EPL.)

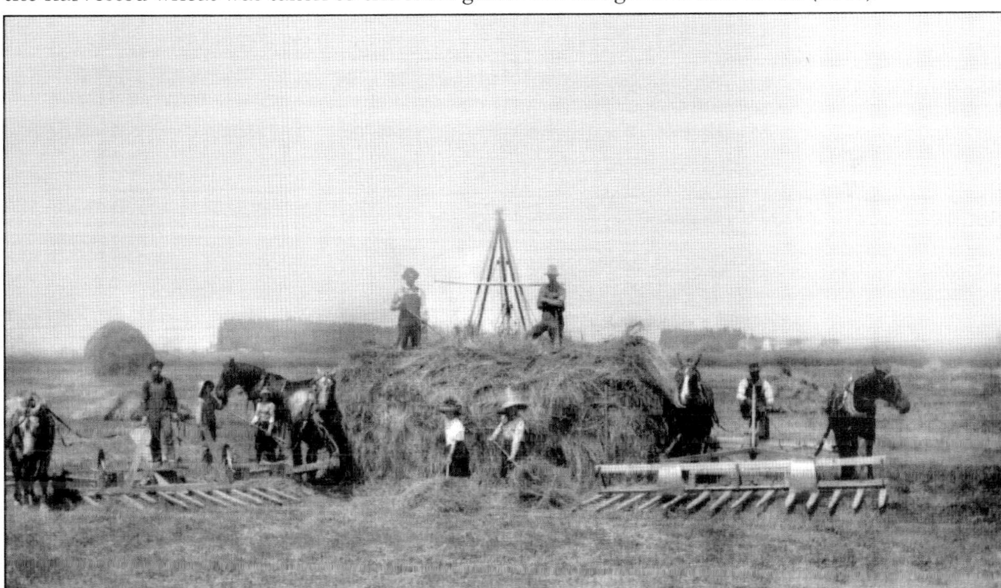

Hay bailing is pictured at Joe Preece's ranch, located across from the old Denmark Hall on Denmark Road in the Kittitas Valley. Born in England in 1852, Preece came to the United States in 1872. After working a variety of odd jobs, he homesteaded a quarter section in the Kittitas Valley and turned the sagebrush into a thriving wheat farm. The girls in the hats are Preece's daughters Mary, Flora, and Selena. (EPL.)

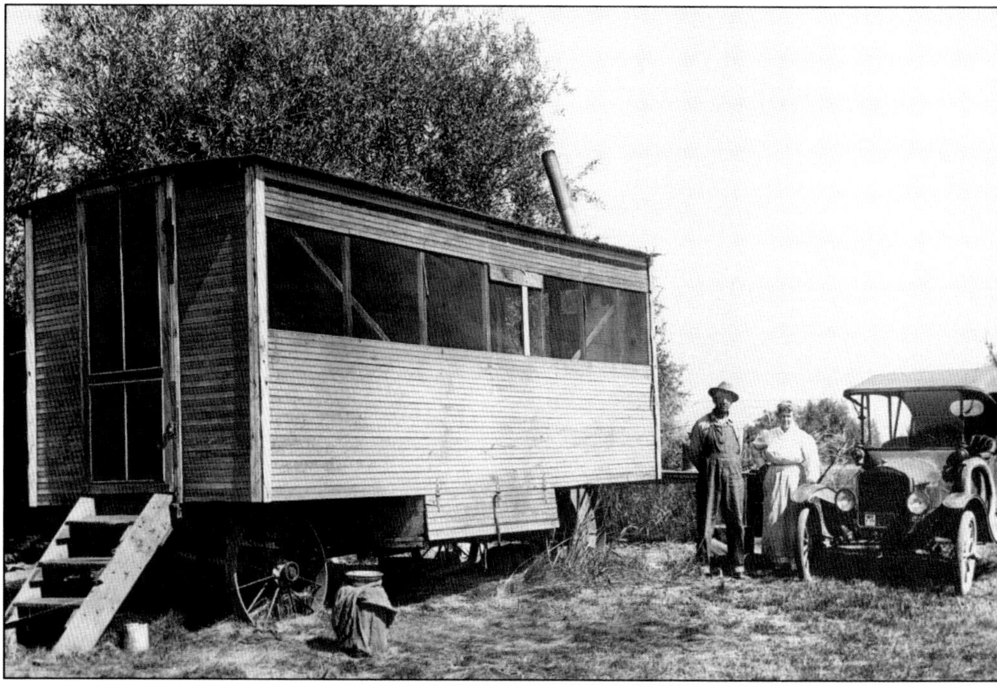

Mary and Dave Parmeter's cook wagon is seen along the Yakima River around 1915. The cook wagon fed the men working on the Cascade Canal, which brought irrigation water into the Kittitas Valley. Aside from the cook wagon, there were tents set up to house the laborers who worked long hours digging and building the canal flumes. (EPL.)

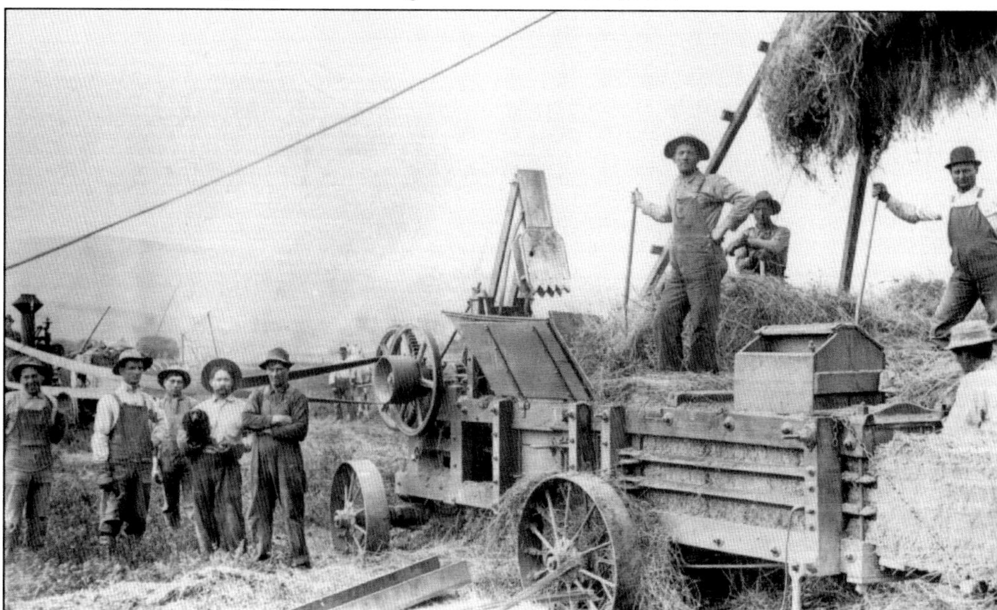

A hay baling crew works in the Kittitas Valley. A tractor was used to turn a belt around a pulley that was attached to the baler to provide power. Men would pitch the hay into the baler, and it would compact the hay into the tightly packed bales. Before machine power, there were horse-powered presses as well as man-powered bale presses. (EPL.)

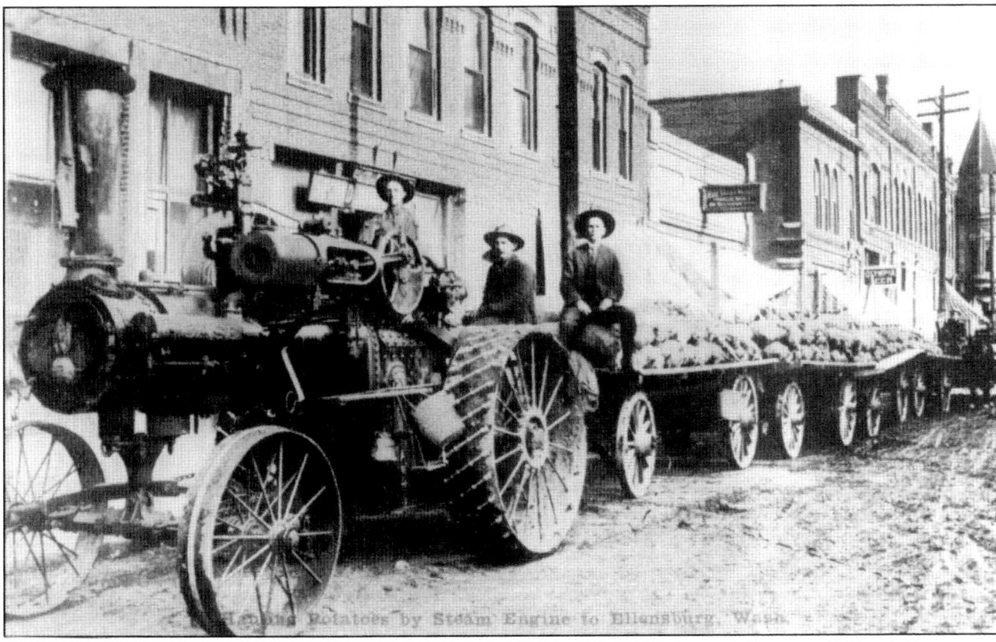

A tractor pulls wagons full of potatoes on Fourth Avenue between Main and Pearl Streets in Ellensburg. Potatoes grow well in the Kittitas Valley, especially once irrigation water was readily available. The Chicago, Milwaukee, & St. Paul Railroad built two potato storage sheds near Kittitas in the 1920s, as did the Northern Pacific Railroad near Thrall. The cupola of the Davidson Building can be seen behind the wagon train. (EPL.)

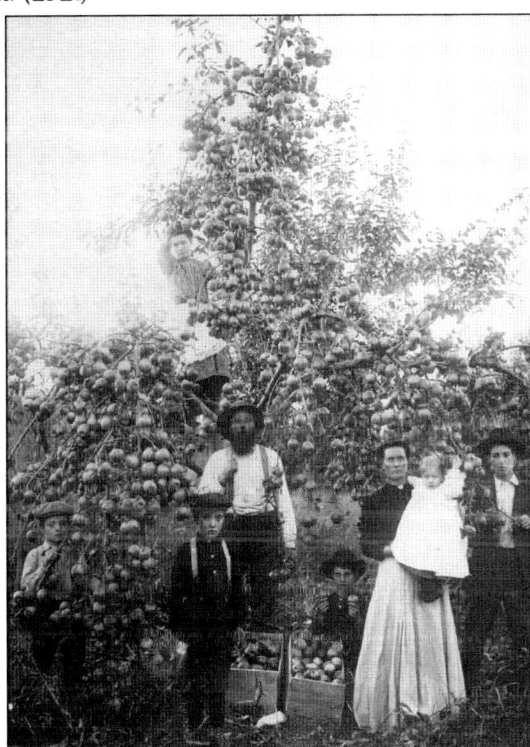

William Sheldon, wife Viola, and six of their seven children stand by one of the apple trees on their farm in the Kittitas Valley. Sheldon owned 1,300 acres of land, 20 of which were part of one of the largest apple orchards in Kittitas County. Sheldon also owned a threshing machine and hay baler and hired his services out to other farmers every fall. (EPL.)

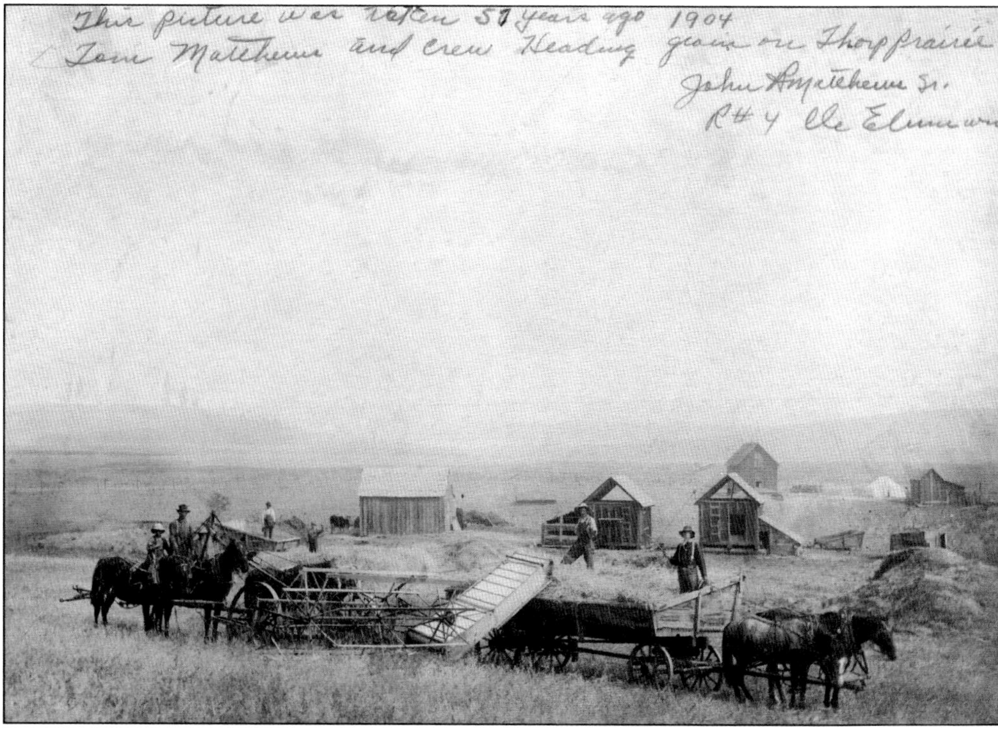

In this 1904 image, Tom Matthews and crew are heading grain on the Thorp Prairie. Heading grain was a process in which the grain header was pushed by horses, cutting the grain, which was then sent up the conveyor ramp into a header box, also pulled by horses. Once the header box was full, it was emptied into a big stack to dry before threshing. (KCHM.)

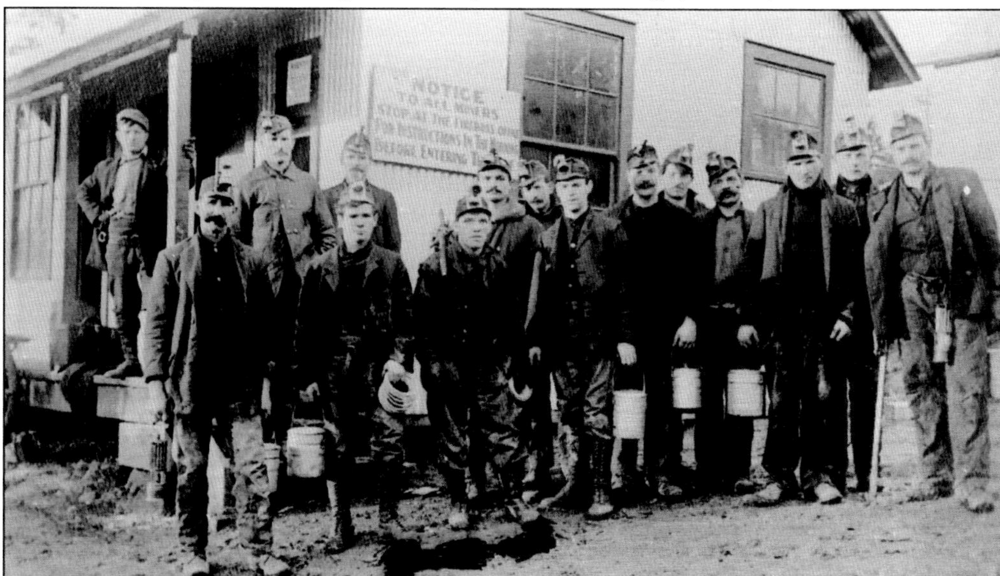

A coal mining crew in Roslyn waits near the fire boss's office for their shift to start. The fire boss would enter the mine, verify whether it was safe or not, and give the miners clearance to go to work. The miners here have their helmets on and lunch pails in hand. (EPL.)

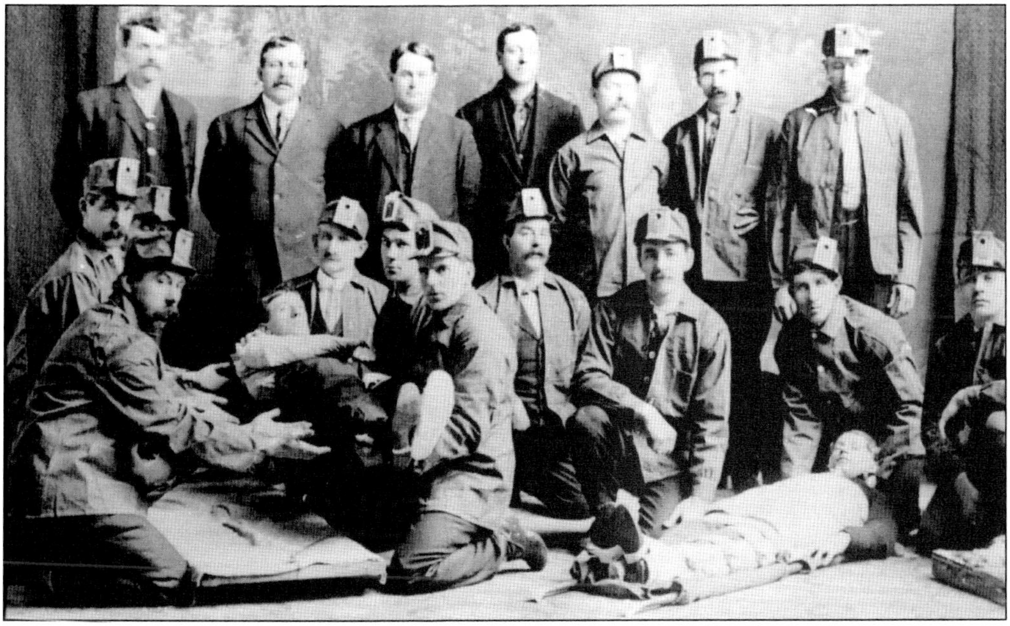

A mine rescue crew poses for a picture in Roslyn with other mine officials. Coal mining was very dangerous, mainly because the tunnel shafts could expose naturally occurring methane gas, which could either ignite and explode or asphyxiate the miners. Rescue crews were trained men who were on call in case of a disaster or if an injured miner needed extracted. (EPL.)

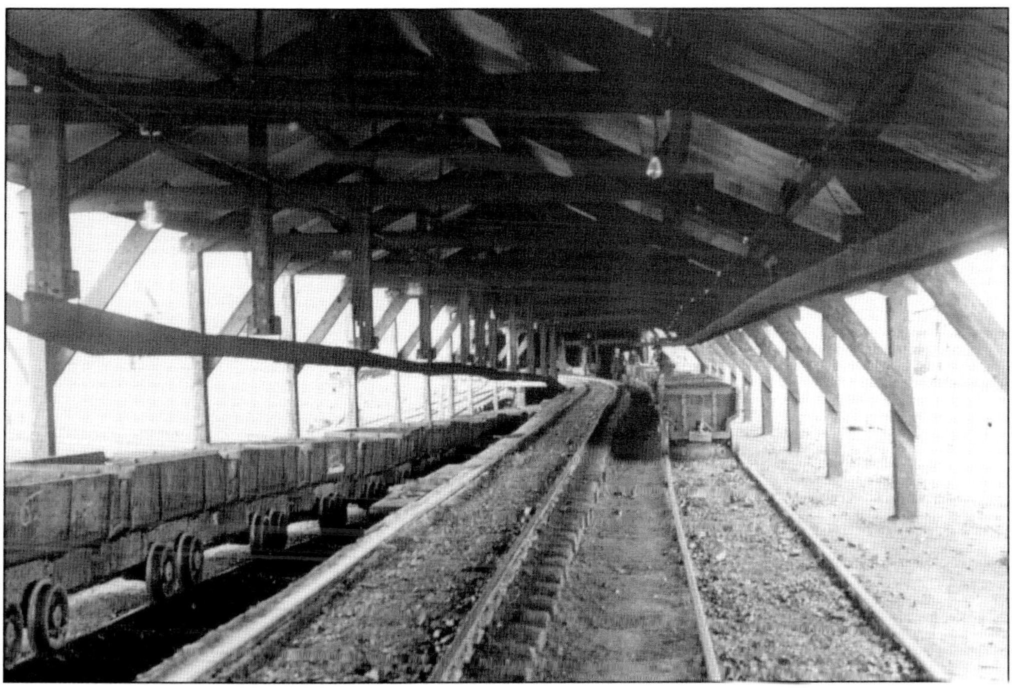

The tipple landing for the No. 7 Mine in Cle Elum is pictured here around 1920. When mining cars surfaced out of the mine, they were taken to the tipple, an elevated building that turned the cars over and dumped the coal into train cars. The mining cars were then sent back into the mines for more coal. (EPL.)

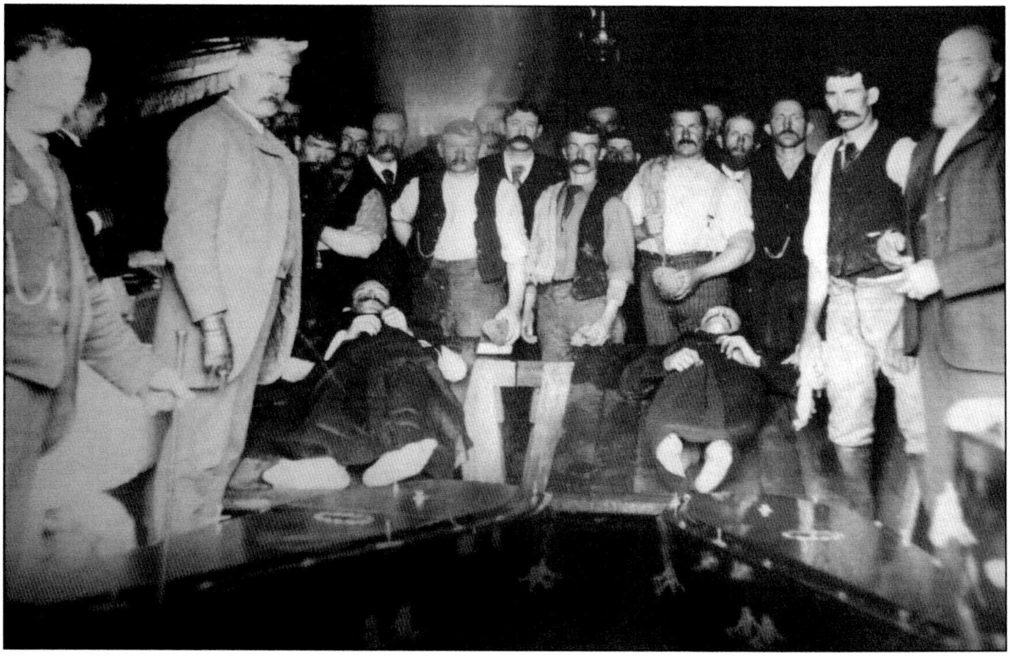

On the afternoon of May 10, 1892, an explosion at the No. 1 Mine in Roslyn killed 45 miners, making it the worst coal mine disaster to date in Washington State. The No. 1 Mine was started in 1886, and by 1892, it had expanded over 2,500 feet into the earth and had seven layers. The mine company had furnaces on the surface, which were in place to ventilate the mines from the dangerous methane gas called firedamp. On that fateful day, miners were drilling between levels when a pocket of firedamp exploded. Pictured here are two of the miners being prepared for burial in a temporary morgue, their coffins by their feet. In the second picture is the burial procession; the wagons in the street are lined up to carry the caskets to the cemetery. (Above, EPL; below, RM.)

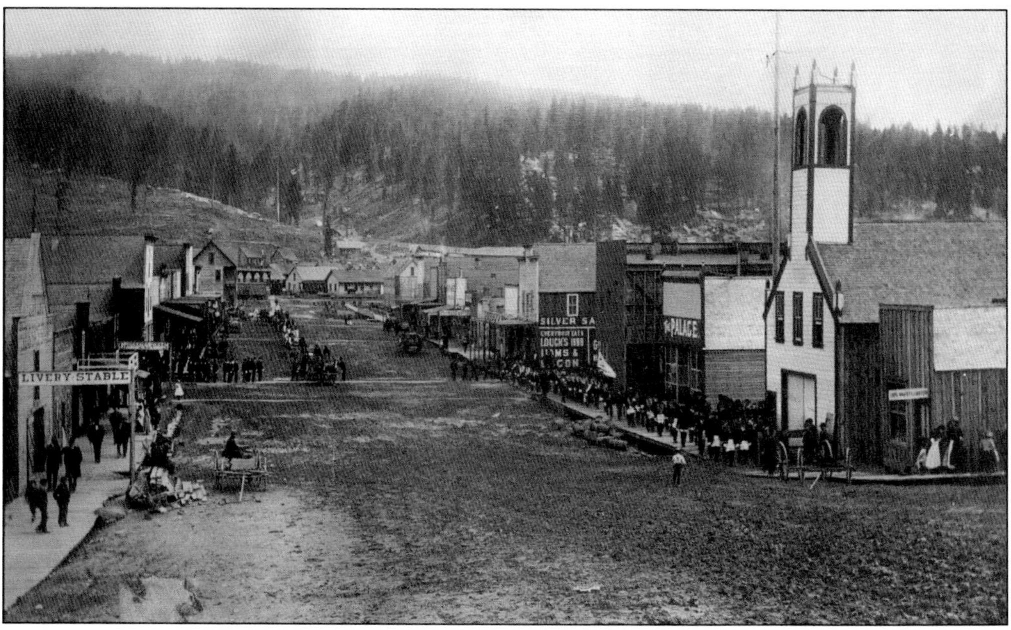

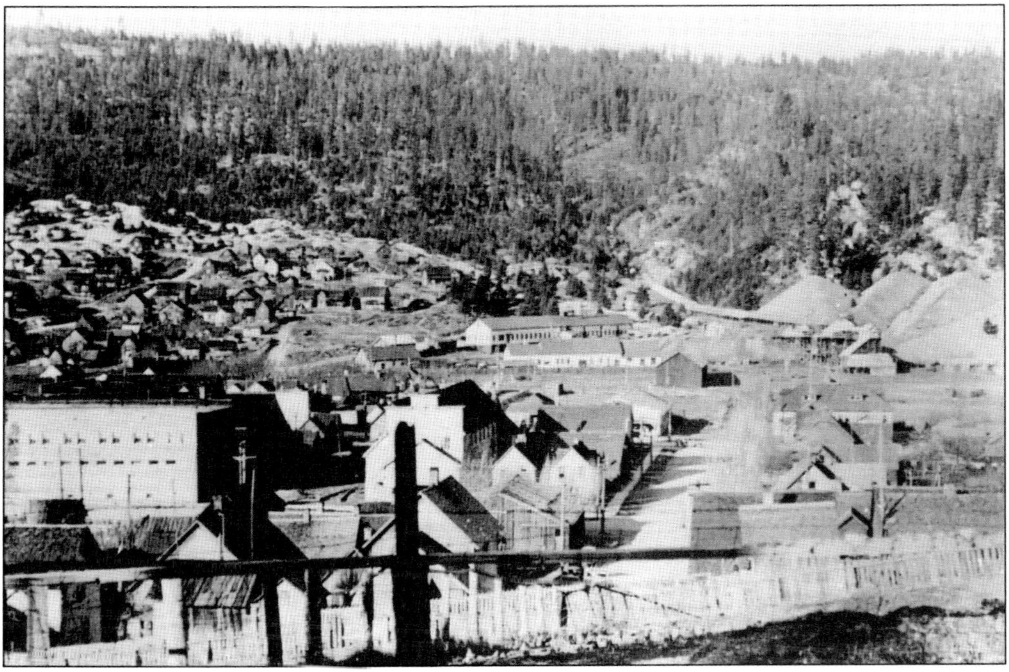

This view of Roslyn looks east down West Dakota Avenue towards the No. 1 Mine. Near the mine entrance are various buildings belonging to the Northwestern Improvement Company, and the mine trailing piles can be seen at right. This was one of the first mines opened in Roslyn and was in operation from 1886 to 1927. (EPL.)

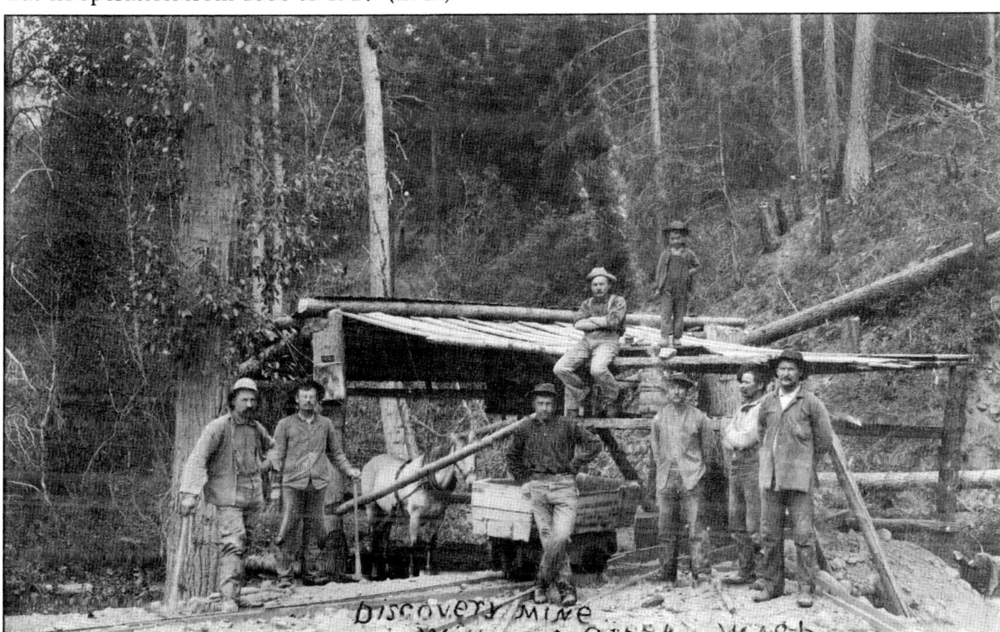

The Discovery Mine along Williams Creek was above Liberty in the Swauk Mining District. When gold was discovered near Swauk and Williams Creeks, prospectors from all over the region convened on the area. To settle tensions and protect miners, the Swauk Mining District was formed early on. It recorded the mine claims and kept records of the mines in the district. (KCHM.)

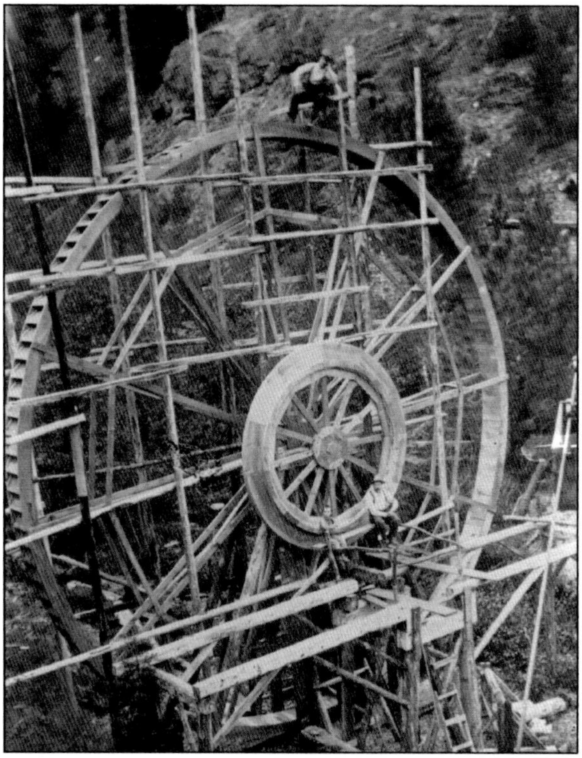

A large arrastra and waterwheel in the Swauk Mining District are pictured near Blewett Pass around 1890. Water from a creek turned the wheel, which turned a shaft that crushed gold-laden ore to separate the metal from the ore. At the base, a large grinding rock was drug along another flat rock, breaking up the ore and making it easier to mine the gold. (EPL.)

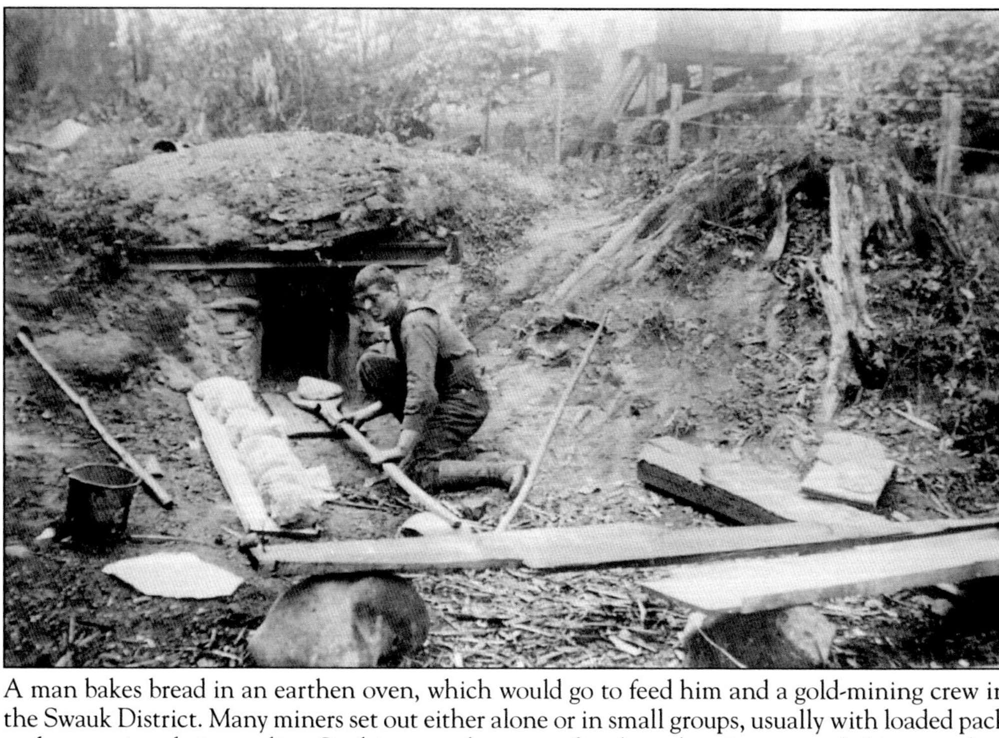

A man bakes bread in an earthen oven, which would go to feed him and a gold-mining crew in the Swauk District. Many miners set out either alone or in small groups, usually with loaded pack mules carrying their supplies. Cooking was done over fire, but when it came to baking, earthen ovens were often used. (EPL.)

Six

TRANSPORTATION

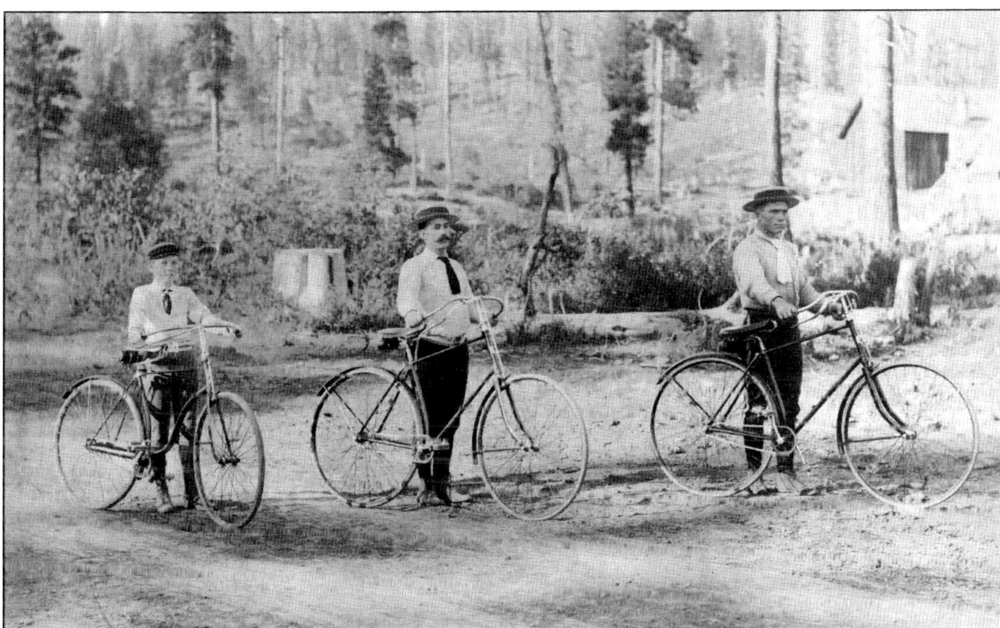

John Donovan (center) and two boys stop with their bicycles along the road between Roslyn and Cle Elum around 1890. The distance between Roslyn and Cle Elum is about three miles, and for those who did not have a horse, a bike was the next fastest mode of transportation. (RM.)

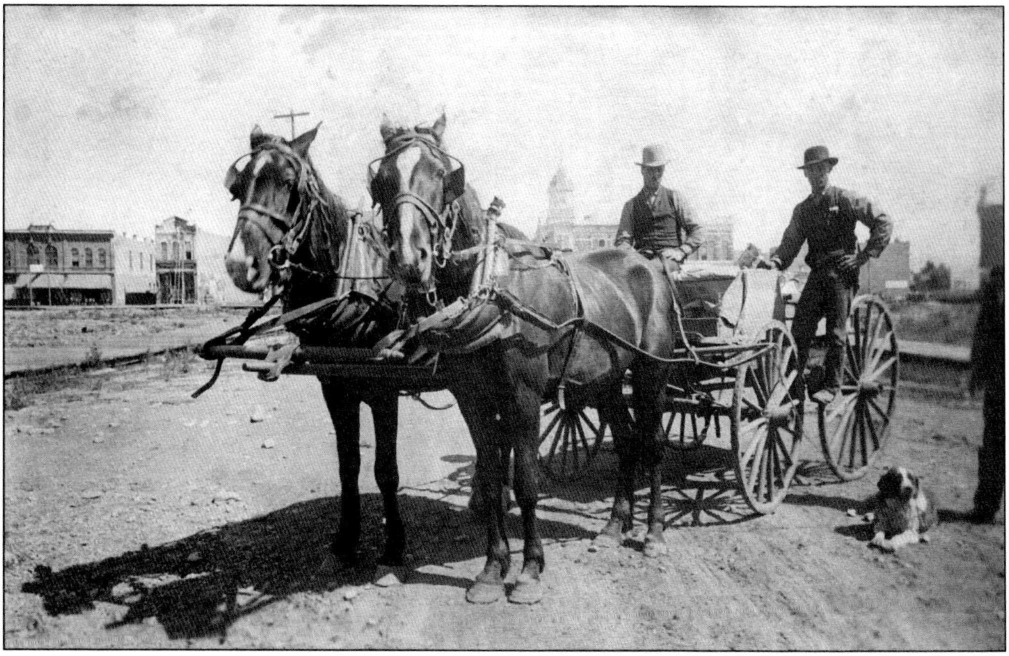

Taken not long after the Ellensburg fire of 1889, this photograph shows the first milk wagon used in the area. Sitting near the intersection of Pearl Street and Second Avenue, these men are in front of the newly constructed buildings along Third Avenue. On the edge of the picture at right is the Cadwell Building, which houses the Kittitas County Historical Museum today. (KCHM.)

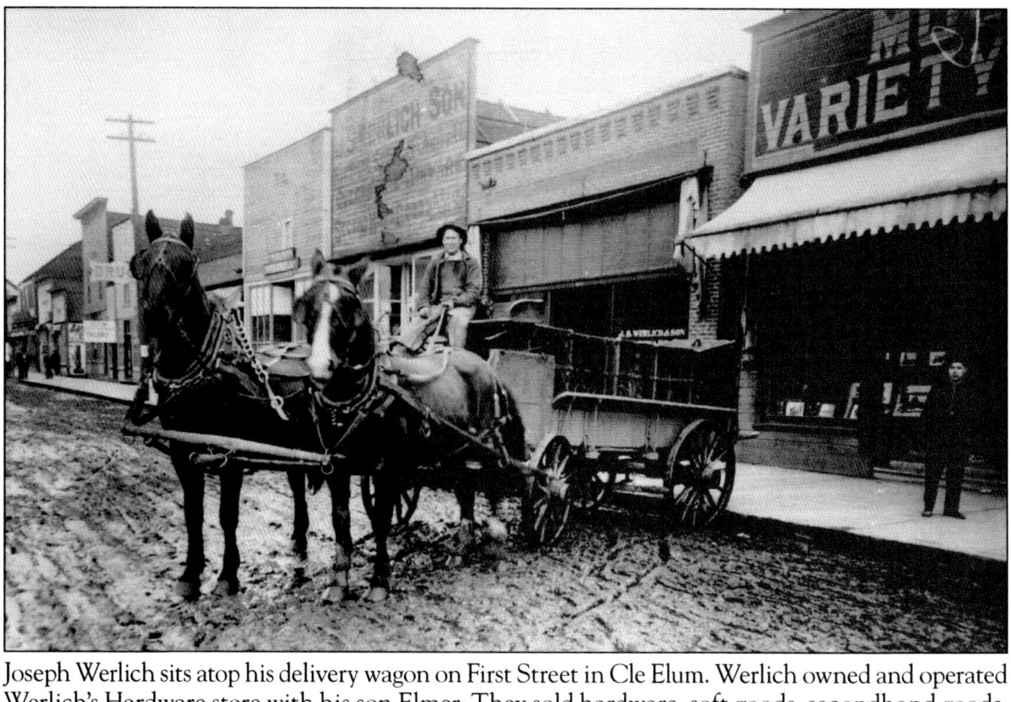

Joseph Werlich sits atop his delivery wagon on First Street in Cle Elum. Werlich owned and operated Werlich's Hardware store with his son Elmer. They sold hardware, soft goods, secondhand goods, and more. Werlich eventually sold his store and moved to Yakima County. The brick portion of his store still stands at 117 East First Street. (EPL.)

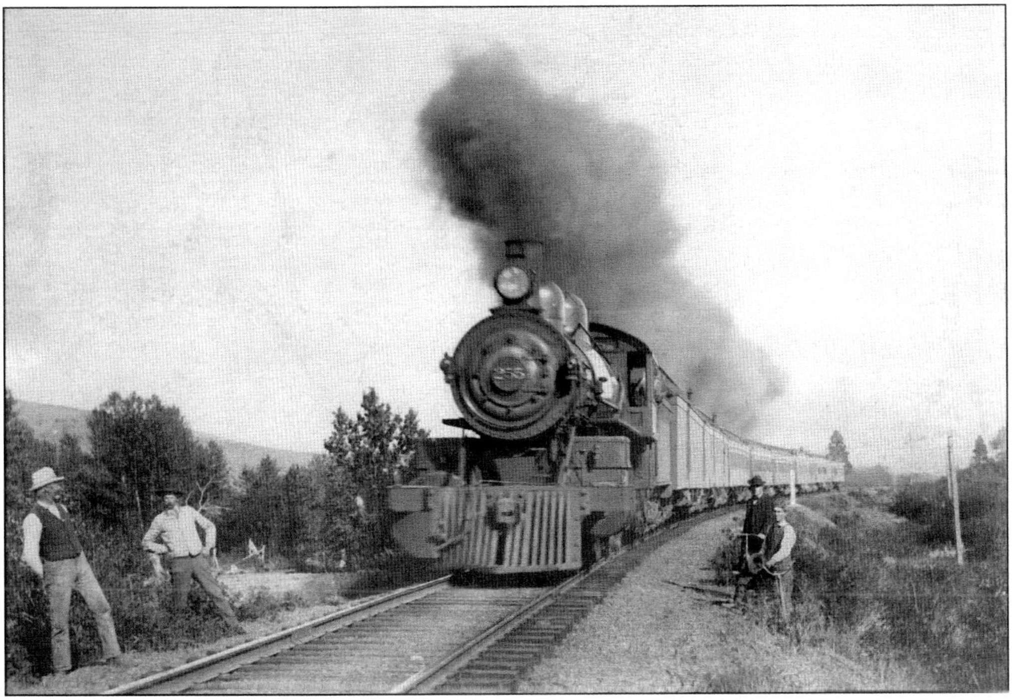

A Northern Pacific Railroad locomotive steams into Thorp from Ellensburg. In 1895, a train depot was built in Thorp, and the town grew around it, initially with a maintenance shop, warehouses, and shipping facilities for the railroad. The town was platted around the depot, and people began moving into the area. (KCHM.)

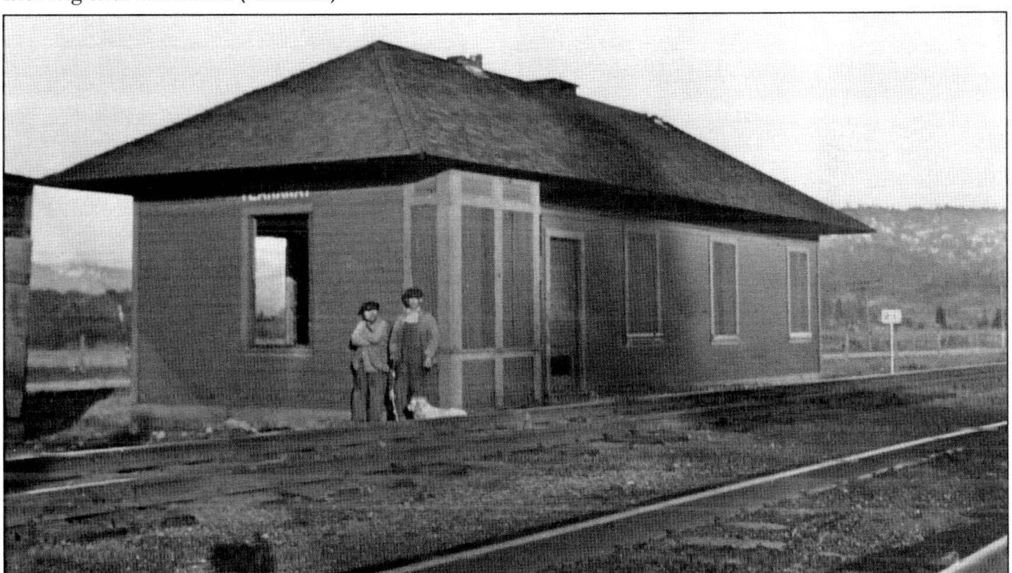

This train is pictured near the flag stop at Teanaway along the Northern Pacific line. Flag stops were not depots; a telegraph operator usually worked at a flag stop, giving instructions to the engineer, and passengers could also be picked up on an as-needed basis from flag stops. Early on, due to the mining and logging in the area, Teanaway had a small townsite near the present junction of Highway 10 and Highway 97 east of Cle Elum. (CWU.)

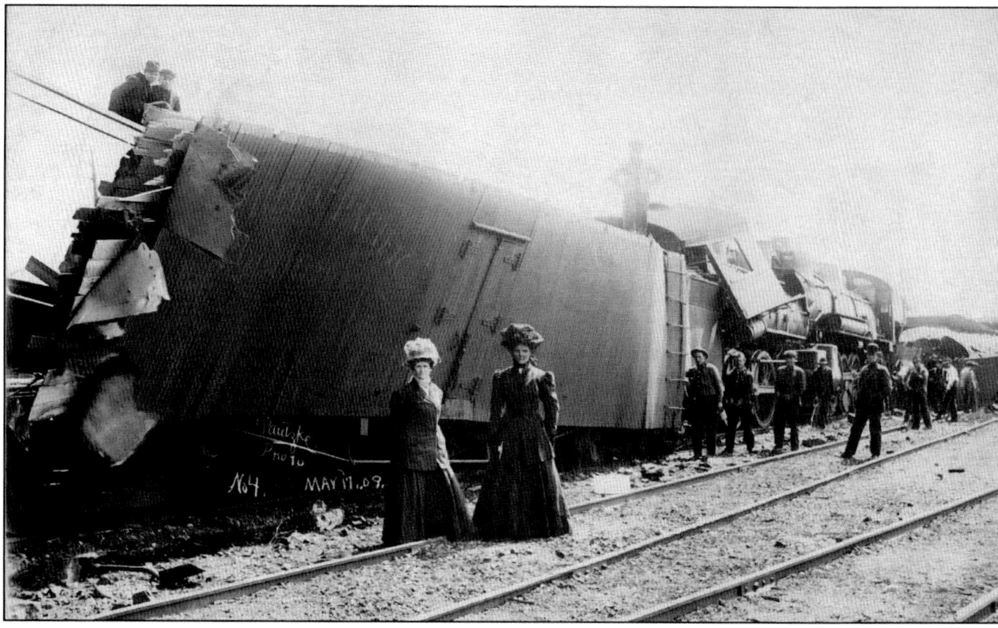

Two Northern Pacific train locomotives collided head-on near Dudley, a flag stop along the rail line between Thorp and Bristol, in the early hours of May 17, 1909. Both trains had been told to hold the main line, so neither made the switch to the sidetrack. The eastbound train hit the stopped westbound train at roughly 30 miles per hour. The engineer on the eastbound train died in the wreck. (KCHM.)

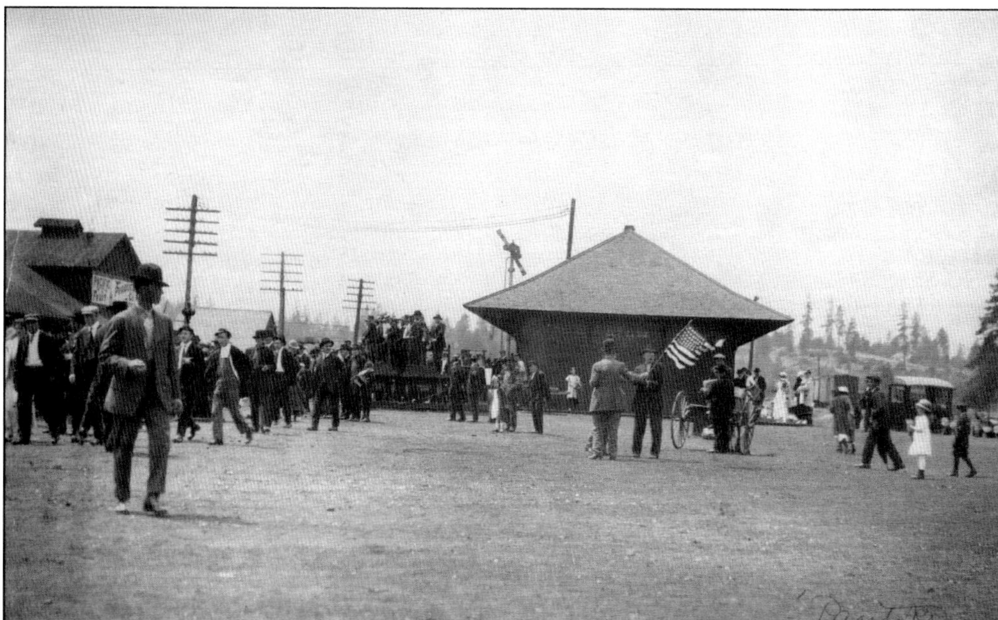

The Northern Pacific's Cle Elum depot is shown here as it appeared in 1918. Looking east, this photograph shows two men holding an American flag and a large group of people gathered at the depot. It is possible that the crowd is waiting for a train car carrying World War I troops on their way to Camp Lewis, which passed through here about this time. (CWU.)

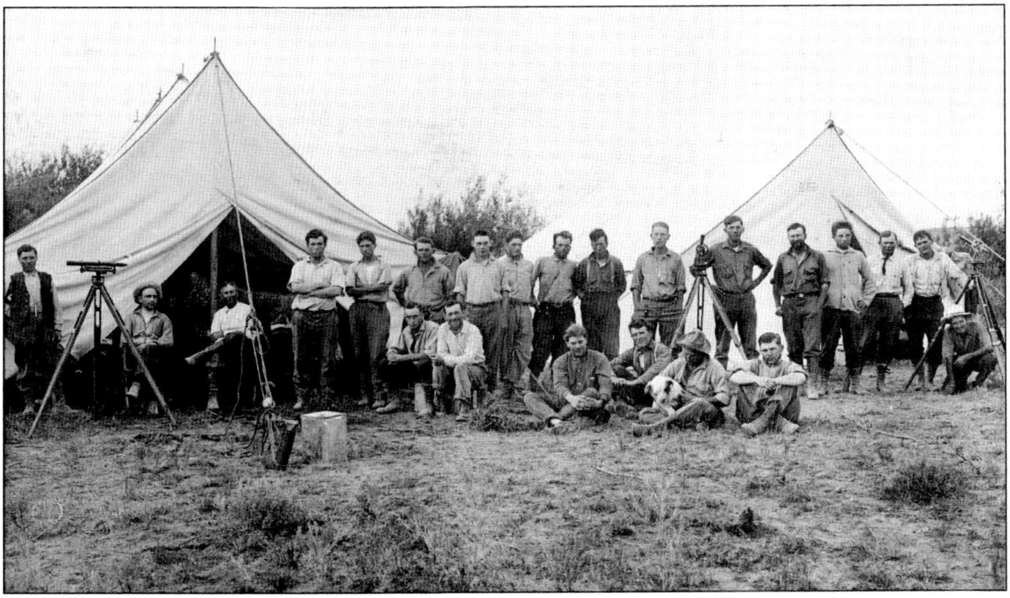

A survey crew for the Chicago, Milwaukee & St. Paul Railroad poses for this picture in 1912. When the rail line was constructed through the county, the railroad hired locals to help with general labor and other work. In this photograph, Ernest Pautzke, son of photographer Otto Pautzke, stands behind the survey tripod on the right. (EPL.)

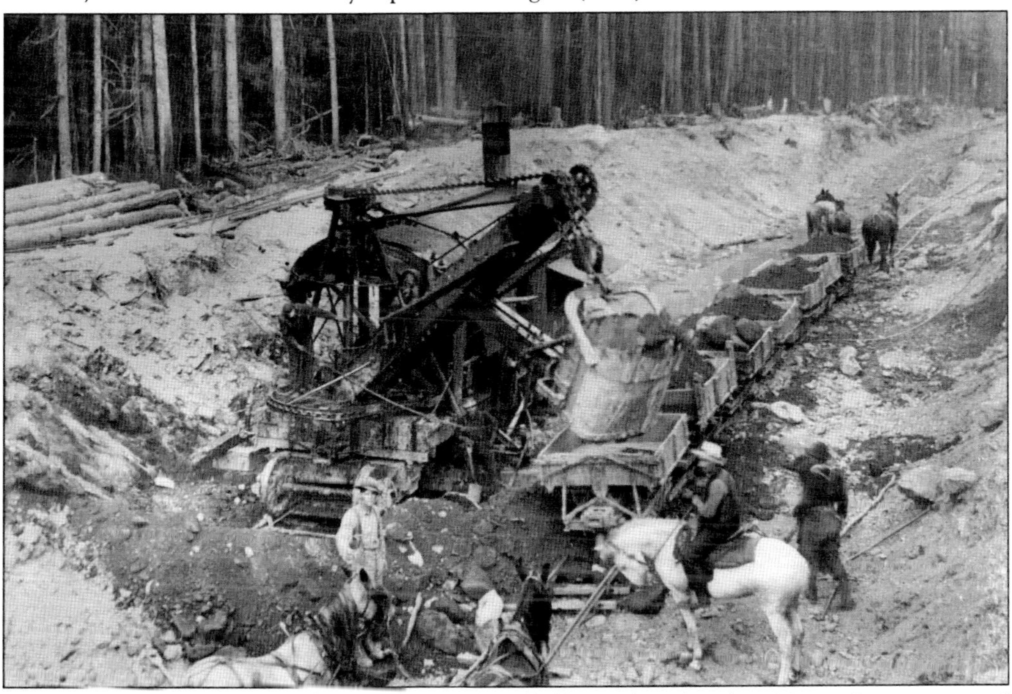

Workers cut a path for the Chicago, Milwaukee & St. Paul Railroad in Upper County around 1907. Bringing the rail line from Chicago to Seattle was a massive undertaking and cost of over $60 million, the equivalent of about $1.5 billion today. Even though the railroad lacked modern equipment and relied heavily on horse labor, the line was completed in three years, which is considered an amazing feat to this day. (EPL.)

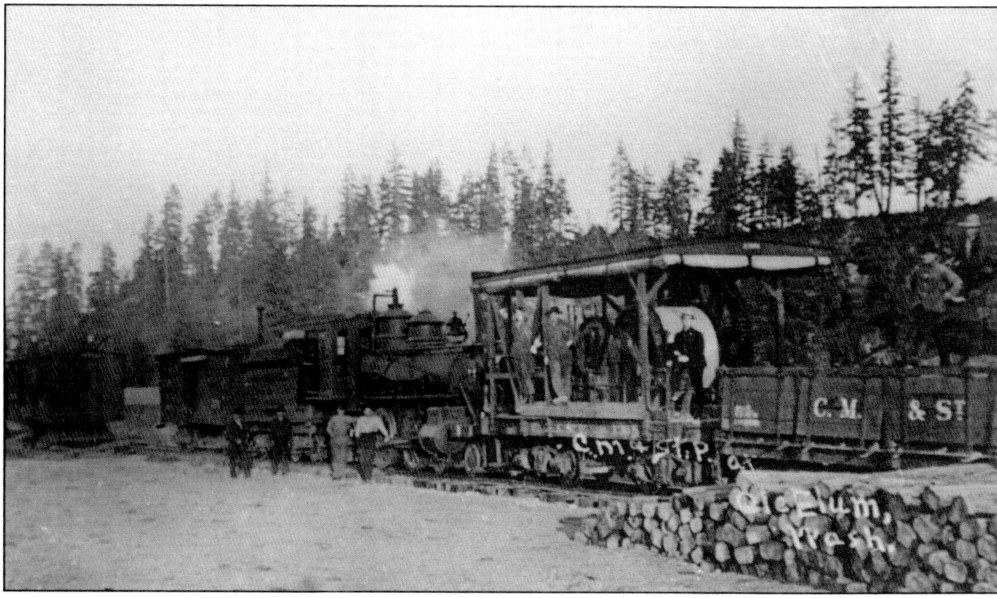

Pictured is the Chicago, Milwaukee & St. Paul Railroad construction crew near South Cle Elum in the early 1900s. Cle Elum had the Northern Pacific Railroad, so the CM&StP ran their line on the south side of the Yakima River through South Cle Elum. The pile of railroad ties at right is ready to be put to use. The CM&StP line was completed by 1910. (EPL.)

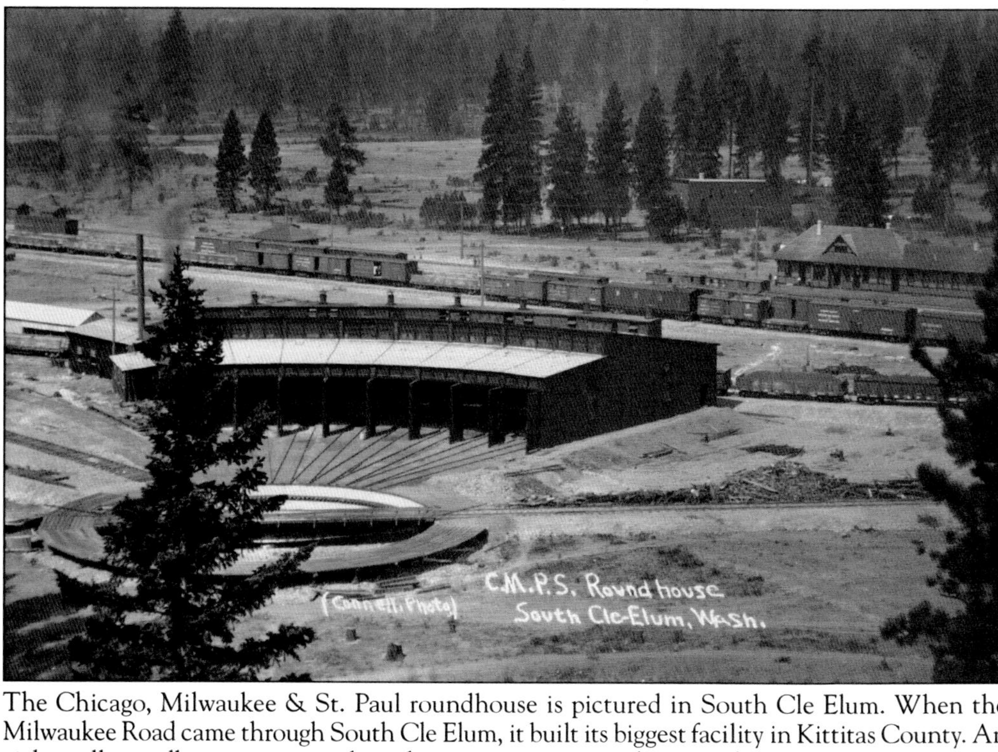

The Chicago, Milwaukee & St. Paul roundhouse is pictured in South Cle Elum. When the Milwaukee Road came through South Cle Elum, it built its biggest facility in Kittitas County. An eight-stall roundhouse, water tanks, ash pits, maintenance shops, and other buildings made up the yard. The roundhouse was used extensively until the entire Milwaukee Road was electrified, making it obsolete. At right is the South Cle Elum depot. (EPL.)

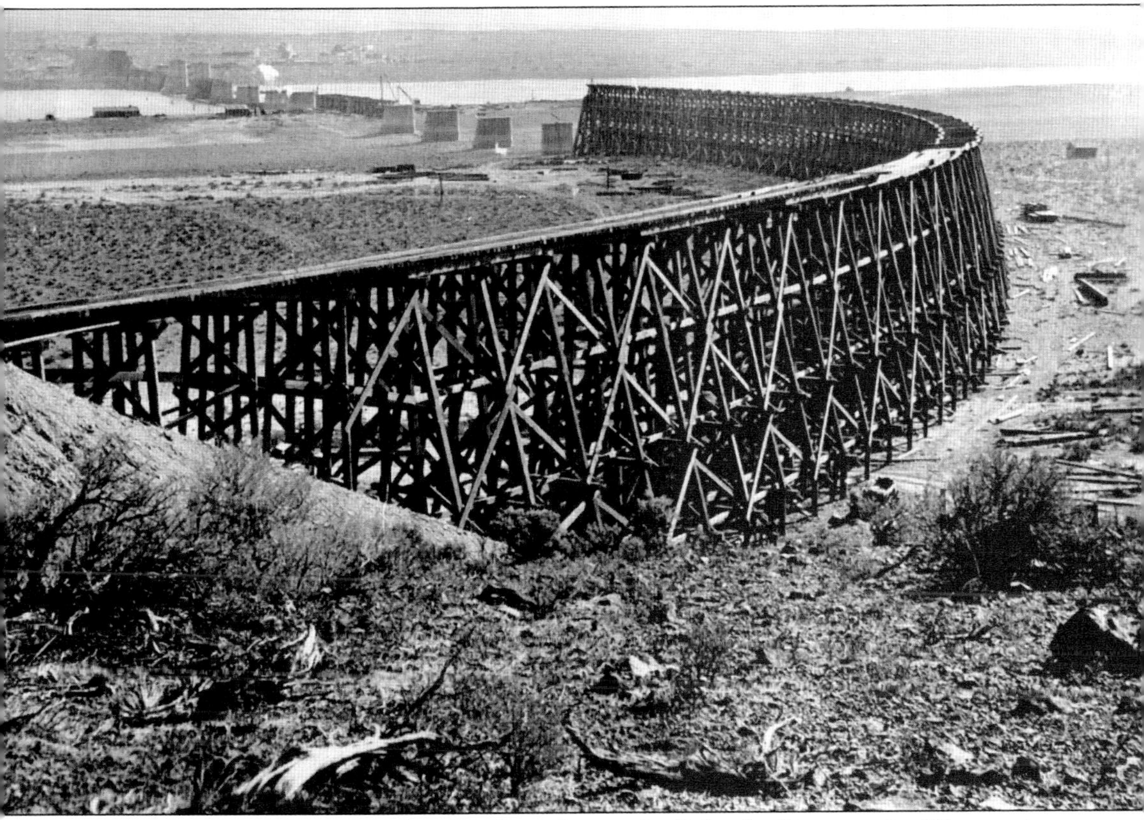

The Chicago, Milwaukee & St. Paul Railroad trestle over the Columbia River south of Vantage is under construction in this photograph, taken before 1909. Built before any river dams, while the river was much lower than it is today, the trestle was elevated to avoid the river flood plain and allow boats to pass under it. The Columbia River was used extensively by steamboats during this era because the river was easily navigable and unobstructed for the most part. Supplies for this bridge were brought downriver via steamboat, usually after they were shipped in and unloaded from other rail lines. Across the river in Grant County, the town of Beverly sprung up in 1905, mainly to house the workers building the Milwaukee Road. The railroad ceased to operate along this line in the 1980s, and the railroad line became the John Wayne Pioneer Trail. The bridge is closed to pedestrians today, but it still exists, as does the town of Beverly, which has its own zip code and a post office. (EPL.)

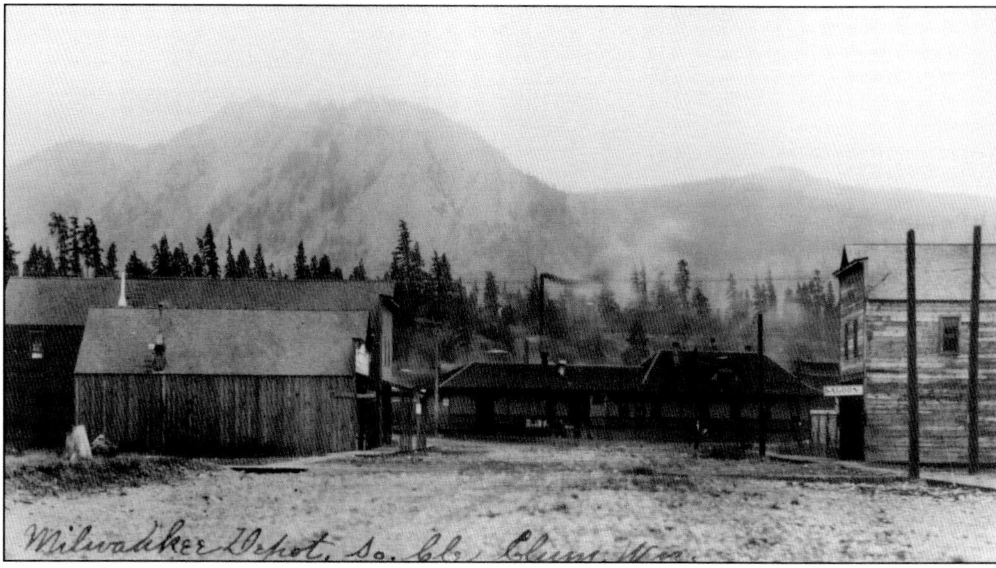

The South Cle Elum train depot, which was along the Chicago, Milwaukee & St. Paul rail line, is shown here in 1912. This photograph was taken from the north, looking south down Main Street towards Peoh Point and the South Cle Elum Ridge. At right is Alvin M. Gerber's saloon, as well as E.A. Ryan's barbershop. (EPL.)

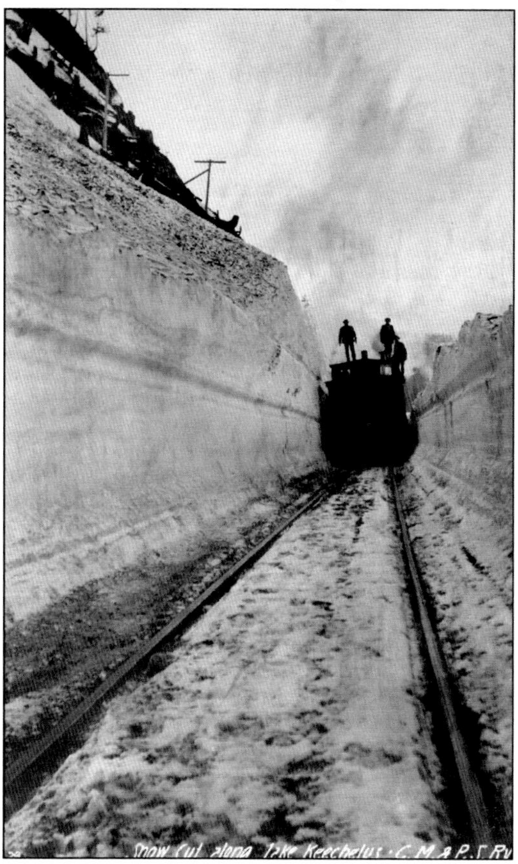

One major problem the railroads dealt with was the immense amount of snow that falls in the Cascade Mountains. Keeping the tracks clear was a constant necessity because the rail lines were then the main transportation between Kittitas County and the Puget Sound. The railroad had a snowplow, called a rotary, which had a 12-foot-diameter cutter wheel that cut the snow and spit it out the side. (KCHM.)

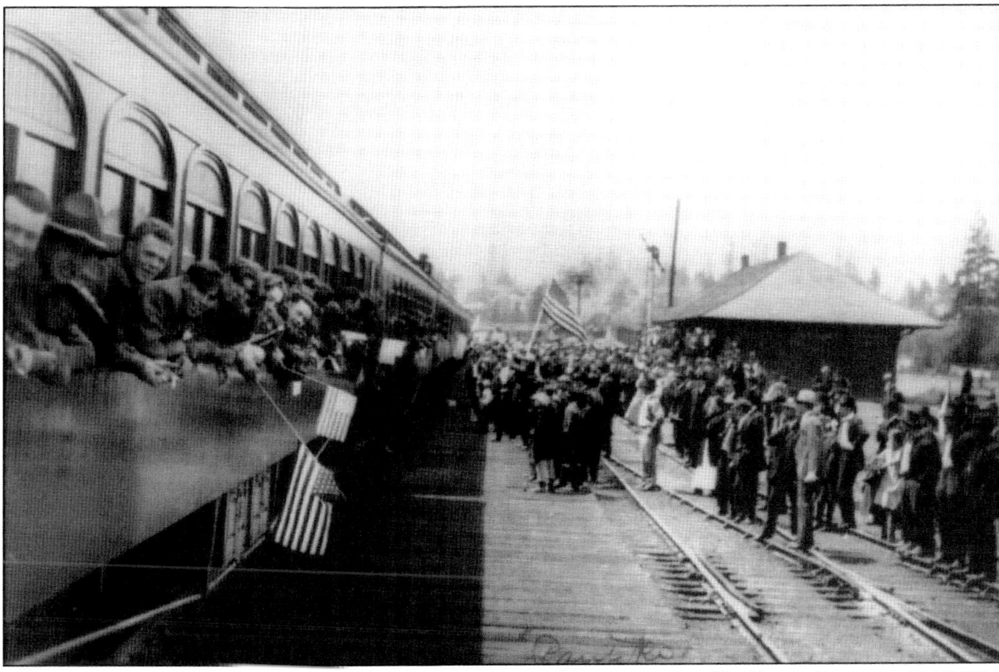

A Northern Pacific train full of World War I troops is seen at the Cle Elum depot in 1917. The troops were passing through Cle Elum on their way to Camp Lewis, which later became Fort Lewis. Many people from Cle Elum, Roslyn, and the surrounding area turned out to support the troops. (EPL.)

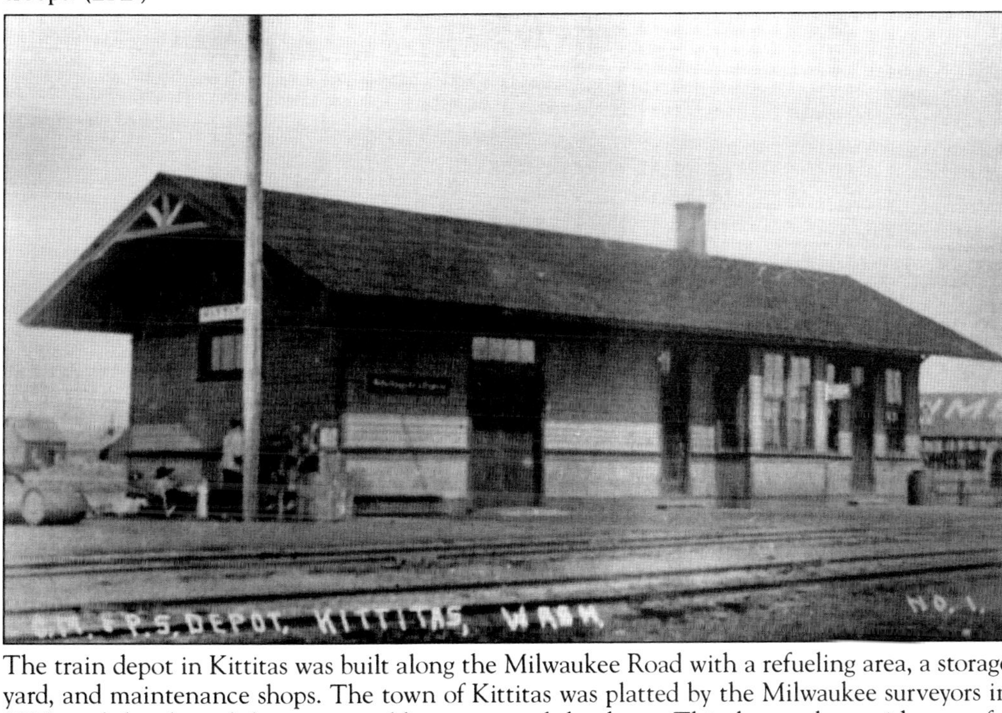

The train depot in Kittitas was built along the Milwaukee Road with a refueling area, a storage yard, and maintenance shops. The town of Kittitas was platted by the Milwaukee surveyors in 1908, and they hoped the town would grow around the depot. This depot, along with part of a refueling water tower, still stands in Kittitas along the John Wayne Pioneer Trail. (EPL.)

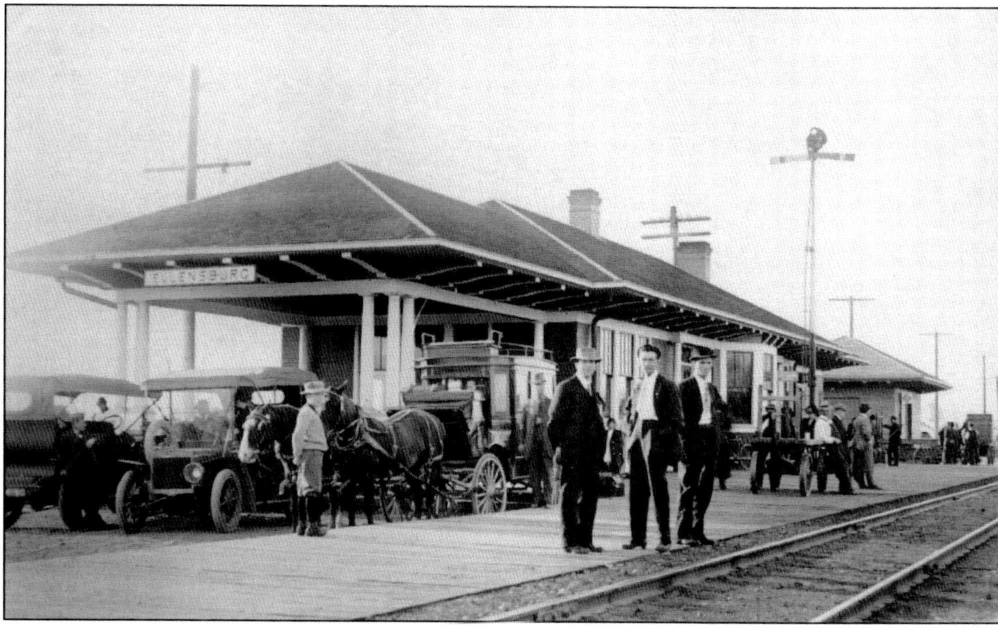

The Chicago, Milwaukee & St. Paul depot in Ellensburg was located on Fourteenth Street at the north end of Main Street. There is an empty lot where this depot once sat just across the road from Kiwanis Park. This was a popular depot, especially with college students who could board here and travel to the Puget Sound area. (EPL.)

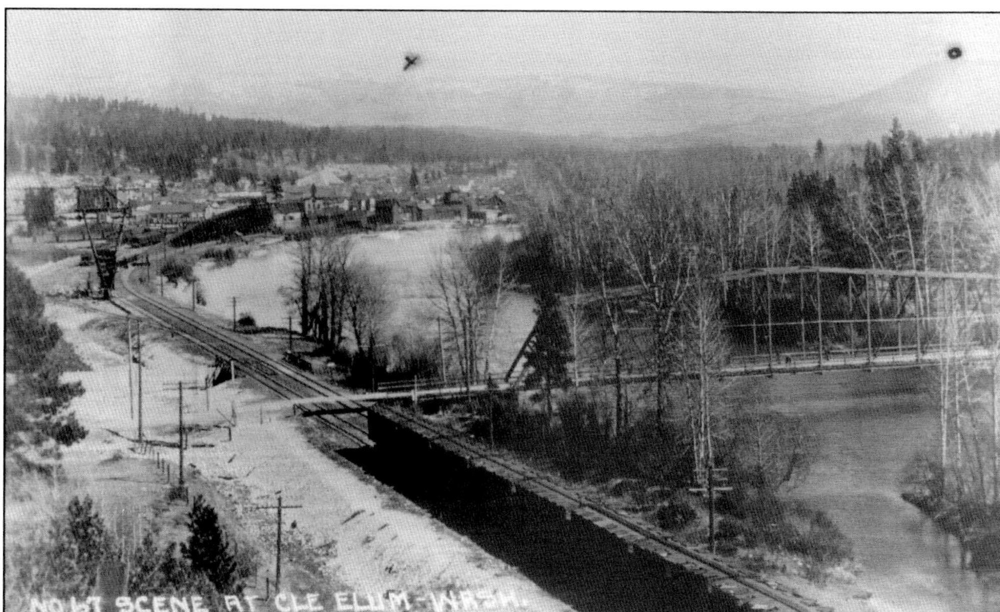

A postcard shows Cle Elum along the Yakima River. South Cle Elum is to the right, located across the bridge over the Yakima River. The tracks belong to the Northern Pacific Railroad, and the large ramp along the tracks is where the coal was loaded onto train cars. The author of the postcard put an "X" over Table Mountain and an "O" over Lookout Mountain. (EPL.)

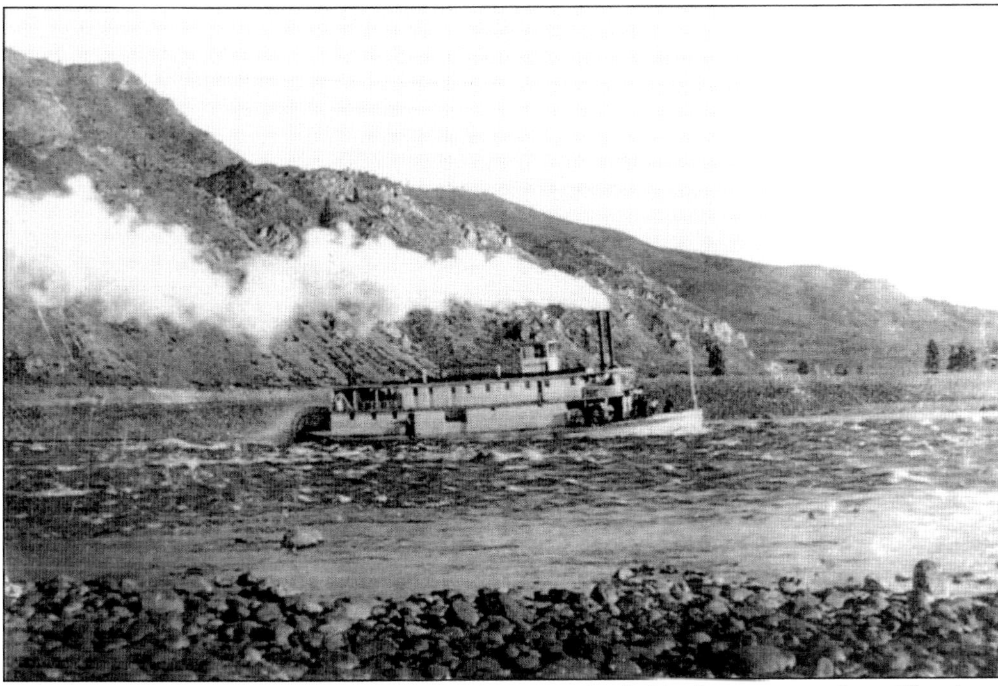

This stern-wheeler, named the *City of Ellensburg*, was funded by businessmen from Ellensburg. This steamer began running about 1887, hauling goods up the Columbia River from the docks at Moses Coulee. No railroad ran to Wenatchee, so the best method of transporting goods north was the river. When the railroad did arrive in 1893, the businessmen sold the boat and left the lucrative business. (EPL.)

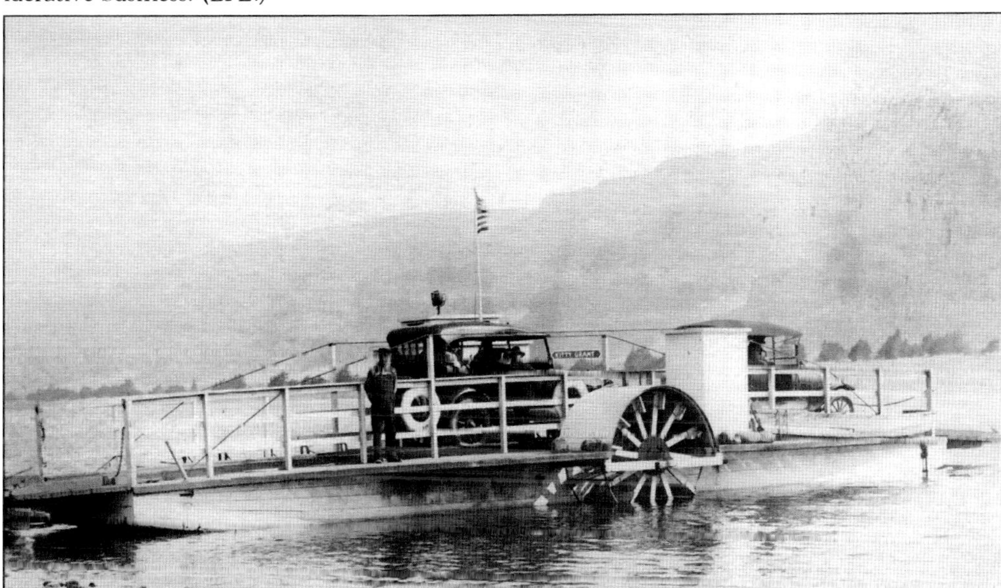

At the eastern terminus of Kittitas County is the Columbia River, where it borders Grant Count. Before a bridge was built in 1927, the only way to cross the river at this junction was by ferry. Initially run by the Van Slyke family, the ferry operations were taken over by Kittitas and Grant Counties in 1917. The Kitty-Grant ferry operators had a house in Vantage that they shared. (KCHM.)

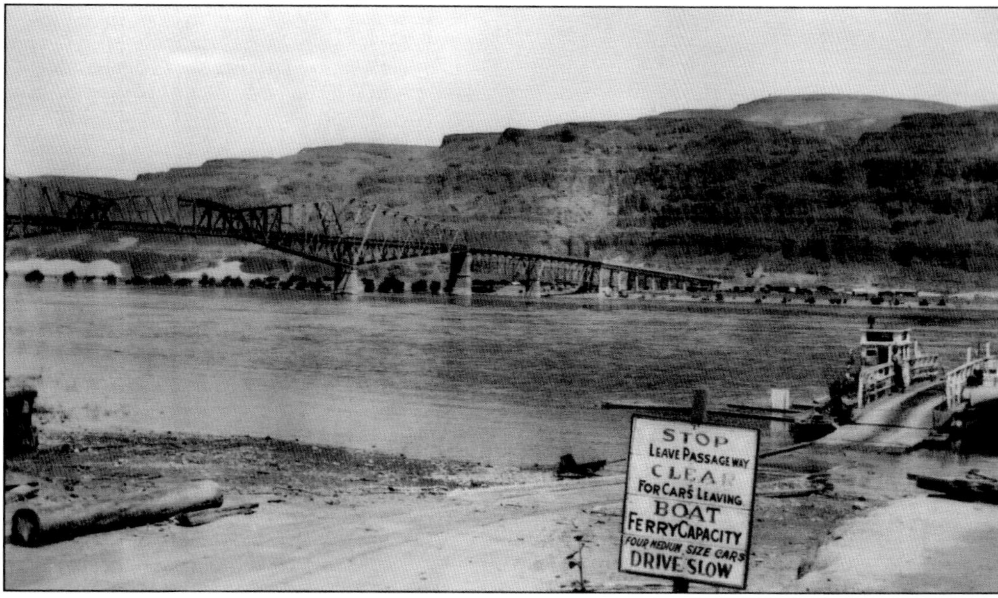

It was the end of an era when the Vantage Bridge was completed in 1927; it made the once necessary Kitty-Grant ferry system obsolete. The span connected the Sunset Highway (later Highway 10, then Interstate 90) with Grant County for the first time. This bridge was used until 1962, when a new bridge was built to better withstand the rising water levels behind Wanapum Dam. (EPL.)

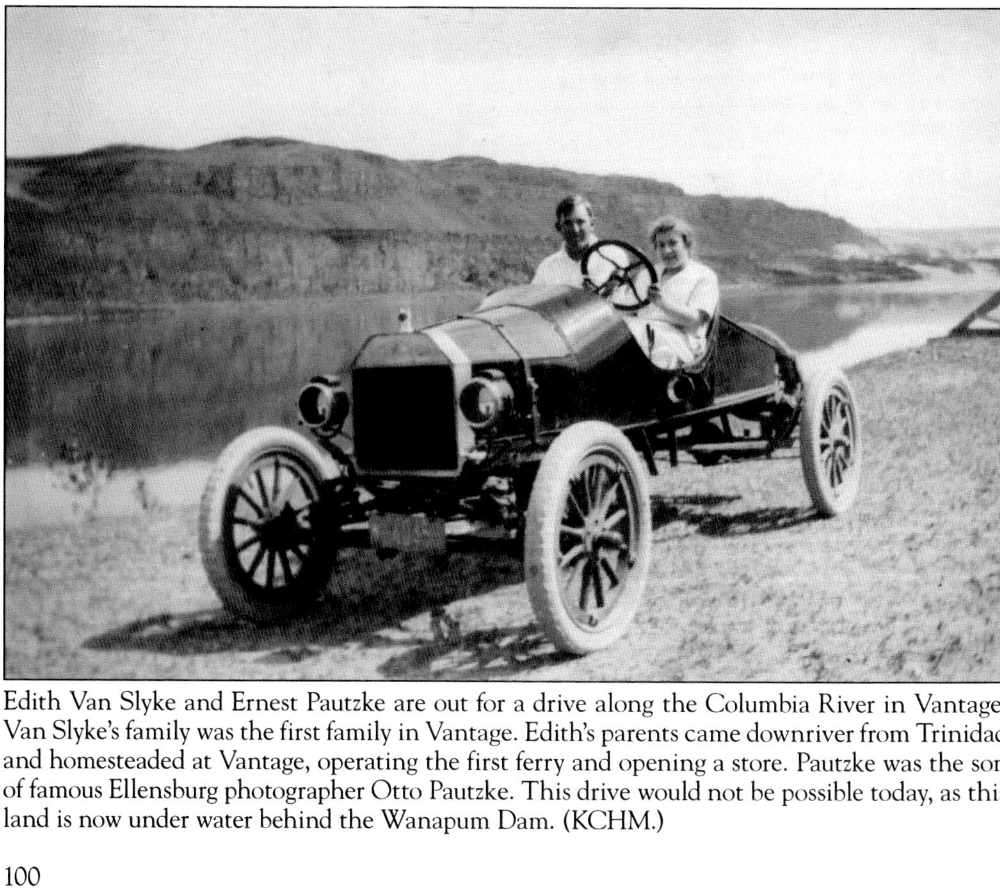

Edith Van Slyke and Ernest Pautzke are out for a drive along the Columbia River in Vantage. Van Slyke's family was the first family in Vantage. Edith's parents came downriver from Trinidad and homesteaded at Vantage, operating the first ferry and opening a store. Pautzke was the son of famous Ellensburg photographer Otto Pautzke. This drive would not be possible today, as this land is now under water behind the Wanapum Dam. (KCHM.)

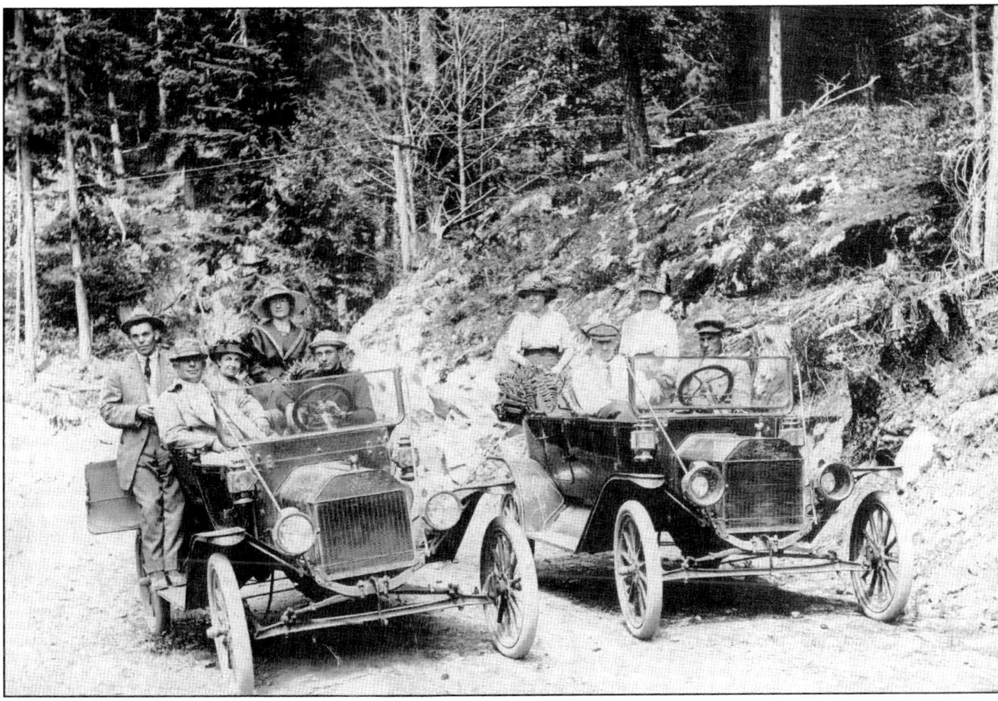

Two cars are out for a leisurely drive in Teanaway around 1910. In the car to the left are Frank and Maggie Fitterer and Philip and Emma Fitterer with Clarence Fitterer behind the wheel. In the car to the right are T.R. Jacobsen and family. Frank and Philip were brothers, and they began Fitterer Brothers Furniture store in Ellensburg in 1896, which is still in business today. (KCHM.)

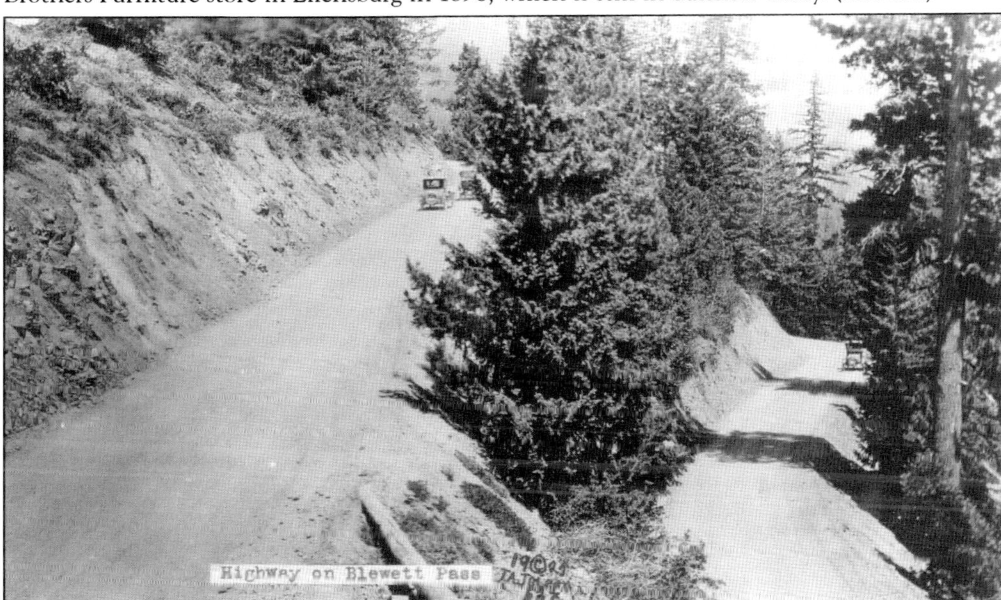

The northern border of Kittitas County follows the top of Blewett Pass. Initially a wagon road known as Swauk Pass, Blewett Pass became part of the Yellowstone Trail when the advent of cars required a more navigable road. Pictured is one of the many switchbacks on the road to the old Blewett Pass, which was about five miles west of the current pass. (KCHM.)

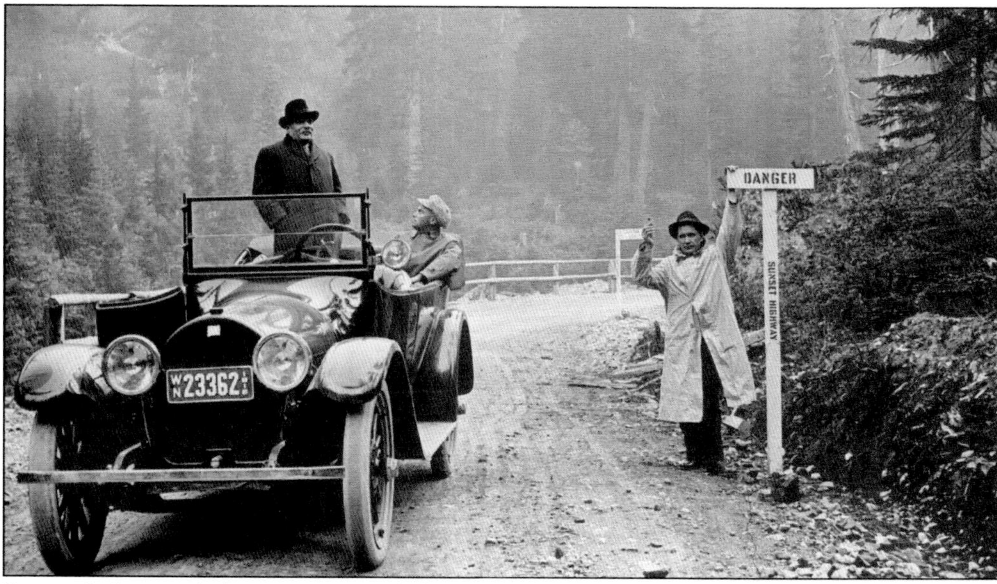

First an Indian trail, then a wagon road, this path winding through Snoqualmie Pass was the early Sunset Highway, pictured in 1916. The Washington State Highway Department began in 1905, and among the many routes needing improvement through the state was the Sunset Highway. Grading, road signs, ditches, and guardrails were completed by this time, but the road was often muddy or impassible in the winter months. (CWU.)

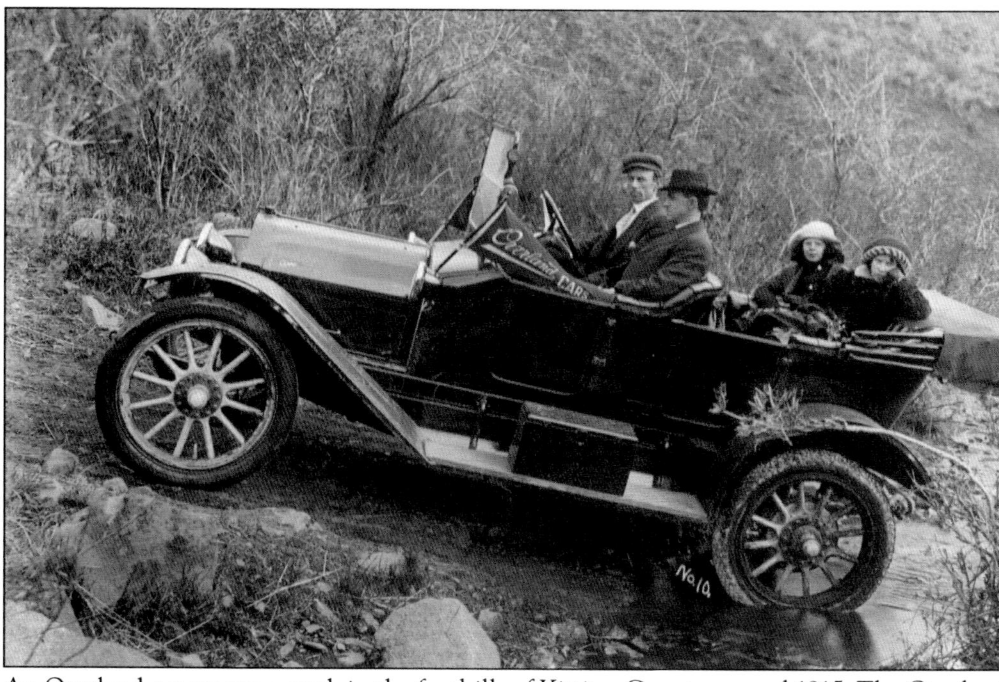

An Overland car crosses a creek in the foothills of Kittitas County around 1915. The Overland Automobile Company started in 1903 and produced cars, trying to rival other early automobile manufacturers. This touring car, driven from right-hand side as many were then, was complete with a folding windshield. The company ceased making cars in 1926, and today, the Overland is valuable collector's item. (EPL.)

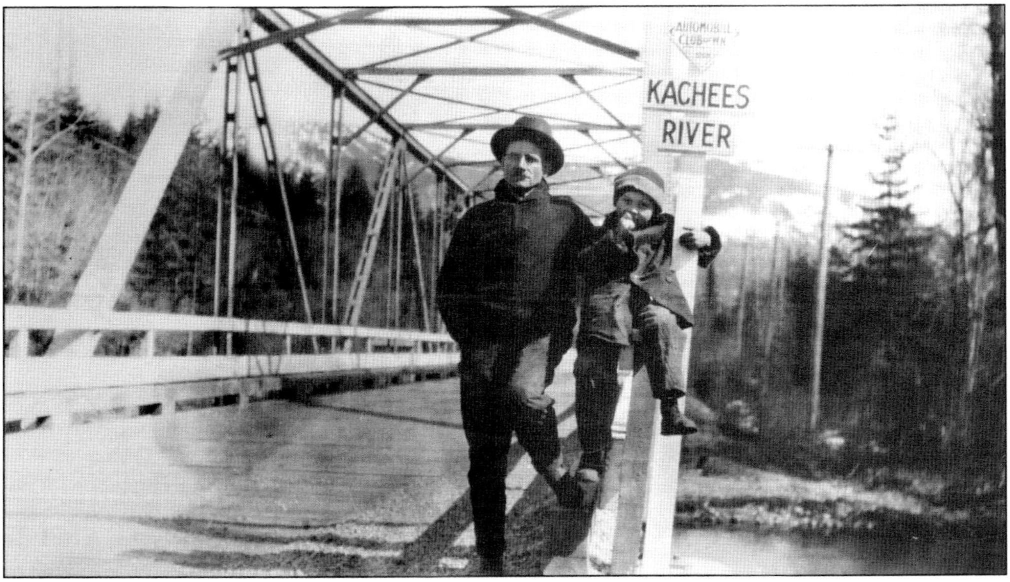

This bridge spanned the Kachess River, which flows from Lake Kachess to Lake Easton, near Snoqualmie Pass. When the wagon road over the pass needed to be improved, work began on Sunset Highway, which was completed in 1915, making travel much quicker. Cars on Interstate 90 follow this same road through the pass today and drive over a modern bridge near this site. (KCHM.)

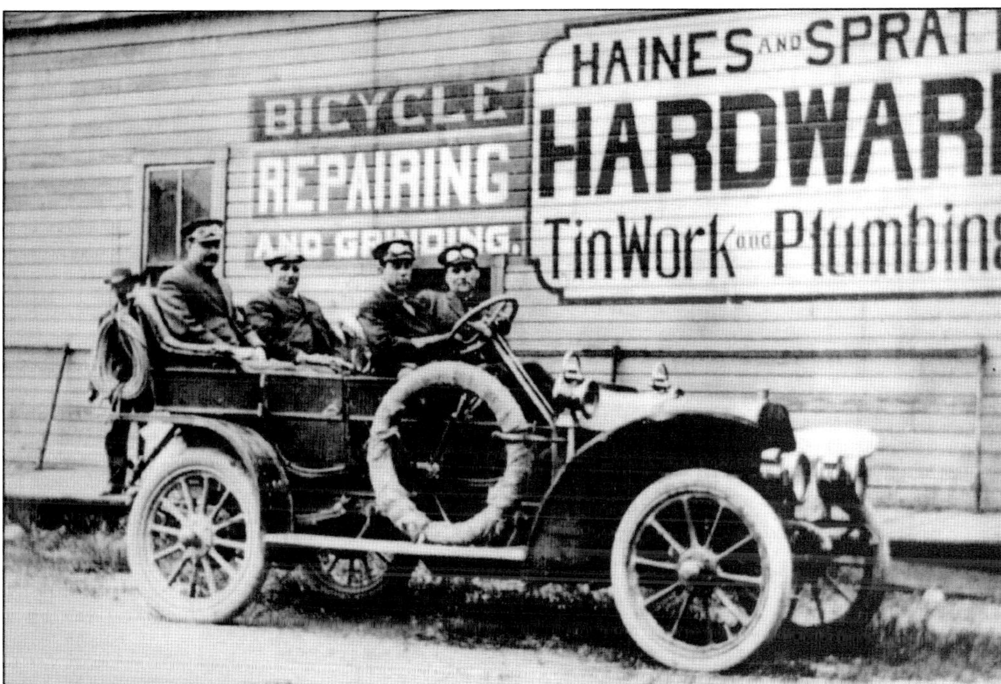

A touring car sits by Haines and Spratt Hardware in Cle Elum around 1908. The First Street store claimed that they had "the largest and best stock in our line." Early car travel was not easy; the men wore goggles since the car lacked a windshield, and the roads were dusty. The coil of rope probably also came in handy on roads where horses were more common than automobiles. (EPL.)

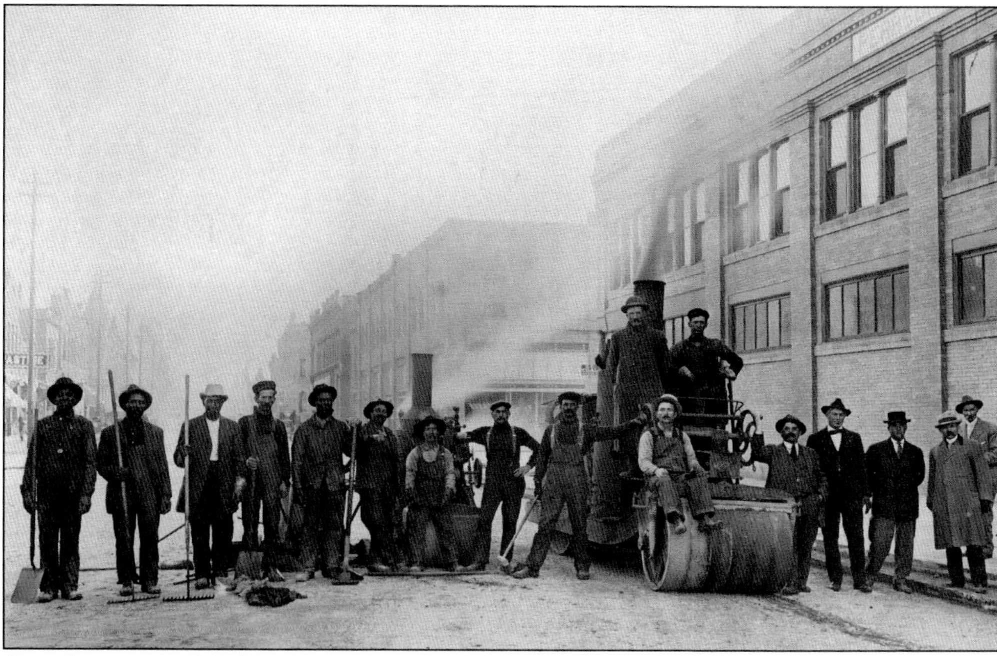

A road crew poses for this 1910s picture on Fourth Avenue in Ellensburg. Ellensburg, as did other cities, undertook major road grading and paving projects in the early decades of the 20th century, mainly because of the growing use of automobiles. At right is the Pearson Building, constructed in 1908. It houses the Palace Restaurant today. (KCHM.)

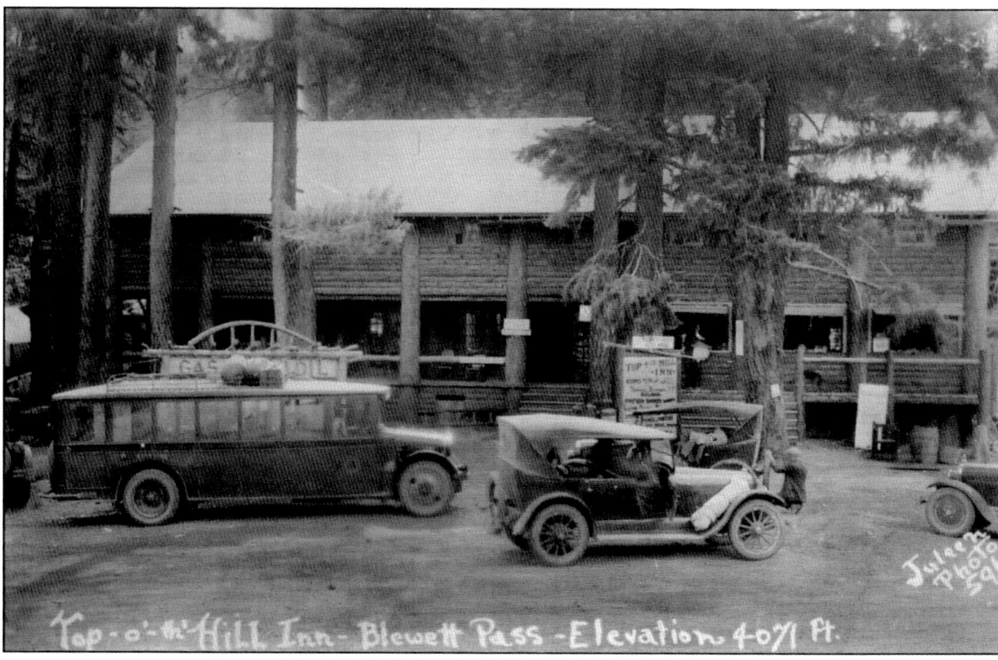

The Top-O'-Th'-Hill Inn at old Blewett Pass was a popular stopping-off point on the long drive between Cle Elum and Wenatchee. The inn offered rooms to rent, hot meals, gasoline, and groceries for travelers. People would even travel by bus to stay at the lodge. Note the Wenatchee Department of Public Works bus seen here. (EPL.)

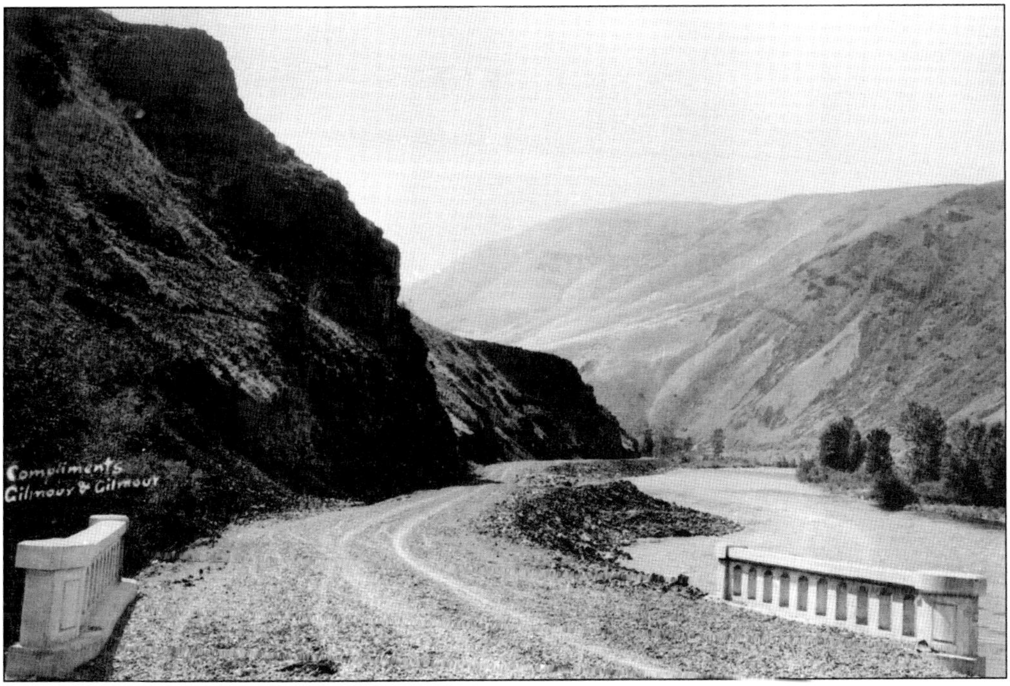

The road along the Yakima River Canyon is heading south from Ellensburg. Before Interstate 82 was completed between Ellensburg and Selah, this road connected Ellensburg to Yakima County. The road has since been widened and paved, but the drive today looks very similar otherwise. Gilmour Grocery in Ellensburg distributed this photograph postcard. (EPL.)

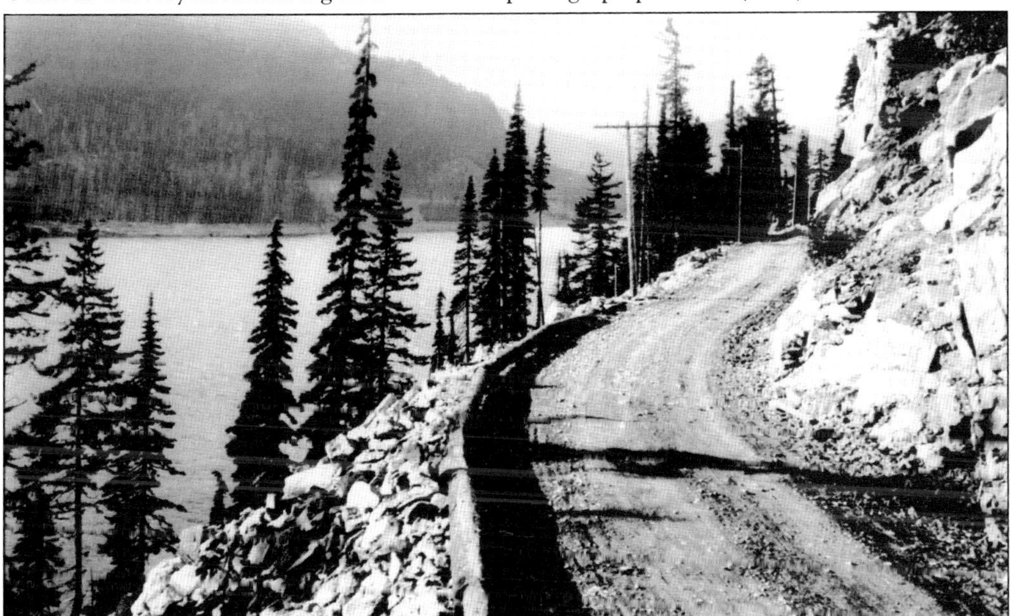

Pictured is the early road between Snoqualmie Pass and Easton as it traveled along the ridge above Lake Keechelus. When Ellensburg pioneer Tillman Houser came to the Kittitas Valley in 1868 from Renton, it took him 15 days. Subsequent travelers improved the road as more wagons traveled it, and this is how it looked to early automobile drivers. (EPL.)

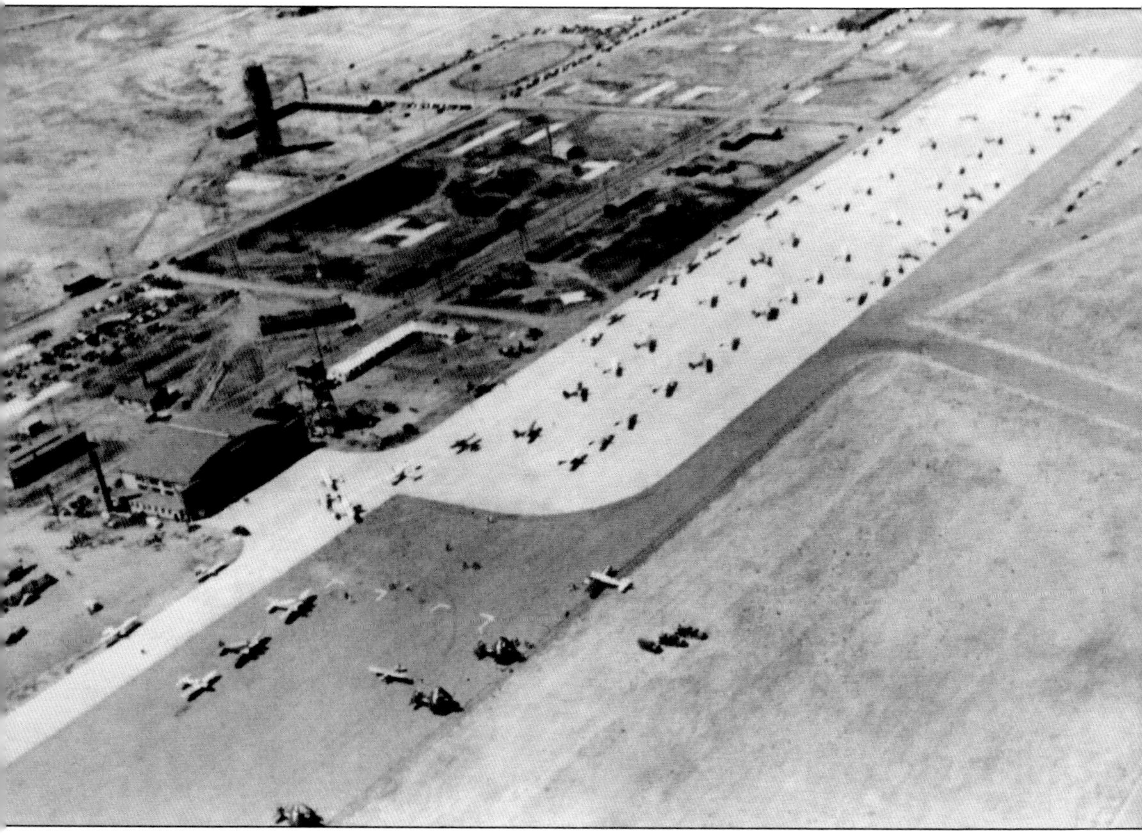

An aerial view of Bower's Field Airport, located north of Ellensburg, is shown during the World War II cadet training program. The airport was much smaller than this in the 1930s, but leading into and during World War II, Ellensburg was picked as one of a few inland locations for an air base. Work began, and the small airstrip was soon converted into this large airport. (EPL.)

Seven

Recreation and Celebration

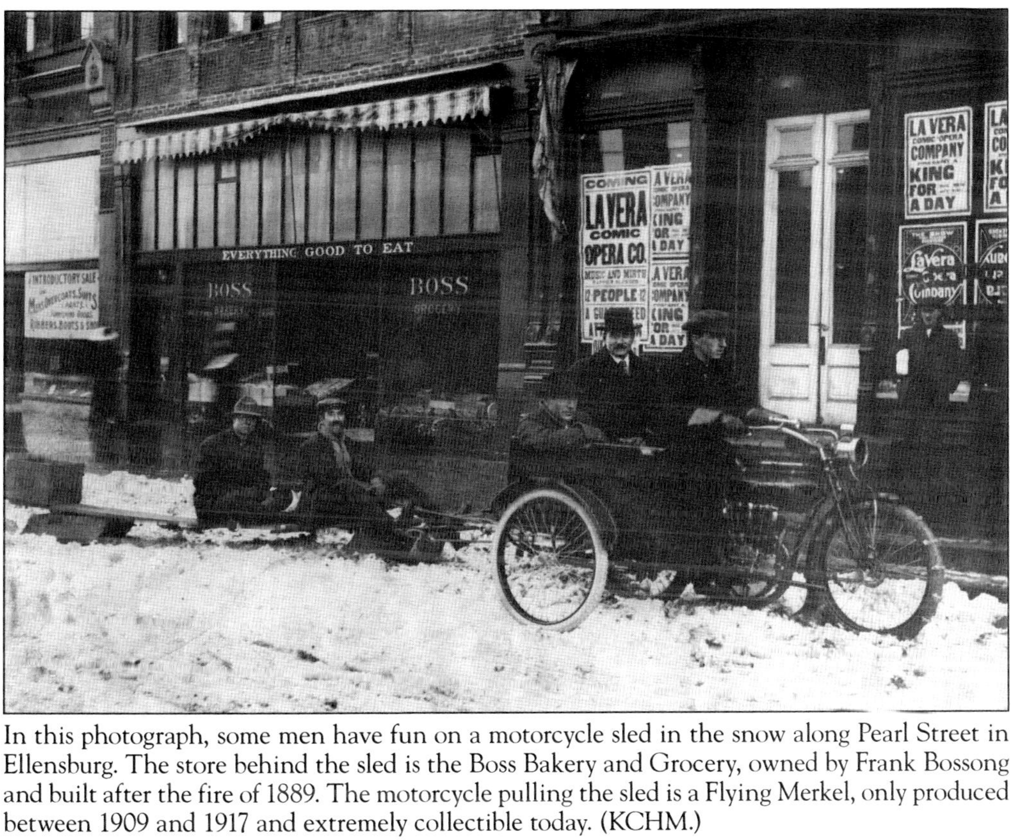

In this photograph, some men have fun on a motorcycle sled in the snow along Pearl Street in Ellensburg. The store behind the sled is the Boss Bakery and Grocery, owned by Frank Bossong and built after the fire of 1889. The motorcycle pulling the sled is a Flying Merkel, only produced between 1909 and 1917 and extremely collectible today. (KCHM.)

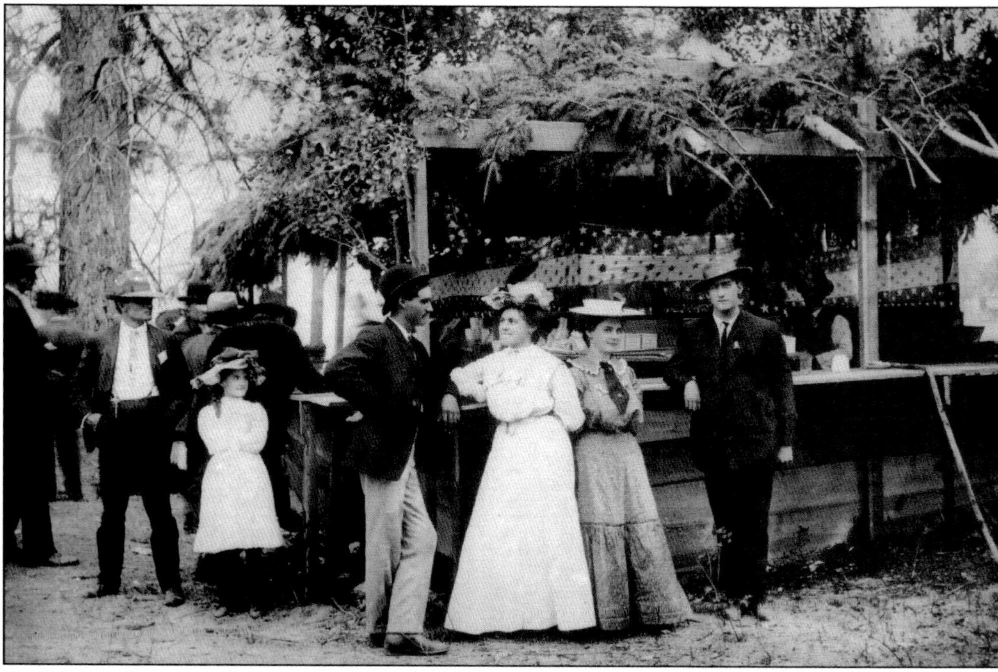

Fred Connell and Stella Wagner (center) stand at the Modern Woodmen of America refreshment booth (the same booth on the cover of this book) in Thorp in 1903. The couple looks at each other under the watchful eye of a young girl. The MWA meeting was a popular social event for many people in Kittitas County. (EPL.)

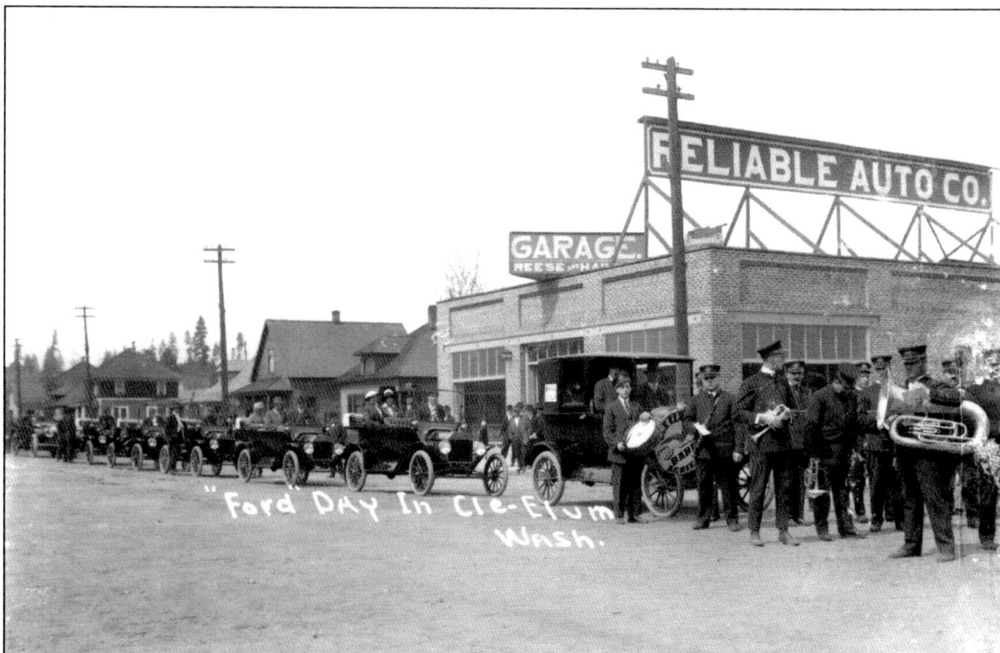

A parade of Ford automobiles line East First Street in 1915, led by the Cle Elum Eagles Marching Band. The lead car in the parade is a 1915 Model T Touring car with a price tag of $765, which seems like a good deal, but today, the cost was the equivalent of about $17,000. (EPL.)

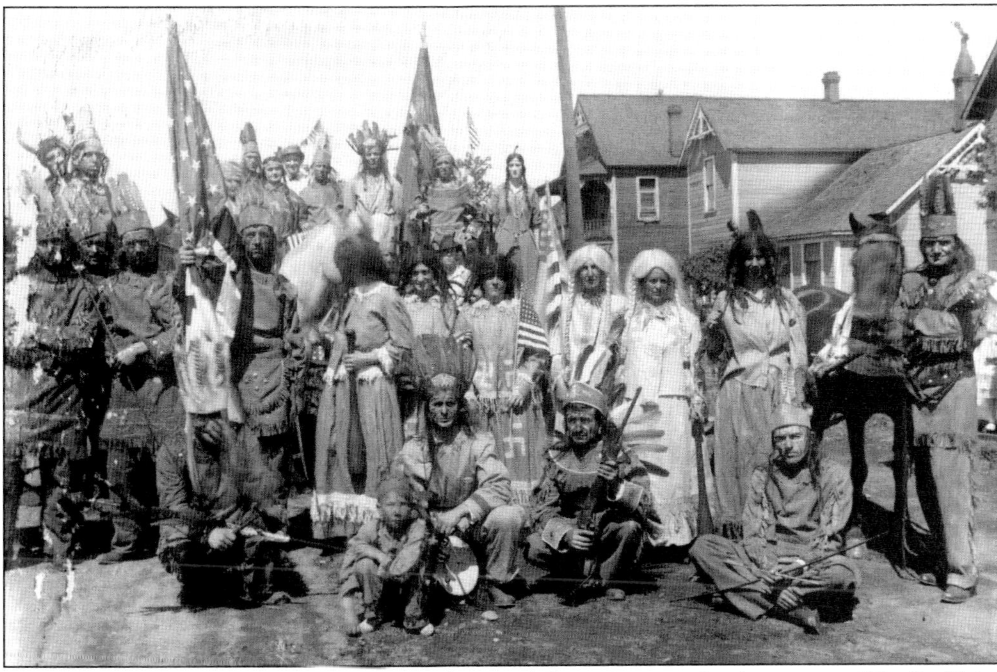

A group of Cle Elum Red Men Lodge members in full regalia pose for this picture. The Red Men are the oldest American fraternal organization, dating back to the Sons of Liberty and the Boston Tea Party in the 18th century. While the face paint, feathers, and clothing appear to be mockery of Native Americans, the organization states that they do so out of respect and patriotism for early America. (EPL.)

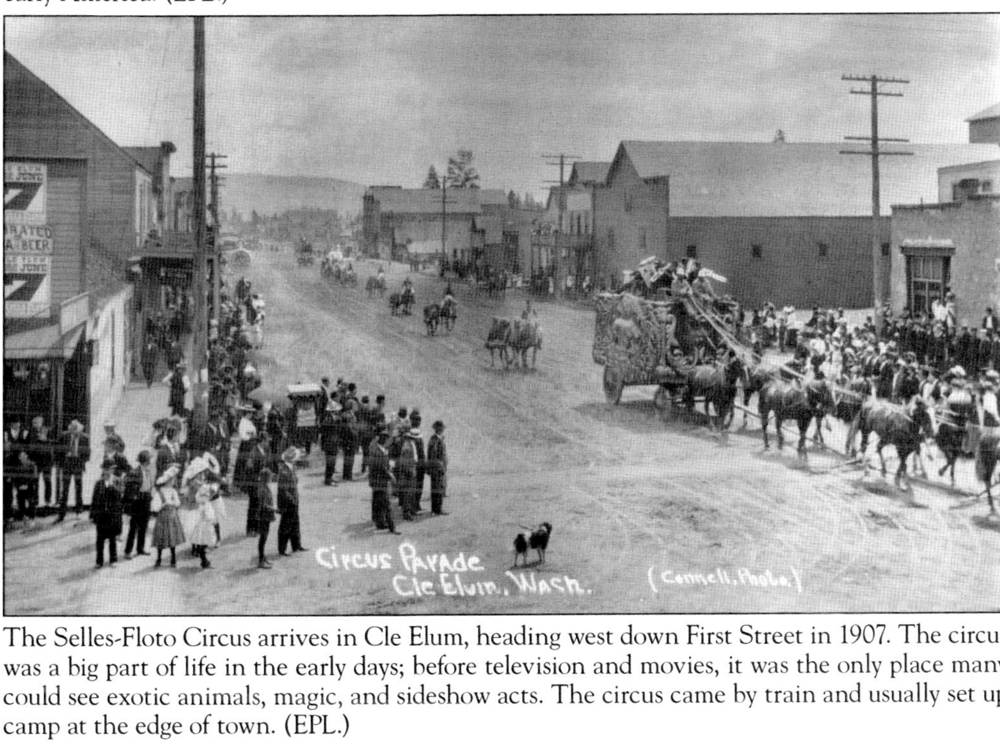

The Selles-Floto Circus arrives in Cle Elum, heading west down First Street in 1907. The circus was a big part of life in the early days; before television and movies, it was the only place many could see exotic animals, magic, and sideshow acts. The circus came by train and usually set up camp at the edge of town. (EPL.)

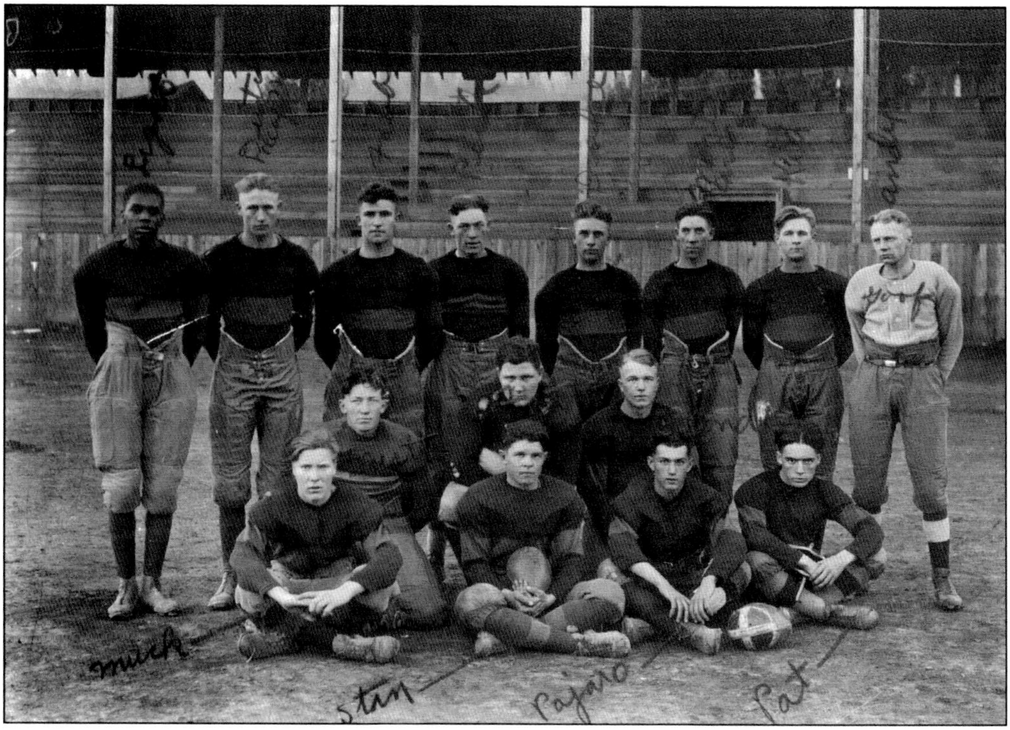

In many towns in the early 20th century, school athletics were a major source of entertainment. Pictured here is the 1923 Roslyn High School football team posing in front of the grandstands of the community field, where everything from sporting events to community gatherings took place. The grandstands are long gone, but the field is still in Roslyn and is called Pioneer Park today. (CWU.)

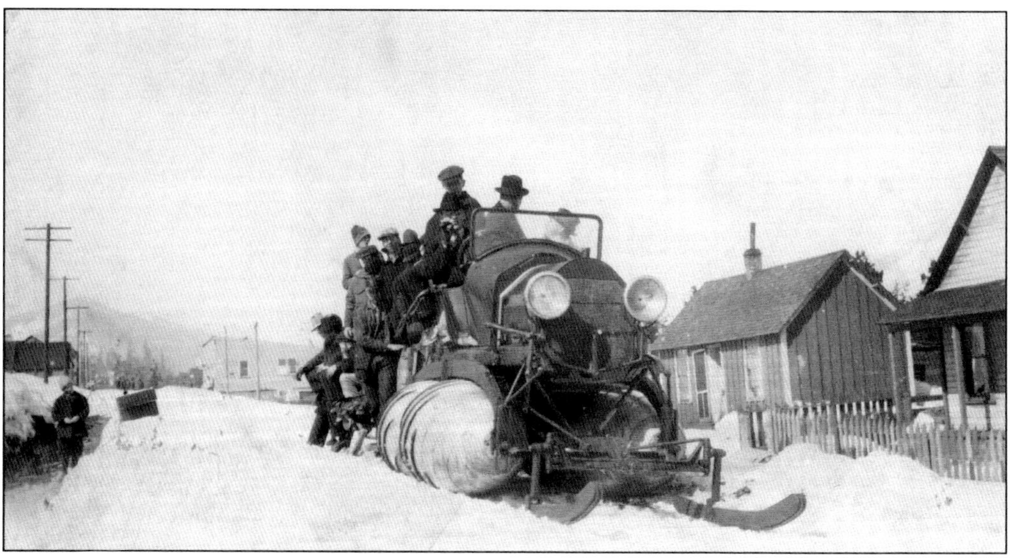

Men and boys crowd together on Easton's first snowmobile around 1925 as it heads down Railroad Street. Auger-like cylinders, or screws, on both sides of the vehicle spun, propelling the vehicle through mud and snow with ease. While effective, these vehicles were expensive and only usable a few months out of the year. (CWU.)

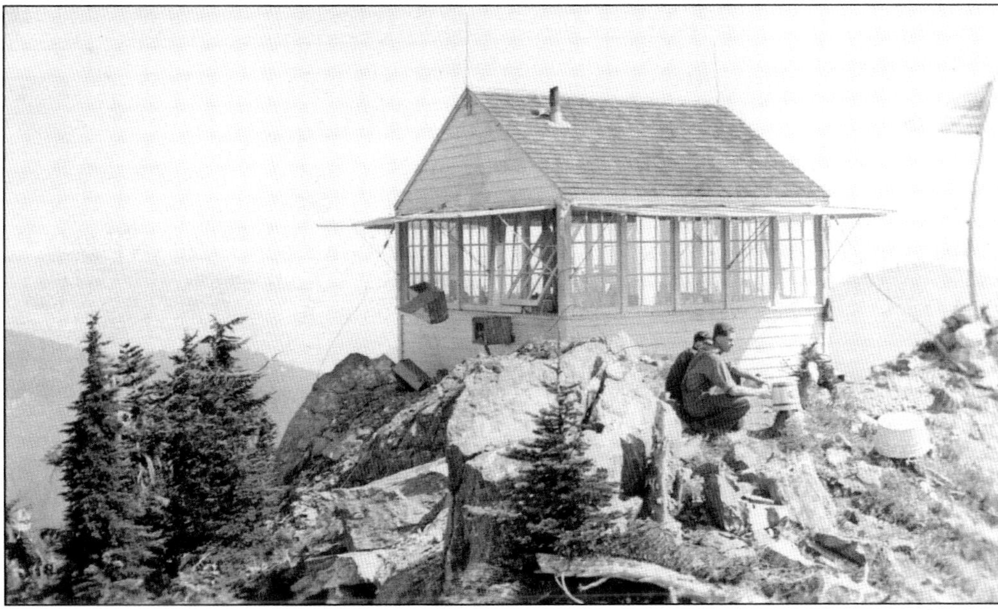

A fire lookout building sits atop Thorp Mountain, which is west of Salmon La Sac overlooking Lake Kachess. The US Forest Service paid lookouts to live in buildings like this during the summer months to keep a watchful eye out for forest fires. This photograph shows how the lookout appeared in 1935; it still stands today and is accessible via US Forest Service trails. (CWU.)

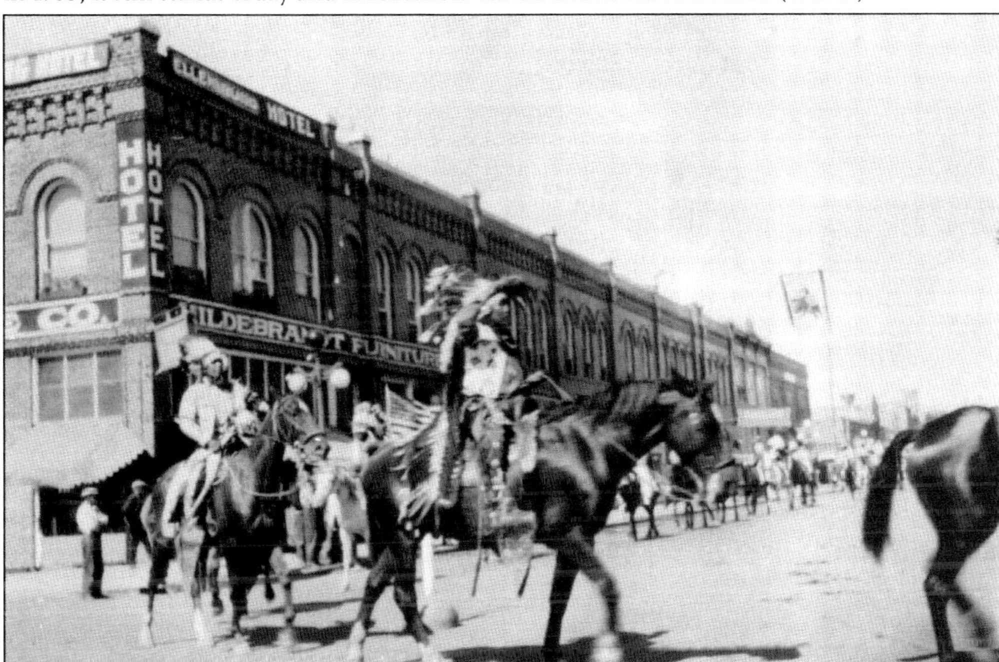

A Yakama Nation procession is pictured in the Kittitas County Fair and Rodeo Parade in Ellensburg. Every Labor Day weekend since 1923, Ellensburg plays host to the fair and rodeo. Here, the parade comes down Main Street and turns left onto Third Street. The Shoudy-Cadwell building is behind on the corner. (EPL.)

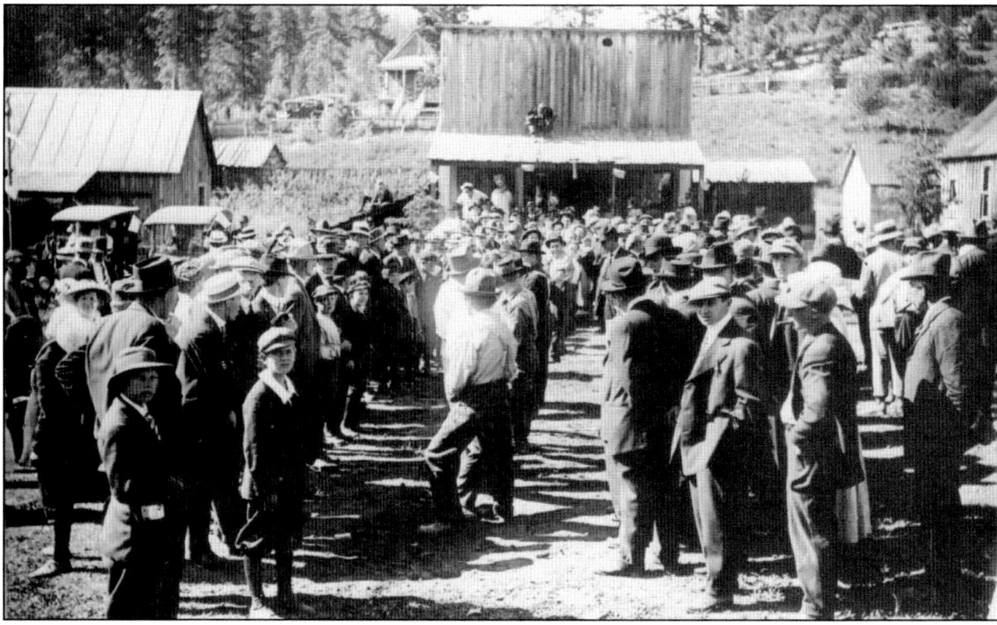

A group gathers in Liberty with the men in the middle doing some sort of dance or participating in a game. The building in the middle of the photograph was the town store, which burned down sometime after this picture was taken. The Liberty School is on the hill to the left of the store. It was later moved down the hill and converted into a town hall. (EPL.)

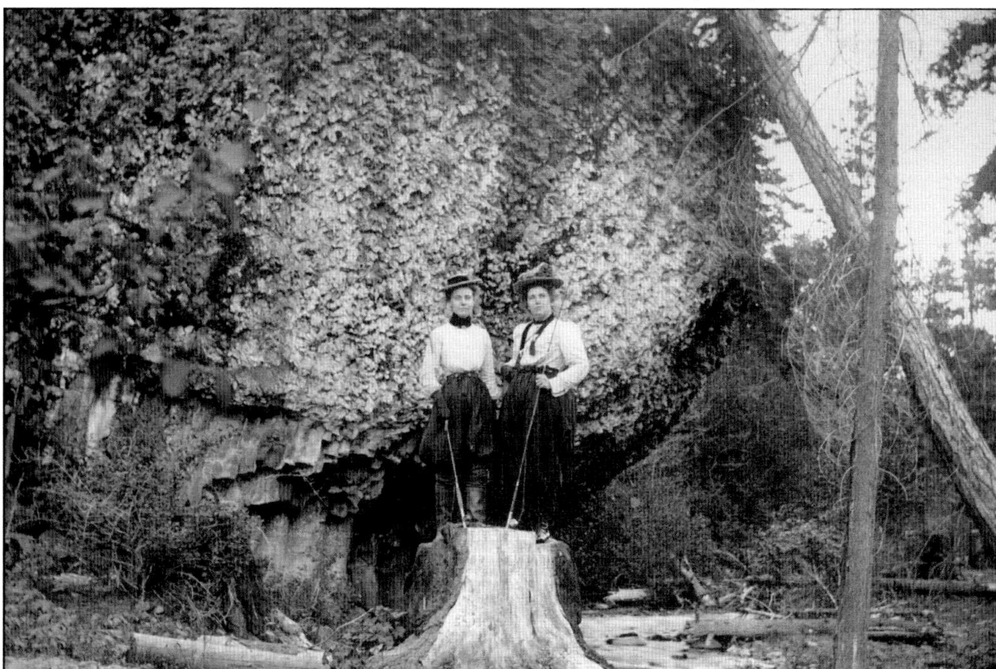

Ellen Pautzke (right) and an unidentified friend take a break from fishing to pose for a picture taken by Ellen's husband, Otto, somewhere in the county foothills. Between the creel over Ellen's shoulder and the gloves on the women's right hands, it is fair to say that these women were serious about fishing. (EPL.)

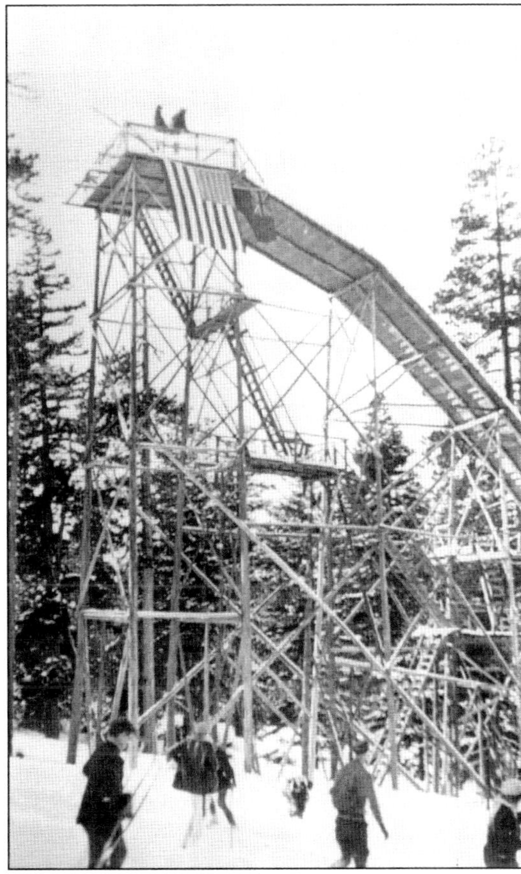

The Cle Elum Ski Club was started by John Bresko in 1921. A large ski jump was constructed on a hillside east of town, as were groomed skiing trails. The Cle Elum Ski Club was the only organized skiing in the state at that time, which made it popular with people all over the region. During the winter weekends, the club saw hundreds of skiers take to the hill. The ski club also hosted events and competitions; the largest one in 1931 had roughly 8,000 spectators turn out to watch the ski jumping. The club saw moderate success until the mid-1930s, when the Depression sank in and the Washington State Highway Department began keeping the road to Snoqualmie Pass cleared all winter. (EPL.)

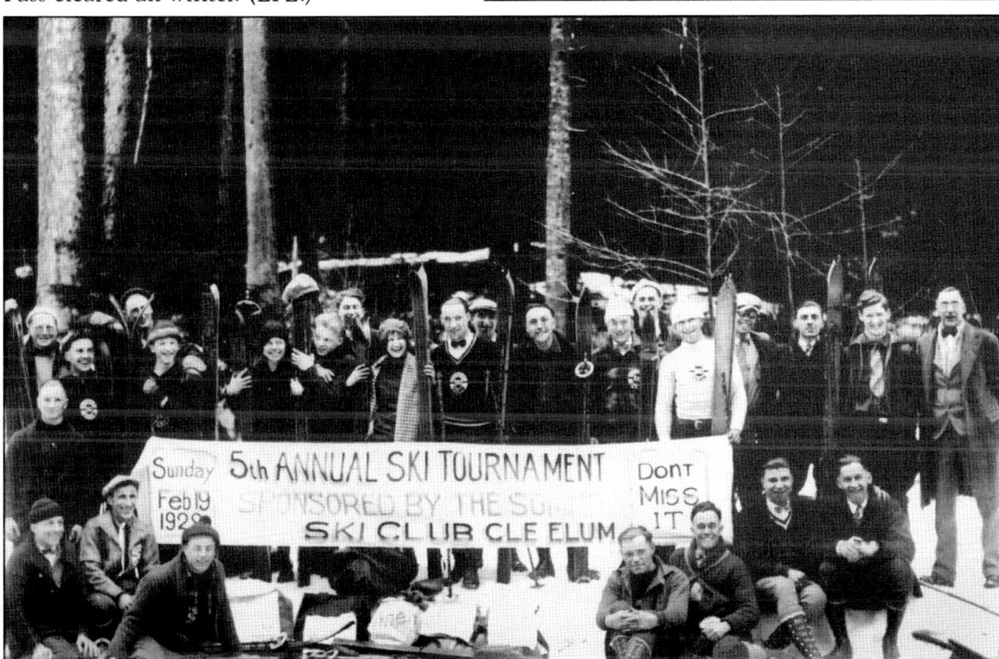

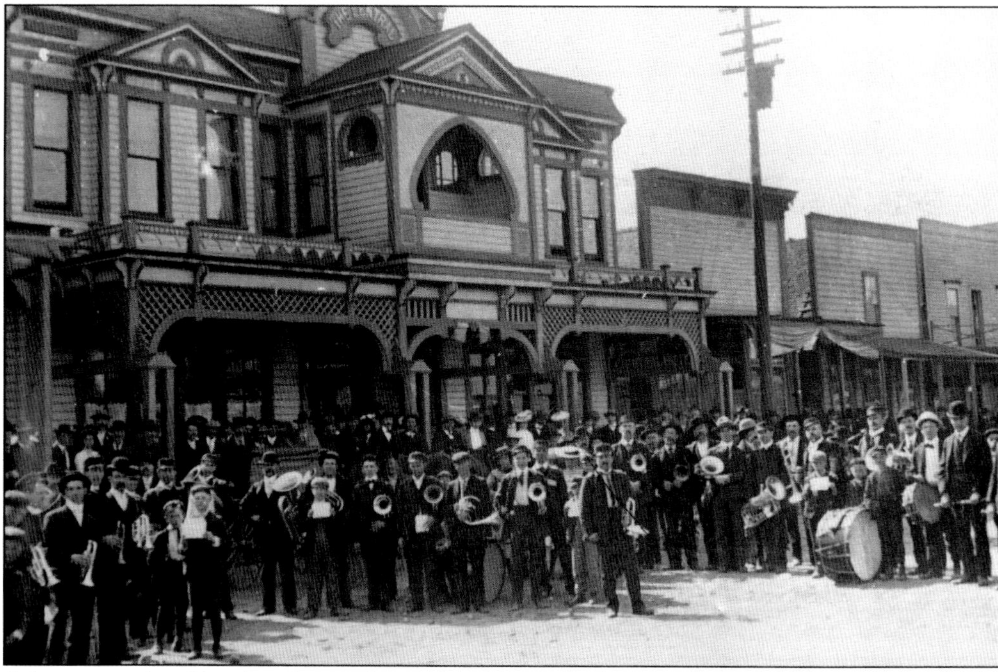

A large crowd and band gather in front of the Central Hotel in Cle Elum in 1905. The Central Hotel, located on Pennsylvania Avenue, was a popular stop for travelers on the Northern Pacific Railroad. Down the street to the right, just out of the frame, was the Reed House Hotel, built by town founder Walter J. Reed. (EPL.)

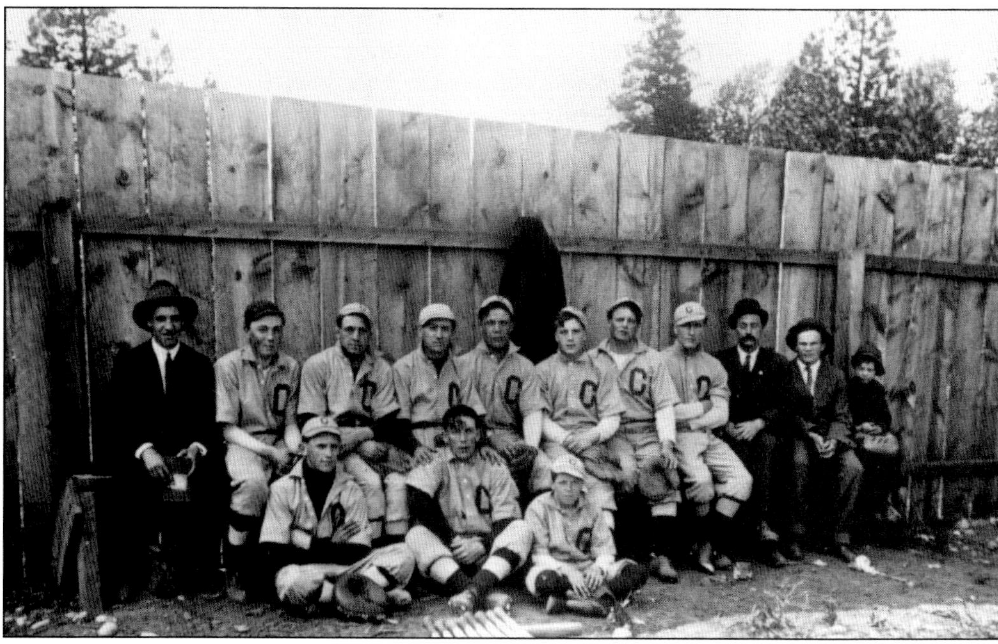

The Cle Elum baseball team is pictured here in the early 1900s. Early on, every city had at least one baseball club (some had more) that traveled locally and played other city teams. Nearly the entire town would turn out to watch the games, and it was big news and bragging rights for the winning team. (EPL.)

Tom Whited sings for the campers while his wife, Vernita, plays piano at the Lazy F Ranch in the Manastash, near Ellensburg. Tom and Vernita were managers of the dude ranch from 1943 to 1947. The Lazy F Ranch is still open today, hosting a variety of camps throughout the year. (EPL.)

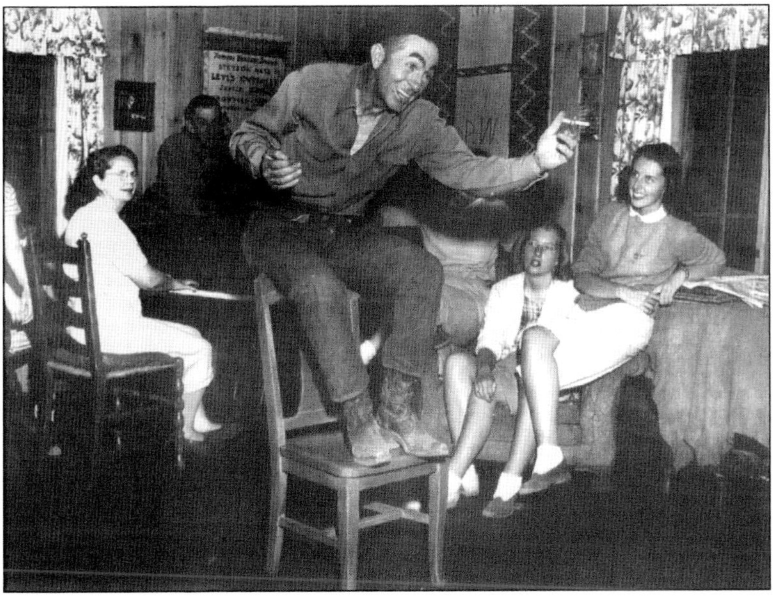

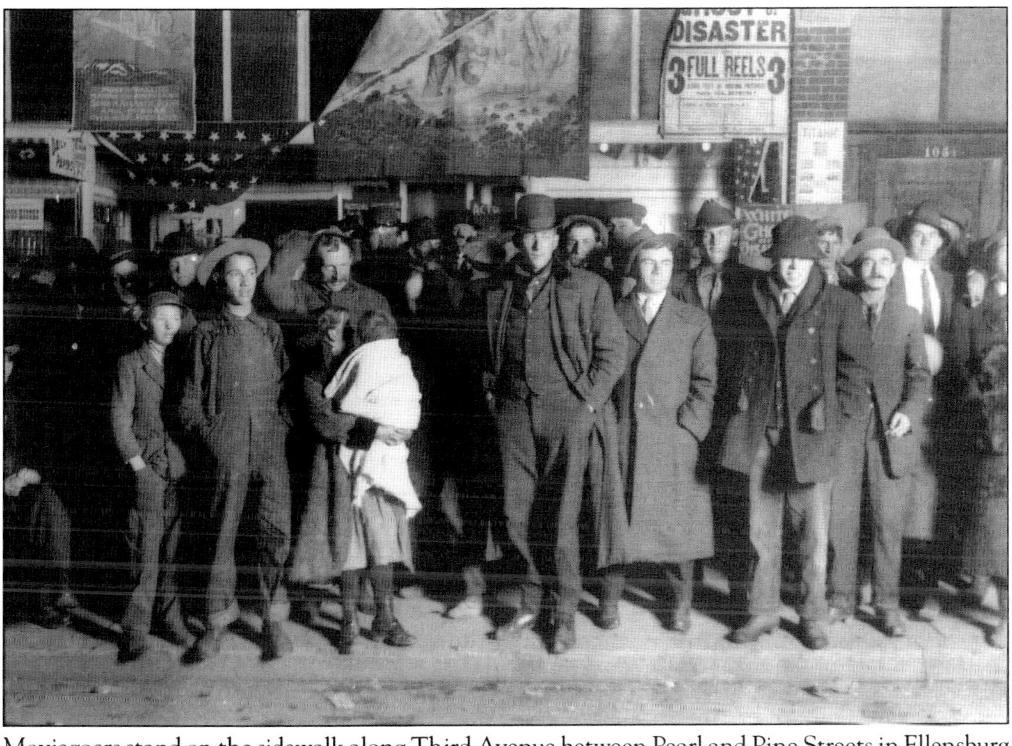

Moviegoers stand on the sidewalk along Third Avenue between Pearl and Pine Streets in Ellensburg in 1913. During this time, movies were in their early stages; note the poster that boasts three reels of moving pictures. The film was the *White Ghost of Disaster*, a film about the *Titanic* sinking, which had occurred the previous year. (EPL.)

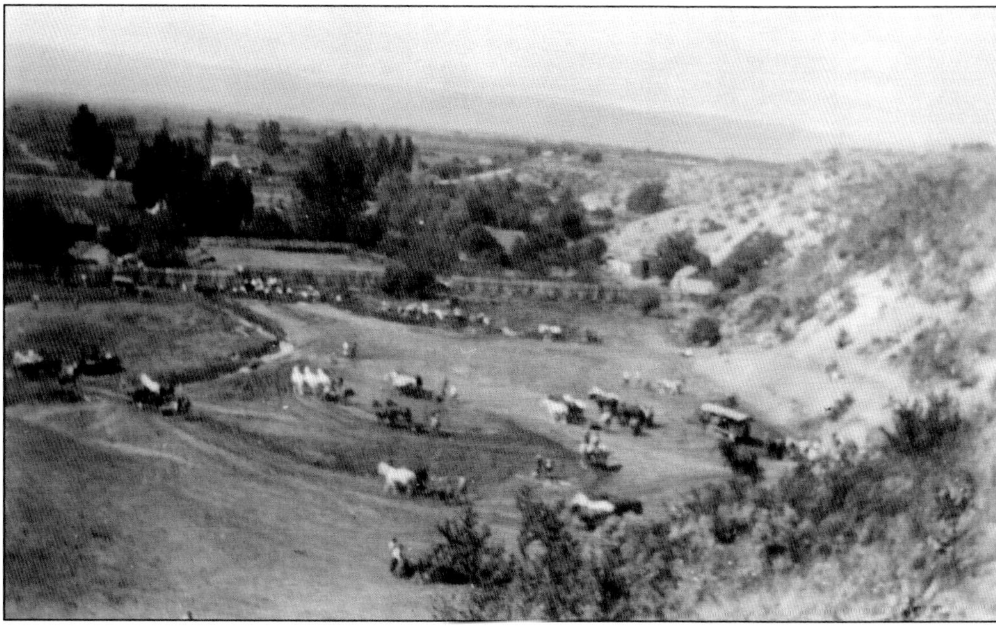

Kittitas County decided to build fair and rodeo grounds in 1922 and began acquiring the land at the base of Craig's Hill in Ellensburg. On June 14, 1923, businesses closed, and Ellensburg had a community day where the over 600 volunteers showed up to help clear the land, reroute Wilson Creek, cook food for the other volunteers, and help in any way. Many stayed overnight and completed the work the next day. Once the 18-acre site was ready, work began on the construction of grandstands, fences, a one-third-mile circumference racetrack, and other fair buildings. By September of that year, the rodeo arena and grandstands were complete, and the first Ellensburg Rodeo took place. (EPL.)

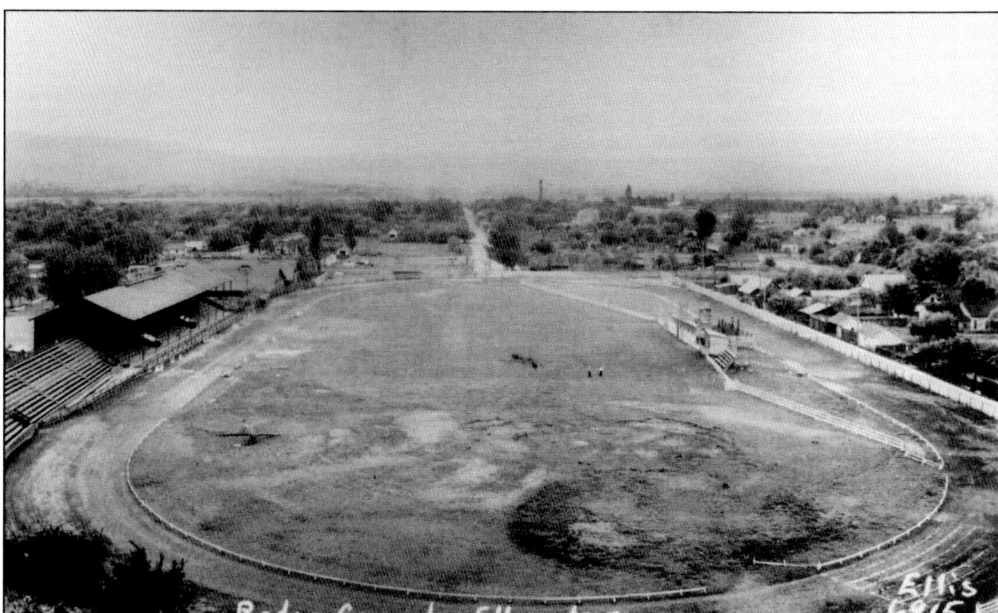

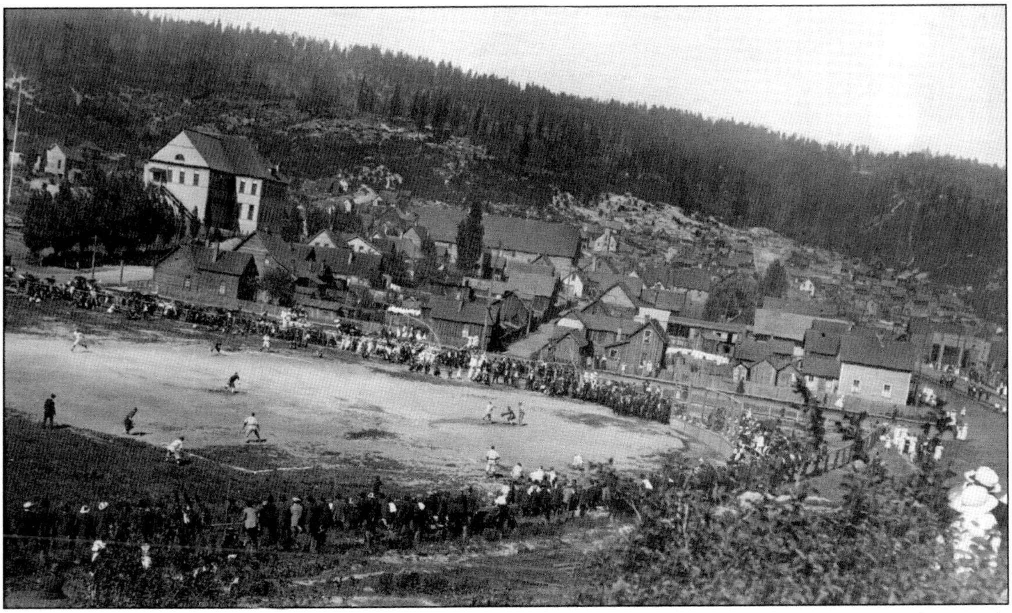

A baseball game is played in front of a large crowd on the community field in Roslyn. Roslyn High School is on the hill in the background. At far right, the tracks of the Northern Pacific Railroad branch run down Washington Avenue. Supplies and workers were brought in on these tracks, and coal from the mines in Roslyn, Ronald, and Jonesville was taken out. (RM.)

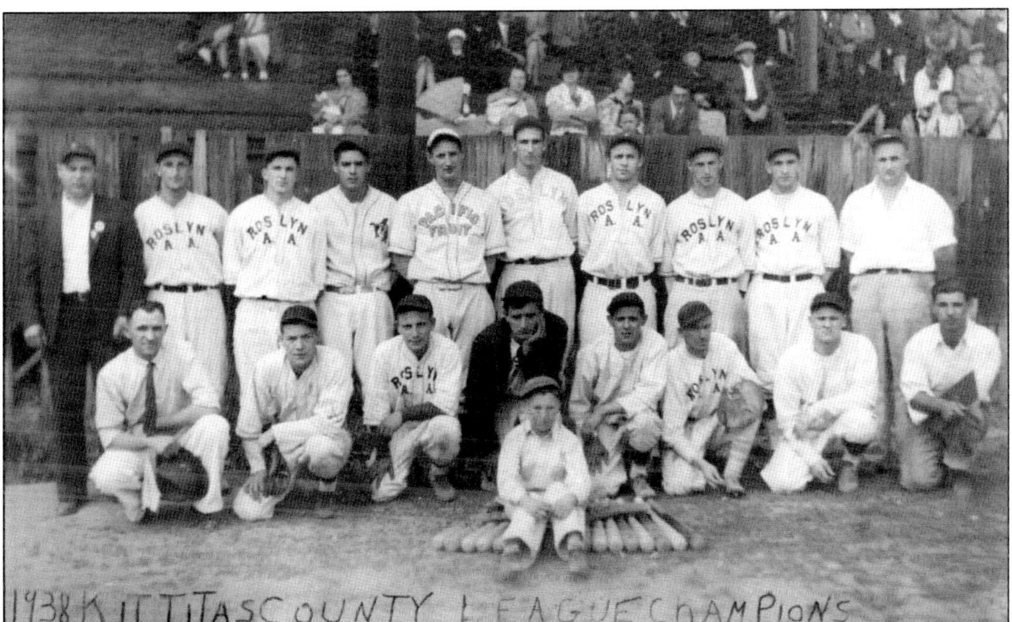

Roslyn's baseball team was hard to beat, as there were many strong young men living in Roslyn at the time. Standing in front of the grandstands in Roslyn, the 1938 Roslyn baseball team poses after winning the Kittitas County League Championship. Following this season, two of the star players tried out for the Yakima Pippins of the Western International League. (RM.)

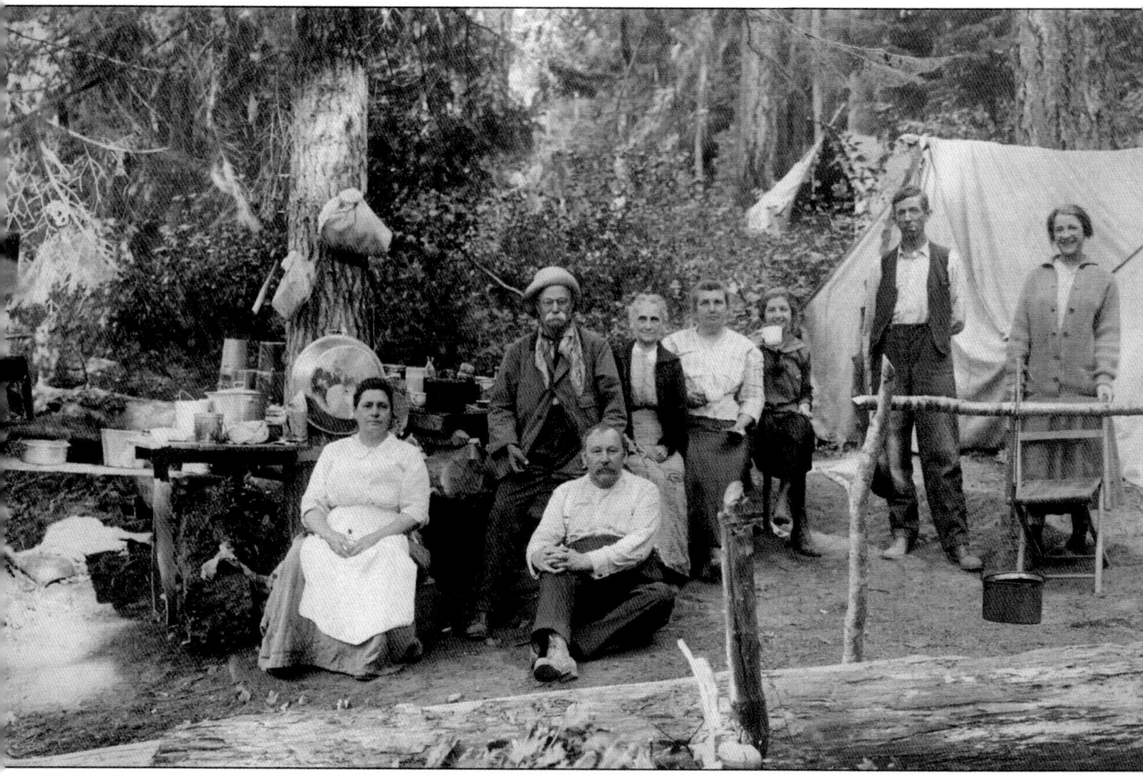

During the hot summer months in Kittitas County, people used to flee into the cool forested hills and camp, much like some people do today. In this 1900 photograph are Ellensburg residents camping in the foothills above the Kittitas Valley. From left to right are Mary Mires, Austin Mires, Otto Pautzke, Elizabeth Claydon (Ellen's mother), Ellen Pautzke, Kitty Wright, A.M. Wright, and Charlotte Wright. (EPL.)

Eight

County Views

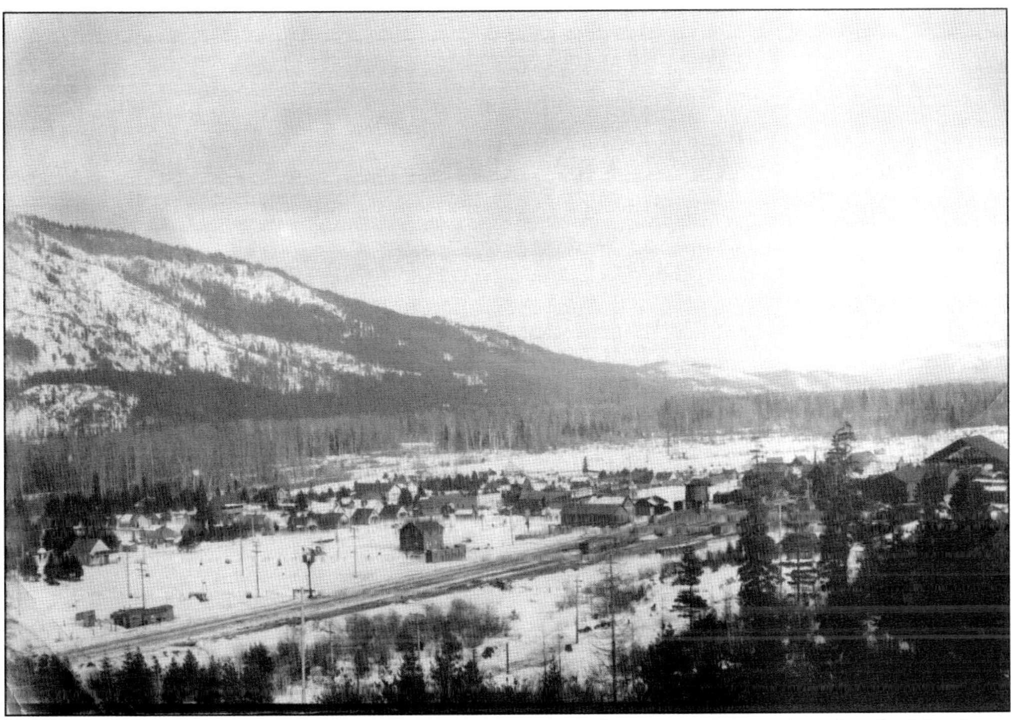

In this image facing southeast across Easton sometime after 1909, the rail line for the Northern Pacific runs on the edge of town. At the very bottom of the photograph, along the base of the hill, was the Milwaukee Road, which ran parallel to the Northern Pacific through Easton. At left and behind the water tank, the facade of the Johnson Brothers General Store is just visible. (KCHM.)

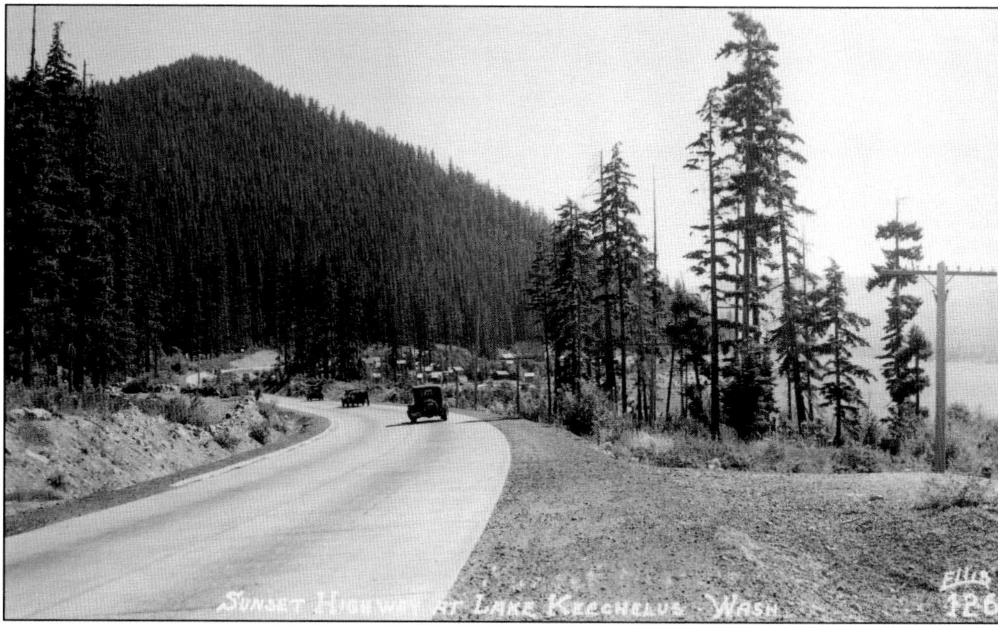

After making the long drive from Seattle over Snoqualmie Pass, the first main stop along the Sunset Highway was on the shores of Lake Keechelus. These cars, heading east, are approaching a small townsite that sat along the lake. The large building in the middle is the Keechelus Inn. When the road was widened and became Interstate 90, these buildings were removed. (KCHM.)

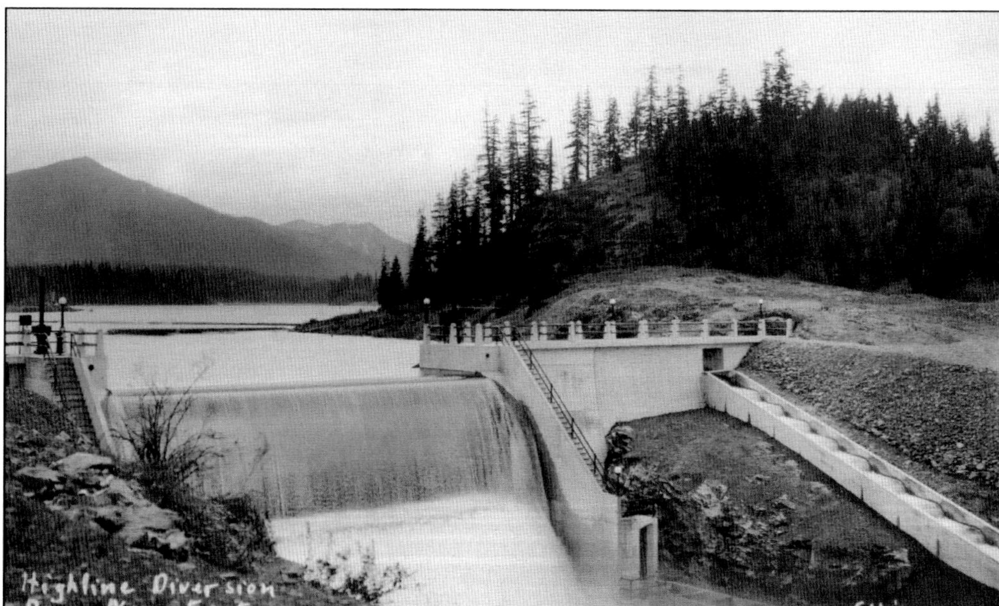

The irrigation water used in the Kittitas Valley originates in the large lakes of the Cascade Mountains. At the end of Lake Easton is a dam, officially called the Easton Diversion Dam, but also dubbed the Highline diversion dam on this photograph because it diverted water into the Highline irrigation canal. The Easton Diversion Dam, which is 248 feet long and 66 feet high, was completed in 1929. (KCHM.)

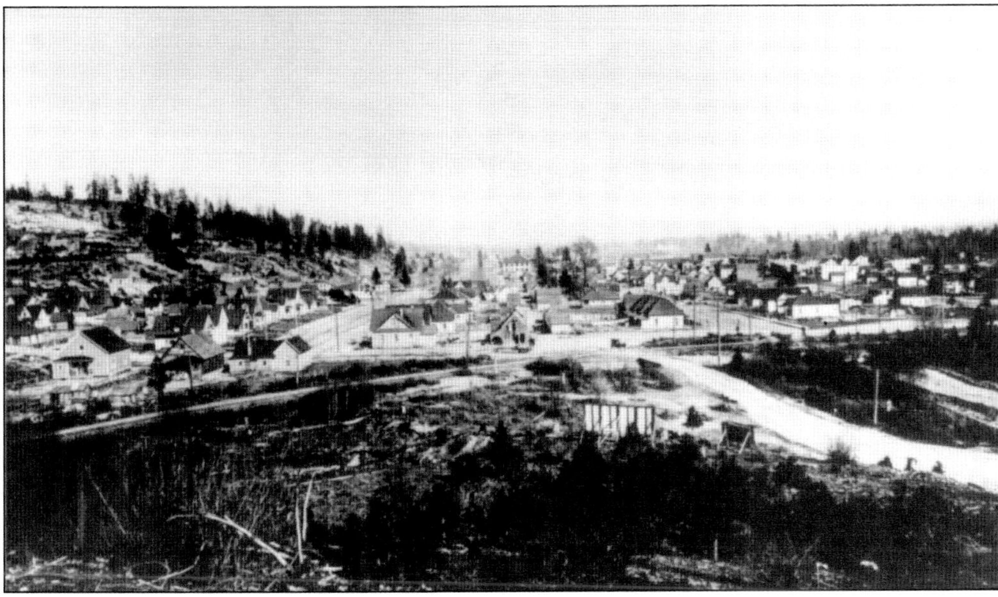

This view looks east over Cle Elum. West Third Street is on the left, and West Second Street is on the right. The road coming down from Roslyn is at right, and the railroad line that ran up to Roslyn and Ronald can be seen across the middle of the photograph. The old Cle Elum High School is in the middle of the photograph. (EPL.)

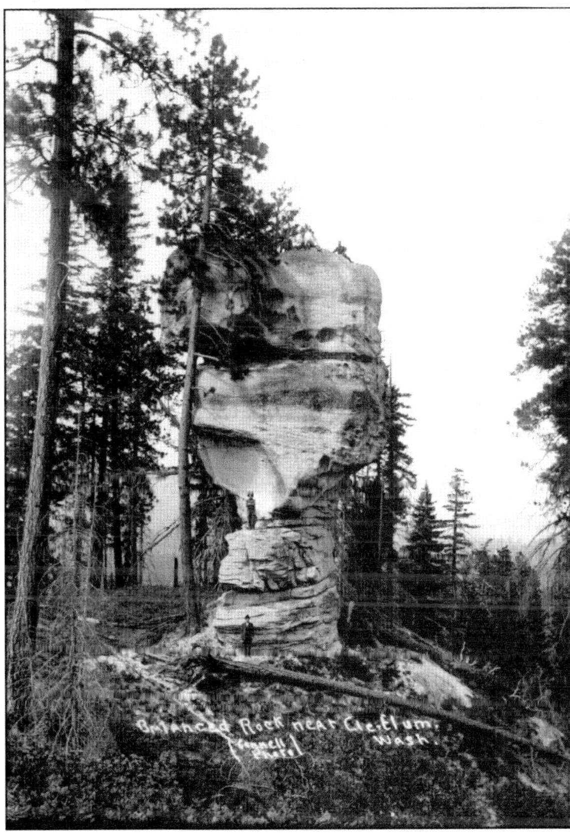

This amazing rock tower known as Balanced Rock is in the hills above Cle Elum, somewhere near the Teanaway Valley. It was a popular spot to visit in early days, and many pictures of this formation, along with many other unique sandstone rock formations, are in the town archives. The exact location of this formation is not available. (EPL.)

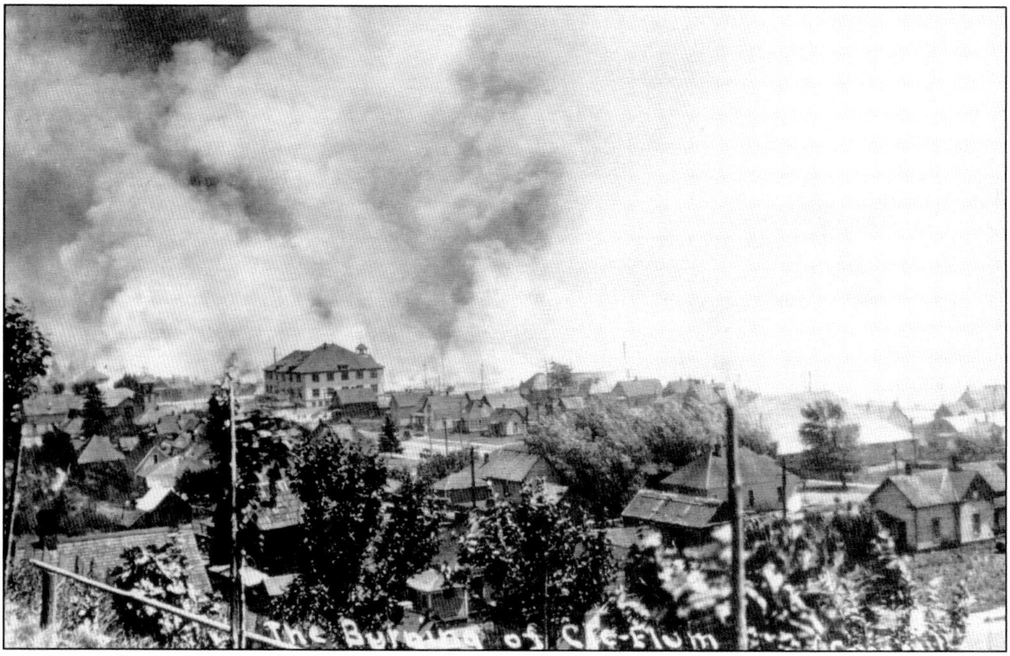

On June 25, 1918, a large fire burned more than 29 city blocks of Cle Elum, destroying over 30 businesses, including a sawmill and three churches, as well as 205 houses. The fire started between the Rose Theater and the Moss store; the two buildings were only separated by a foot of space and a pile of old boards and other garbage had collected there. Likely the result of a cigarette tossed into the pile, the flames spread quickly with the wind. After burning for nearly four hours, the fire was suppressed by both the fire department and lack of fuel. The fire rendered about 1,800 people homeless, most of them miners and their families. The Northwestern Improvement Company and the Independent Coal & Coke Co. offered assistance, as did the Cle Elum branch of the Red Cross. (Above, EPL; below, CWU.)

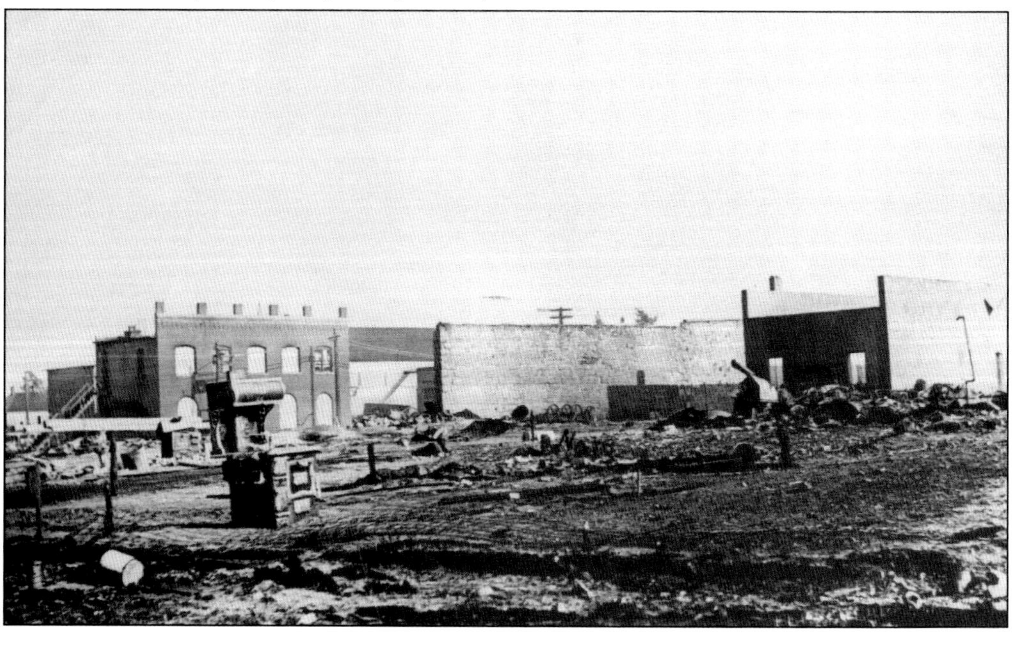

The sign on this building reads, "Wild Cat Dance Hall," during a Fourth of July celebration in Liberty around 1915. One of the banners states, "It's the quality of Cascade-Pride that made it famus [sp] state wide," referring to the Cascade Pride Malt Beverage that was available for 5¢. The dance hall later became the Liberty Community Hall. (EPL.)

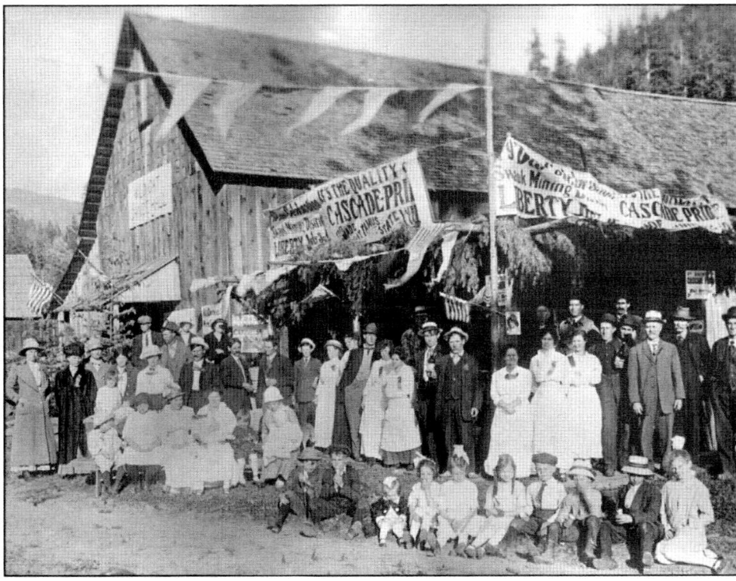

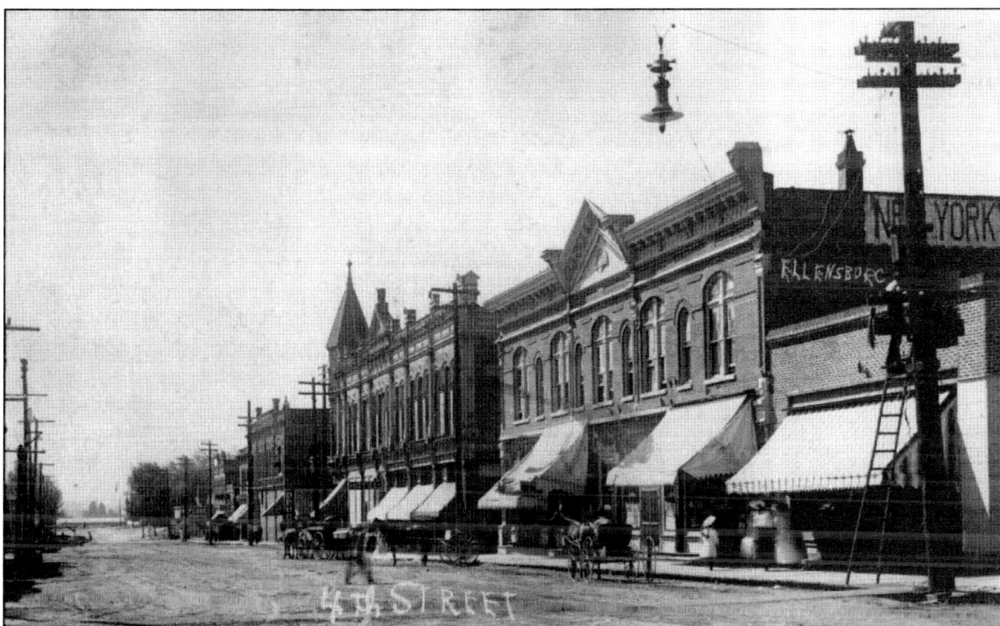

A 19th-century view of Fourth Avenue in Ellensburg is looking west towards Pearl Street. The brick structure at far right was part of the Masonic Temple that burned in the 1889 fire, but it was left in place and made part of the new building. Except for the structure across from the Davidson Building's cupola and some roadwork, this view has not changed much in over 100 years. (EPL.)

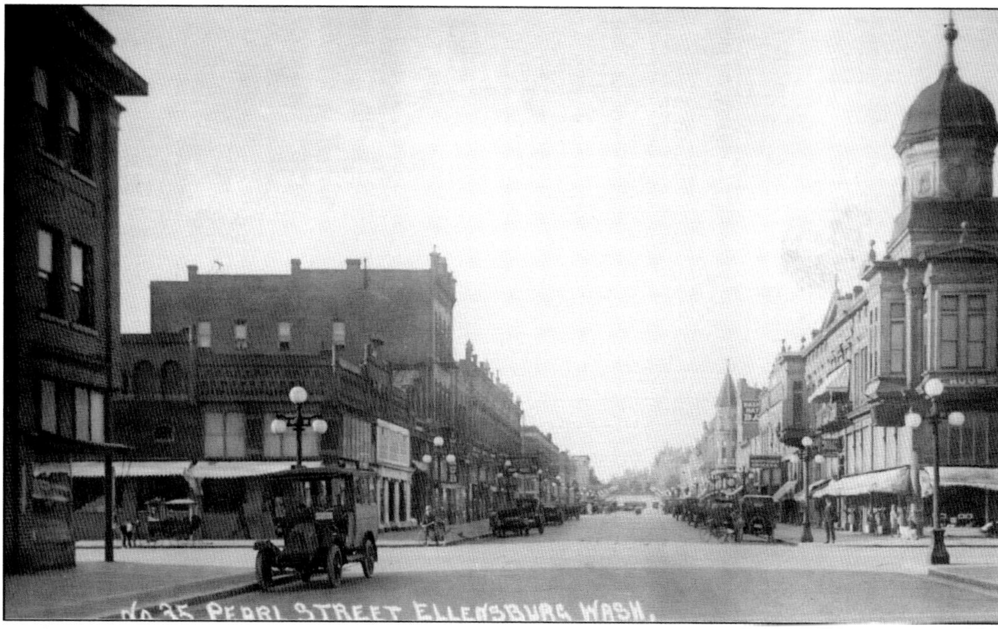

Looking north on Pearl Street across Third Avenue in Ellensburg, this photograph shows how quickly automobiles changed the landscape. Only a decade before, the roads were dirt, and horses, not cars, filled the streets of town. At left is the three-story St. Regis Hotel, and kitty-cornered from the hotel at right is the Kreidel Building, which still stands but has since removed the cupola. (EPL.)

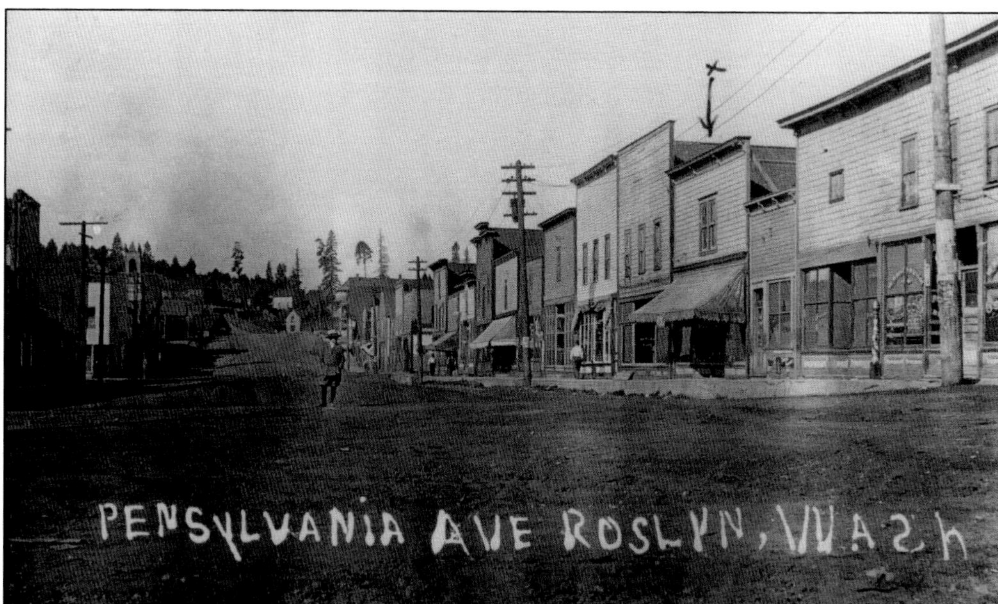

A young boy poses for a picture in the middle of Pennsylvania Avenue in Roslyn around 1900. Looking west from First Street, men stroll the sidewalks along the north side of the street. Behind the second telephone pole from the right is a mural on the side of the current Roslyn Café. (EPL.)

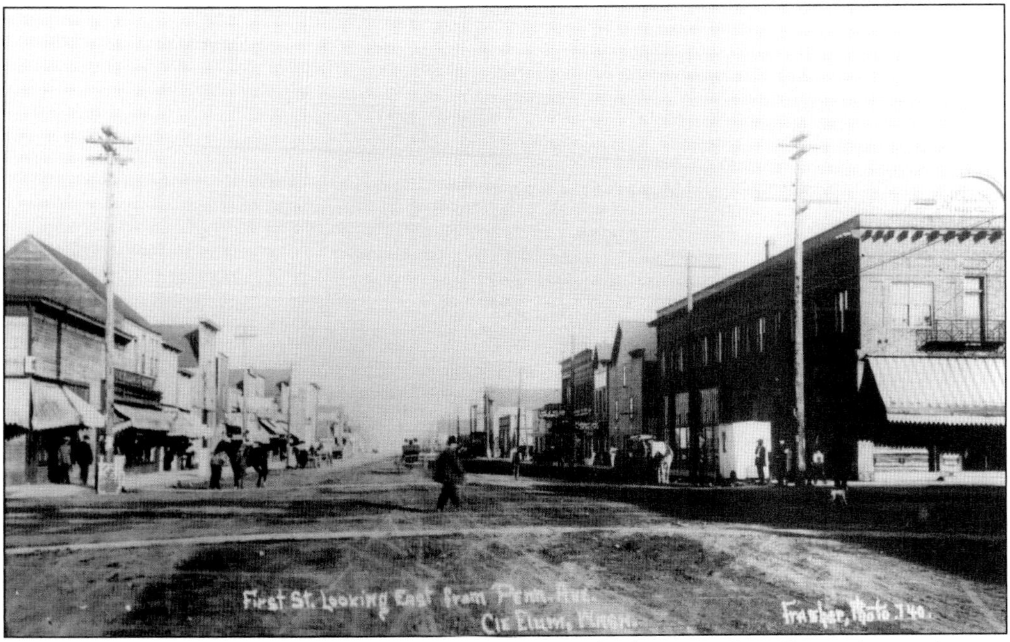

People and horses line the sides of Cle Elum's First Street, looking east from Pennsylvania Avenue in this 1910 photograph. At right was the Central Hotel Annex, built in 1909 by A. Sasse when his business outgrew the original Central Hotel building. Almost every structure on the north side of the street (left) was burned in the 1918 fire. (EPL.)

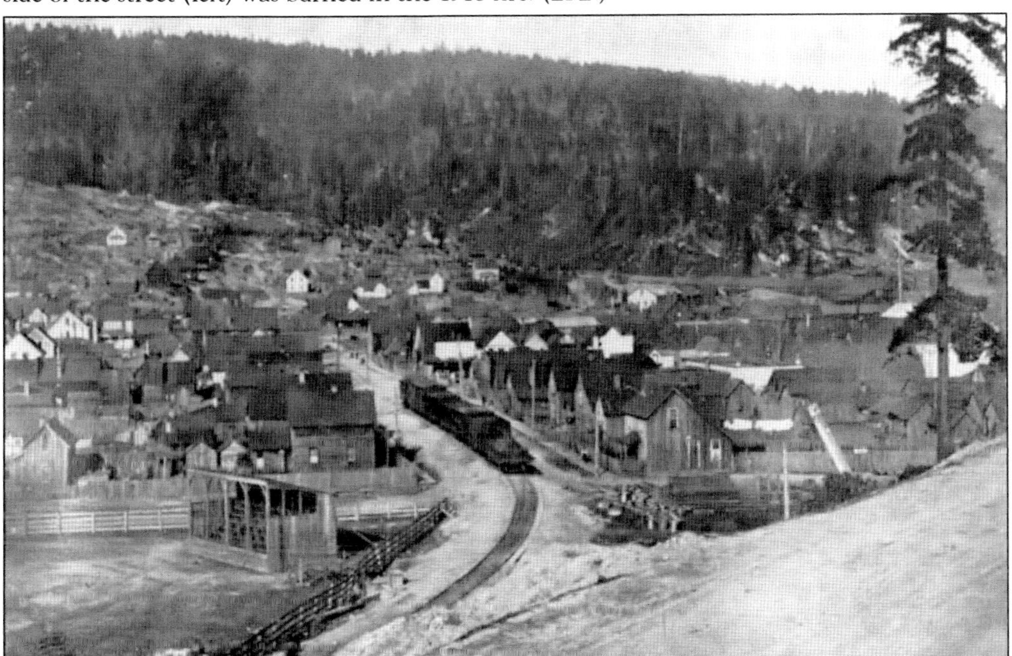

The Northern Pacific Railroad spur that carried coal from the mines ran down the middle of Washington Avenue in Roslyn. Looking east from the hill above the community baseball field, the No. 1 Mine is located in the draw above and to the right of the train. The tracks are no longer there, but the Coal Mines Trail follows their course today. (EPL.)

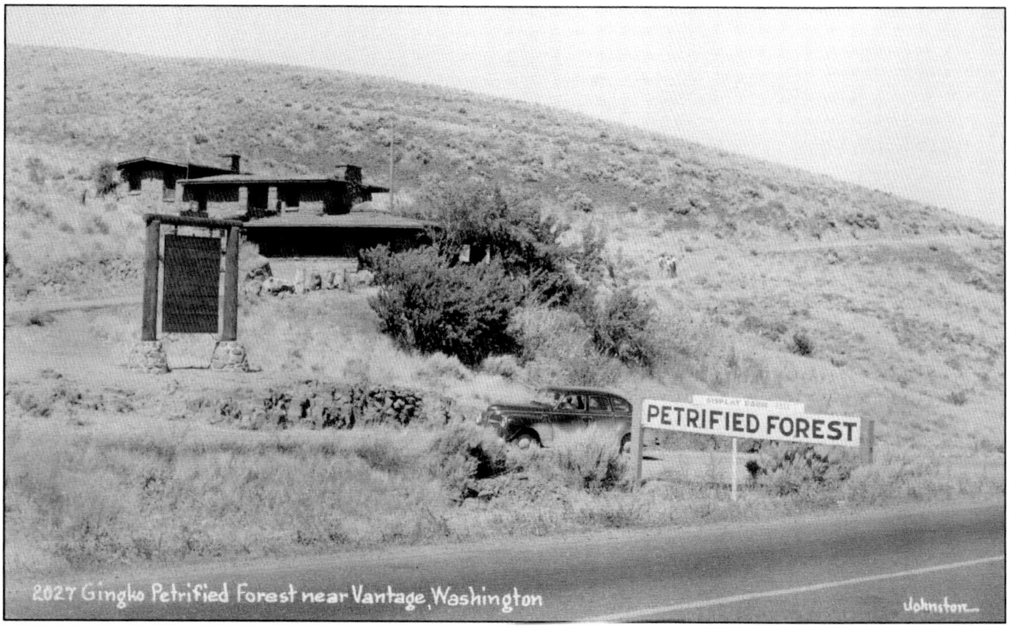

On Vantage Highway, between Ellensburg and Vantage and then the main highway, is the Ginkgo Petrified Forest State Park. Located just outside of Vantage, the park is build around a large fossilized forest discovered in the early 1930s. From the visitor center, an interpretive trail leads guests through the park's many petrified wood outcroppings. (EPL.)

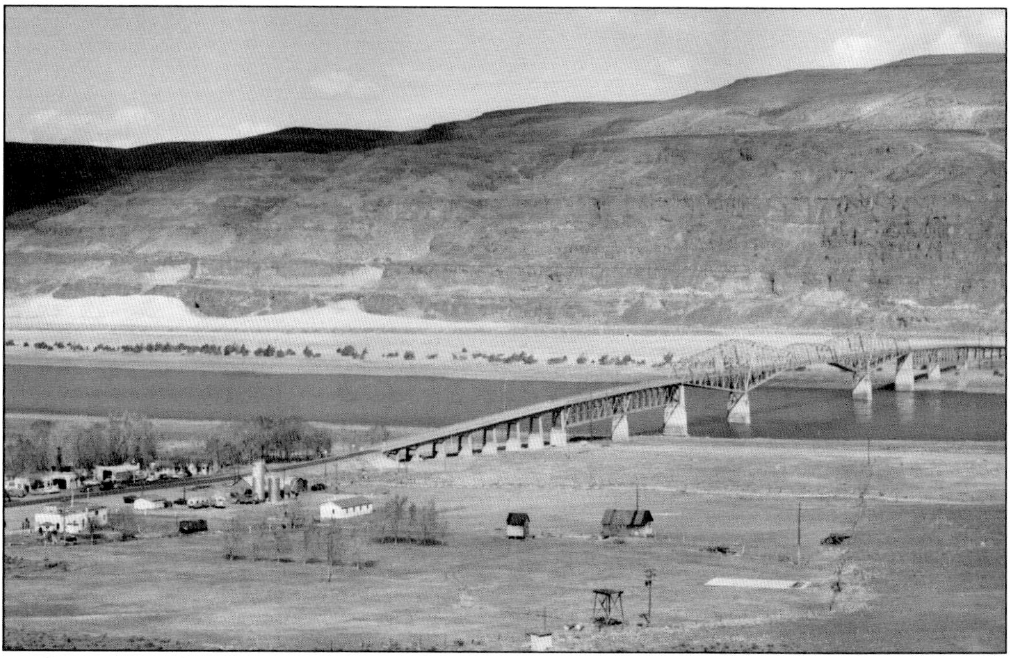

Looking across the Vantage Bridge towards Grant County, it is remarkable to see how much different the area looked in 1927. This bridge replaced the ferry system at Vantage and served many travelers for almost 40 years. This bridge was replaced by a higher one in 1962 for the construction of Wanapum Dam, which created a reservoir that covered most of this land and would have submerged parts of this bridge. (EPL.)

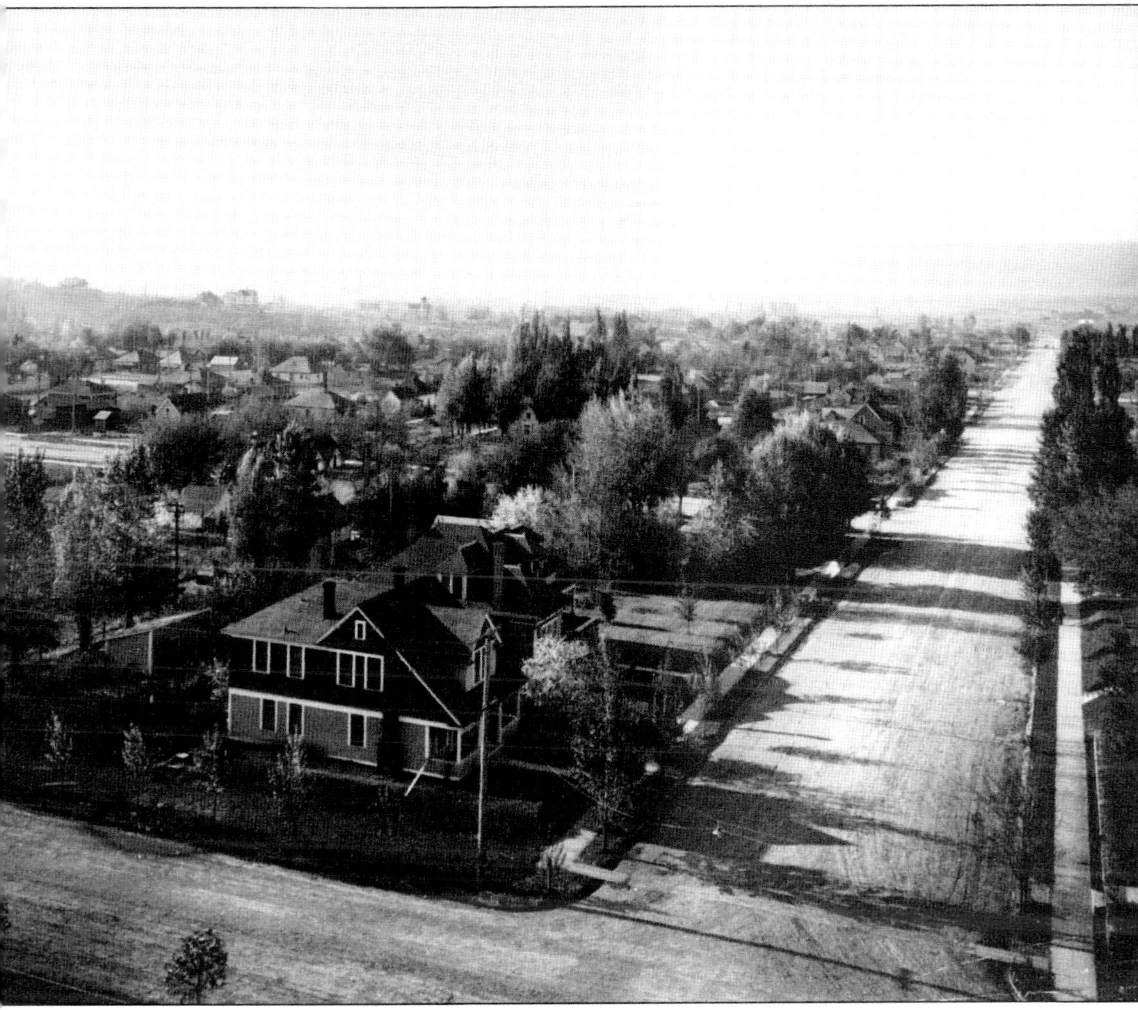

The parting image is a view down Anderson Street in Ellensburg from the Barge Hall tower on the Central Washington University campus. Taken by Asahel Curtis in 1912, this photograph shows how much the barren landscape had transformed in just over 20 years, compared to the images on page 13. On the far left is Craig's Hill with the Castle Building on the right. (EPL.)